NASCAR NEXTEL CUP SERIES 2005

2005 NASCAR NEXTEL CUP SERIES AWARDS CEREMONY

Waldorf＝Astoria, New York, N.Y.
December 2, 2005

ACKNOWLEDGEMENTS

NASCAR NEXTEL Cup Series 2005

UMI PUBLICATIONS, INC. STAFF

Chairman and Publisher:
Ivan Mothershead

President:
Bill Seaborn

Vice President and Associate Publisher:
Rick Peters

Controller:
Lewis Patton

Vice President & National Advertising Manager:
Mark Cantey

Advertising Executive:
Paul Kaperonis

Managing Editor:
Ward Woodbury

Associate Editor:
Ritchie Hallman

Art Director/Publication Design:
Brett Shippy

Manager of Information Systems/Publication Design:
Mike McBride

Treasurer and Director of Customer Services:
Mary Flowe

Executive Secretary and Customer Services Representative:
Renee Wedvick

UMI Publications, Inc., is pleased to present "NASCAR NEXTEL Cup Series 2005," the official chronicle of the 2005 NASCAR NEXTEL Cup Series season. And what a great season it was.

Congratulations to Tony Stewart and his entire team from Joe Gibbs Racing on their second NASCAR NEXTEL Cup Series championship. Tenth in the point standings in mid June, Stewart began an astounding run that vaulted him to the top of the standings in just eight races, where he remained following all but one of the remaining events.

The second Chase for the NASCAR NEXTEL Cup was another thrilling conclusion to the season that came down to four worthy competitors battling it out for the title in the last race of the year.

Young talents emerged in the form of first-time winners Carl Edwards, Kasey Kahne and the 2005 Raybestos Rookie of the Year, Kyle Busch. And we fondly bid farewell to veterans Rusty Wallace and Ricky Rudd, both of whom called this season their last year of full-time competition.

In sum, the 2005 season was another outstanding example of why NASCAR NEXTEL Cup Series racing is one of the most popular and exciting sports offered anywhere.

Just as NASCAR, in conjunction with its many partners and sponsors, has presented the very best in motorsports competition, we at UMI Publications have continually strived to produce the very best books for you to enjoy. That would not be possible, however, without the assistance of many talented and dedicated people. Therefore, we would like to recognize those who helped bring it all about.

To our friends at NASCAR, we once again offer our heartfelt appreciation. Thanks especially to Brian France, Mike Helton, George Pyne, Jim Hunter, Mark Dyer, Liz Schlosser, Jennifer White, Herb Branham, Paul Schaefer and Catherine McNeill, for their help and guidance throughout the year.

For 11 years, our managing editor, Ward Woodbury, has overseen the production of this book, and this year we gave him the task of writing the story of the 2005 season. We thank him for his unique and insightful perspective, and his continued dedication to this project.

No story like this would be complete without pictures to bring it to life. Therefore, we would like to recognize the hard-working and gifted photographers who make it possible. Special thanks to the staff of CIA Stock Photography — Don Grassman, Ernie Masche, Gary Eller, Tom Copeland and Andrew Copley — along with our friends Action Sports Photography — Walter Arce, Matt Thacker, Russell LaBounty, Alan Smith, Jared Tilton, Tina Snyder, Tami Kelly-Pope and Debbie Palonen — for providing us with some of the very best imagery available in the sport. We thank them all for their extreme talents and tireless efforts.

Most of all, we'd like to thank you, the fans of NASCAR NEXTEL Cup Series racing, for your support over the years. We're proud to say that NASCAR has the greatest fans of any sport. This book is for you, and we hope you enjoy it as much as we enjoyed bringing it to you.

FOREWORD
NASCAR NEXTEL Cup Series 2005

Another fantastic season, with another fantastic finish. That's my one-sentence description of the 2005 NASCAR NEXTEL Cup season. The subsequent 256 pages will provide a more in-depth look at the 36 races that made up the season, and how the second year of the Chase for the NASCAR NEXTEL Cup format played out.

By all indications, this was another banner year for our sport. As always, attendance figures were impressive. TV ratings were on the rise, both for the 26 races that preceded the Chase and the 10 thrilling races that made up the Chase.

We went down to the season finale at Homestead-Miami Speedway with four drivers still eligible to win the championship — a dramatic way to wrap up the season, to say the least.

When it was over, we had a champion to be proud of — Tony Stewart.

There was justice in that. Tony, who also won the championship in 2002, was one of the dominant drivers throughout 2005. And in addition to winning our series title, he also got the individual race victory he has always wanted more than any other — Indianapolis.

What a highlight that was. But it really was a full season of highlights, starting with four-time series champion Jeff Gordon winning the Daytona 500.

This was a season for the veterans. Rusty Wallace provided us with a farewell to remember, making the Chase in his final season of competition. Mark Martin, who also made the Chase, started the year by saying he was also retiring, before deciding to stay for one more season, a development we welcome.

It was a season for emerging new stars named Carl Edwards and Kyle Busch. Edwards, in his first full-time season, qualified for the Chase and stayed in the title hunt all the way to Homestead. Busch, younger brother of 2004 series champion Kurt Busch, won two races and the Raybestos Rookie of the Year crown.

Simply put, 2005 was a season to remember. We hope this yearbook helps keep those memories alive.

" We went down to the season finale at Homestead-Miami Speedway with four drivers still eligible to win the championship — a dramatic way to wrap up the season, to say the least."

Sincerely,

Brian Z. France

CONTENTS

NASCAR NEXTEL Cup Series 2005

PREFACE

The winter months gave everyone a chance to step back and reflect upon the season that had just transpired. A year earlier the word most often used to characterize the coming 2004 campaign was "change." The most obvious example of that was the introduction of Nextel Communications as title sponsor of the world's premiere stock car racing series, which required transformation of some kind in nearly all aspects of the sport. Everything from signage to souvenirs were quickly revised, while writers, announcers, sponsors and competitors all practiced diligently their references to the newly-named NASCAR NEXTEL Cup Series.

While all that occurred, more change was taking place at NASCAR headquarters in Daytona Beach, Fla., as Brian France prepared to lead the sport into the future in his first full season at NASCAR's helm. And it didn't take long for the new chairman & CEO to shake things up a bit with his announcement of a major modification of the system used to determine the series champion that had been in place for nearly 30 years. The Chase for the NASCAR NEXTEL Cup would pit at least 10 drivers against each other with 10 races remaining in the season to battle for the right to be named the first NASCAR NEXTEL Cup Series champion.

Kurt Busch prepares for the 2005 defense of his NASCAR NEXTEL Cup championship, earned during his fourth year of full-time competition in the series. His title was the second straight for Roush Racing.

Kyle Busch (left) listens intently to his Hendrick Motorsports teammate, Jimmie Johnson. After capturing the 2004 NASCAR Busch Series Raybestos Rookie of the Year title, Busch, at 19 years of age, is considered a strong contender to take NASCAR NEXTEL Cup Series rookie honors in

Opinions abounded as everyone weighed in on the potential impact of the revised format, but as it played out over the 10-month season early critics were swayed while proponents were affirmed. Going into the final event of 2004, five drivers held a chance of taking the title. When the checkered flag fell on the Ford 400 at Homestead-Miami Speedway in late November, Kurt Busch had finally prevailed by a mere eight points over Jimmie Johnson and just 16 ahead of Jeff Gordon in the most hotly contested championship battle on record.

The inaugural NASCAR NEXTEL Cup Series season was considered a resounding success. Perhaps France himself summed it up best by saying: "2004 is undoubtedly going to go down as either the greatest season we've ever had or one of the greatest seasons."

It came as no surprise then, when France announced prior to the start of the 2005 season that there would be no further changes to the point system and the 10-race Chase for the NASCAR NEXTEL Cup would once again decide the championship. That, however, did not mean that NASCAR would simply sit back and be satisfied with the status quo.

In January, a revision to the procedure that determines starting lineups for races was announced. In essence, the top 35 teams according to owner points would now be guaranteed a place in the starting field. Seven starting positions would be awarded to the fastest qualifiers not among the top 35 in owner points, while the final spot in the field would remain the so-called "champion's provisional."

Further, a new process would go into effect at certain venues that would trim the weekend schedule for NASCAR NEXTEL Cup teams. The new plan called for two 70-minute practice sessions followed by one round of qualifying, after which all cars would be impounded by NASCAR until the race. Only very minor adjustments would be allowed prior to the cars rolling off the starting grid on race day.

The intention of the new format was based largely on cost savings for the teams, effectively eliminating the common practice of having nearly totally different race setups (including engines) for qualifying and the race itself. An additional benefit would come from the fact that a team's time and expenses on the selected race weekends would be cut. The decisions to implement the system lay with officials at the individual tracks, and although seven speedways had already decided to use it as the season opened, NASCAR hoped that it would become universal throughout the series within a year or two.

Although no one could dispute that the 2004 season presented some of the best competition in recent memory (a belief supported by a bevy of year-end statistics) NASCAR sought and found ways that could enhance it even more. So new rules were presented that reduced rear-spoiler height on all cars from the 5½ inches used in 2004 to 4½ inches for all events except those using restrictor

Ryan Newman, responsible for nearly half of the 24 wins compiled by Dodge Intrepids since their introduction to the series in 2001, takes to the track in his brand new Charger, hoping the new body style will help vault him into championship contention after finishing sixth, sixth and seventh in his three seasons of compet

Rusty Wallace signs autographs at Daytona before kicking off "Rusty's Last Call," the former champ's last full season in the NASCAR NEXTEL Cup Series. With 55 career victories, Wallace started the year eighth on the all-time wins list, second only to Jeff Gordon among active drivers.

plates, the theory being that the reduction would significantly decrease downforce on the rear of the cars, in turn putting a premium on savvy setups and driver ability.

To partially compensate for the loss of traction due to less downforce, Goodyear formulated newer, softer versions of their racing Eagles that would "stick" a bit better to the racing surfaces. Off-season testing had some drivers saying that the combination of less spoiler and softer tires made little difference in how the cars felt on the track compared to last year, but all agreed that no one would know the true effect until they were able to experience actual racing conditions.

Also in January, Dodge unveiled the much-anticipated racing version of their Charger model, marking the return of the famous nameplate that chalked up 124 NASCAR race wins from 1966-77. Dodge officials were counting on the new body style to provide an improvement over the Intrepid R/T's record of 24 wins over the four seasons since Dodge's return to the sport.

And if the stable of Dodge drivers ready to race the new Charger was any indication, that improvement would be likely. Ryan Newman, who accounted for 11 of the Intrepid's victories, would once again be joined at Penske Racing South by Rusty Wallace, who was set to begin "Rusty's Last Call," the moniker given to his last full season behind the wheel after a stellar career that had already tallied 55 wins over 21 full seasons. Wallace and Newman would lend assistance to Raybestos Rookie of the Year contender Travis Kvapil who, after four seasons in the NASCAR Craftsman Truck Series that included the 2003 championship, would be taking over the No. 77 Dodge fielded by Penske-Jasper Racing in place of 2004 driver Brendan Gaughan.

Ray Evernham readied his new Chargers for Jeremy Mayfield and 2004 rookie sensation Kasey Kahne, who was chafing at the bit to get back into action and score his first NASCAR NEXTEL Cup Series win after coming one spot shy on five occasions last season. Mayfield would be teamed with crew chief Richard "Slugger" Labbe.

Over at Chip Ganassi Racing with Felix Sabates, the "Three Ms" (Sterling Marlin, Casey Mears and Jamie McMurray) prepared to go back to business, while Petty Enterprises would continue to field the Nos. 43 and 45 Dodges for Jeff Green and Kyle Petty.

The single-car operations of Bill Davis Racing with driver Scott Wimmer and BAM Racing with veteran Ken Schrader readied their new Chargers as well.

The Chevrolet contingent would undoubtedly be led by Hendrick Motorsports teammates Jimmie Johnson and Jeff Gordon, second and third in the final 2004 point standings. Johnson, who led all drivers with eight wins last season, finished the year on a tear with four victories, a second and a sixth place in the final six races. After two straight runner-up seasons, Johnson was more than ready to lay claim to his first series title.

Gordon also finished 2004 on a high note with three straight third-place finishes, setting the table for his "Drive for Five," the name given to his 2005 bid for a fifth career championship.

Rounding out the Hendrick stable would be second-year driver Brian Vickers and 19-year-old Kyle Busch, who would join Kvapil to make up this season's class of Raybestos Rookie of the Year contenders. Busch was seated in the No. 5 Kellogg's Chevrolet, replacing veteran Terry Labonte who was slated to run a 10-race schedule using the number 44, with which he won his first championship in 1984.

Richard Childress Racing would again field the GM Goodwrench Chevrolet for fifth-year driver Kevin Harvick, who welcomed Jeff Burton and Dave Blaney to the team. Childress, who had his eye on Burton for a number of years, quickly snatched him up when the Virginia native left

Mark Martin, who finished among the top five in nine of the last 12 seasons, makes a final bid for a championship in 2005 with his "Salute to You" Tour, named in recognition of the fans that have supported him throughout his NASCAR NEXTEL Cup

Roush Racing before the end of the 2004 season. With Robby Gordon's departure to start his own team, Childress placed Burton in the No. 31 Cingular Chevrolet, while Blaney took the wheel of the newly-numbered 07 Monte Carlo with new sponsor Jack Daniel's. Both Harvick and Childress welcomed the calm and steady demeanors of Burton and Blaney and hoped that would contribute to bringing RCR back to the prominence it enjoyed for more than a decade with driver Dale Earnhardt.

Dale Earnhardt Inc. would return with its tandem of Dale Earnhardt Jr. and Michael Waltrip, but only after major changes among personnel. During the winter, Earnhardt's longtime crew chief, Tony Eury Sr., moved to a management role, while former car chief for the No. 8 team Tony Eury Jr. moved to Waltrip's NAPA Chevrolet. The Budweiser team would now be led by Pete Rondeau in a move that also involved swapping crews between the two DEI teams.

Joe Gibbs Racing would see little change in the teams of former champions Bobby Labonte and Tony Stewart, while adding a third car to the JGR fold. Jason Leffler and sponsor FedEx would occupy the No. 11 Chevrolet, bringing the 30-year-old driver back to the NASCAR NEXTEL Cup Series, where he had run 30 races in 2001 and 10 events in 2003.

Chevrolet drivers Joe Nemechek and Scott Riggs both returned to their respective teams at MB2/MBV Motorsports, where both drivers had shown flashes of promise during 2004, including Nemechek's fourth career win, that coming at Kansas Speedway in October. They would be joined by colorful Boris Said for at least 10 races with backing from Centrix Financial in an

(Above) After a stellar rookie season with four poles and 13 top-five finishes, Kasey Kahne enters 2005 looking for that elusive first win and a chance to compete in the Chase for the NASCAR NEXTEL Cup.

(Right) Carl Edwards turned a lot of heads last season during his 13 starts in Roush Racing's No. 99 Ford, the car he will campaign for the entire 2005 season.

(Far Right) Travis Kvapil, who captured NASCAR Craftsman Truck Series rookie honors in 2001 followed by that series' championship two years later, will compete for the 2005 Raybestos Rookie of the Year title in the No. 77 Dodge for Penske-Jasper Racing.

opportunity that would give the former road-racing champion some more experience on the big NASCAR ovals.

Two single-car operations would also field Chevrolets for 2005, with Bobby Hamilton Jr. driving the Tide Monte Carlo for PPI Motorsports and owner Cal Wells III, while Mike Bliss would take over the NetZero Chevrolet for owner Gene Haas at CNC Racing. Although neither driver had competed for a full season, they, like Leffler, had accumulated enough starts over at least one NASCAR NEXTEL Cup Series season to keep them from competing for rookie honors in 2005.

After back-to-back championships, Roush Racing had to be considered the organization that would lead the way for Ford. Current champ Kurt Busch along with 2003 title holder Matt Kenseth had both shown the strength to win races and the season-long consistency that captures crowns, while the ever-competitive, always intense Mark Martin had no intention of slowing down for his final full season in NASCAR NEXTEL Cup.

Strengthening the Roush stable even further were drivers Greg Biffle and Carl Edwards. Biffle, no stranger to championship campaigns after taking the NASCAR Craftsman Truck Series title in 2000 and the NASCAR Busch Series championship in 2002, finished his sophomore season of 2004 on a high note with a win at Homestead-Miami, his second victory of the season, and was intent upon carrying that momentum well into 2005.

Greg Biffle (left) and crew chief Doug Richert finished 2004 on a high note with a victory at Homestead-Miami Speedway. This year, the former NASCAR Craftsman Truck Series and NASCAR Busch Series champion looks to add a third major title to his resume and continue Roush Racing's championship string.

Edwards, who took over the No. 99 Ford for Roush upon Jeff Burton's departure in August of 2004, showed plenty of promise over the final third of the season with five top-10 runs that included a third place at Atlanta. Many felt his ability behind the wheel along with his back-down-from-nobody attitude would help Edwards make some noise during his first full season of NASCAR NEXTEL Cup Series competition.

Dale Jarrett and Elliott Sadler again teamed up at Robert Yates Racing, with Jarrett determined to join Sadler among the contenders in this year's Chase for the NASCAR NEXTEL Cup after finishing a disappointing 15th in 2004. Sadler ran among the top 10 in points over the entire 2004 season while collecting wins at Texas and California, and he firmly intended to remain in top-10 form to take his second shot at the title.

Rounding out the Ford contingent was Ricky Rudd, set to begin his third season driving for the Wood Brothers. After going winless for the second straight year, Rudd was looking to change all that after rejoining his former crew chief, Michael "Fatback" McSwain, who left Bobby Labonte's team before the end of last season.

With new rules, drivers, team members and sponsors all in place during an off-season that seemed anything but that, everyone turned their attention to Daytona Beach, Fla., where Speedweeks, the traditional launching pad for each new season, loomed. Ready or not, the 2005 NASCAR NEXTEL Cup Series season was about to begin.

2005 NASCAR NEXTEL Cup Series Champion

TONY STEWART

I couldn't be happier about winning the 2005 NASCAR NEXTEL Cup Series championship — not for myself, but for my race team. This year, versus 2002 when we won our first championship, we had fun all year. We got back to why we started racing in the first place, and that's because we love being a part of racing and we love competing.

I'm not the guy who won us this championship — I'm just a piece of the puzzle. The guys on this race team won us the championship, and I'm just really happy for all of them.

Early in the 2005 season, we realized that the Hendrick teams and the Roush teams were really onto something we had not found yet, and we were really behind the eight-ball and had to do our homework. It took awhile to find all the pieces of the whole equation, but around June we really hit on something, and that's when we hit our stride. We had a great test at Michigan that helped us get back on track and with that, we started a string of five wins in

> " These guys have really stuck with me over the years, and I'm grateful for that. So this championship is as much for them as it is for me ..."

seven races. That's what it took to really get us going as a team, and with the confidence we had at that point, we felt like we were contenders again. That's what carried us to the end of the year and got us into the Chase.

The win at The Brickyard was a personal victory for me, but at the same time it was a huge win for the race team. Up to that point, and even now, that was one of the greatest days in my life, but to be able to finish off the season at Homestead and win the championship was the highlight of the year for me and for the entire team.

The great thing about our race teams at Joe Gibbs Racing is that throughout our organization we have very little turnover. Once someone is in our system, they want to stay for a long time. So a lot of the guys on the team have been with me since I started in the NASCAR NEXTEL Cup Series, and that makes a big difference.

That's why, for me, this championship is more special than the first one. In 2002, when I won the championship, I put the team through a lot of turmoil that went on throughout the season. But this year, not having all that controversy and turmoil with the team made it so we could really enjoy this championship a lot more. These guys have really stuck with me over the years, and I'm grateful for that. So this championship is as much for them as it is for me, and I thank them for everything they did to make it happen.

It also means a lot to me to win this championship with my crew chief, Greg Zipadelli. Greg kind of considers me one of his little brothers, and he's like the big brother I never had. It's like a family relationship as opposed to just a working relationship. Greg has helped me

The Home Depot team was superb on pit road all season long and helped Stewart complete a string of 13 straight top-10 finishes during his rise in the point standings. By the end of the year, Stewart had 17 top fives and 25 top 10s, leading all drivers on his way to the championship.

Greg Zipadelli has been a crew chief for seven seasons, all with Tony Stewart and Joe Gibbs Racing. In that span, the team won the 1999 Raybestos Rookie of the Year title, scored 24 victories, has never finished lower than seventh in the point standings and owns two NASCAR NEXTEL Cup Series championships.

through a lot of tough times, just like he would his younger brother. I really can't see us not being together as a driver-crew chief combination. I can't see myself working with anyone else, and I think he feels the same way. We want to do everything we can to protect the relationship we've developed over the years.

I really want to thank Joe Gibbs and his son, J.D. We miss having Joe around. He's been the foundation of this whole program. Joe's strengths are knowing who to hire and how to hire the right people for the right jobs. When he went back to the Redskins, it was something we were all nervous about, but he left us in great hands with his son, J.D., taking over the operation.

Tony Stewart carries the checkered flag at Sonoma, Calif., after his first victory of the 2005 season. That win was followed by four more in the next six races and propelled Stewart to the top of the standings, a position he held following all but one of the final 15 races of the season.

J.D. stepped into that role at a really tough time in our organization. And having to add a third team, that was just more stress and work for him. We had 150 employees at Joe Gibbs Racing in 2002 when we won the first championship. Now we have over 300 employees. So it's quite a bit different now than it was a couple of years ago. We think J.D.'s done an excellent job.

I think we all look at it from the standpoint that if Joe believes in J.D. and believes he can get the job done, we have no reason to doubt that. That was the right call for us, and he's done a great job. J.D. has done nothing short of doing great things with this team.

The same thing goes for all of the people at Joe Gibbs Racing. So many of them work so hard and contribute to the success of our entire operation. Sometimes they don't get all the recognition they deserve, but every person in our organization plays an important role in the overall success of our teams, and without them we couldn't win championships.

Finally, I'd like to thank all of the fans of NASCAR NEXTEL Cup racing. Without a doubt, NASCAR fans are the best of any sport, anywhere. When we climbed the fence at Daytona, at Loudon a week later and then at Indianapolis, that's something the fans have really associated with us. It's brought us a lot closer to the fans, and that's the reason we climb the fence – to get that much closer to the fans. To be able to get right there with them and celebrate with them, that was something that was special for our race team this year. It's kind of a signature deal for us now, and every time we have a victory we're going to do that.

It was really great to see all the support we had at Homestead. To hear the chant, "Climb the Fence," that was just the cherry on top of the sundae, and it really capped off a very awesome year for us.

Tony Stewart hoists the NASCAR NEXTEL Cup Trophy at Homestead-Miami Speedway. Stewart finish 15th in the season finale but still held a 35-point advantage over Greg Biffle and Carl Edwards.

I'm honored to be the 2005 NASCAR NEXTEL Cup Series champion, and I'm going to do everything I can to be a great champion and represent our sport to the best of my ability. I hope to see you at a race sometime in 2006.

Sincerely,

Tony Stewart

DAYTONA 500

February brought an end to the all-too-brief 2004-05 off-season for NASCAR NEXTEL Cup Series teams, as they began to pack up their transporters and rumble down Interstate 95 from their shops in and around the Carolinas toward Daytona Beach, Fla., for the 2005 edition of Speedweeks at Daytona International Speedway.

The annual Budweiser Shootout ignited the action, once again run on Saturday night under the Daytona lights. The format called for 70 laps (175 miles) to be contested by the 12 Bud Pole winners from 2004 and eight former winners of the non-points event.

Drivers drew for their starting positions and Dale Jarrett, last year's winner of this event, took the top spot with Greg Biffle on his right. Jarrett jumped to the lead on the first lap but

Fans packed the grandstands at Daytona International Speedway for the Saturday night kickoff of Speedweeks and the 2005 NASCAR NEXTEL Cup Series season, the annual Budweiser Shootout at Daytona.

BUDWEISER SHOOTOUT
February 12th, 2005

Fin.	St.	Driver	Laps	Led	Status
1	17	Jimmie Johnson	70	16	Running
2	7	Ryan Newman	70	4	Running
3	11	Jeff Gordon	70		Running
4	8	Tony Stewart	70		Running
5	2	Greg Biffle	70	44	Running
6	6	Kurt Busch	70		Running
7	12	Dale Earnhardt Jr.	70		Running
8	14	Mark Martin	70		Running
9	13	Kasey Kahne	70		Running
10	19	Bobby Labonte	70	3	Running
11	16	Joe Nemechek	70		Running
12	9	Ricky Rudd	70		Running
13	18	Casey Mears	70	2	Running
14	15	Rusty Wallace	70		Running
15	1	Dale Jarrett	70	1	Running
16	5	Ken Schrader	70		Running
17	3	Bill Elliott	70		Running
18	10	Jeremy Mayfield	70		Running
19	4	Brian Vickers	46		Rear End
20	20	Geoffrey Bodine	9		Too Slow

Biffle took over the point before the field circled the track for the second time and led the next 43 circuits.

Opting for track position, Ryan Newman decided on two tires during a round of pit stops and assumed the lead, but his strategy prevailed for only four laps before Jimmie Johnson powered past the ALLTEL Dodge and led the final 16 circuits on the way to a convincing win in the caution-free sprint and a hefty check worth nearly $213,000.

The next day's main attraction was Bud Pole qualifying for the Daytona 500, and Johnson continued to show the strength of his Lowe's Chevrolet by posting a lap at 188.170 mph, which bested all drivers except Jarrett, who circled the 2.5-mile tri-oval at 188.312 mph to score his third career Daytona 500 pole. Jeff Gordon turned the third-fastest lap to join Jarrett and Johnson as the only drivers to break the 188-mph mark in qualifying.

Next up on the Speedweeks schedule was Thursday's Gatorade Duel at Daytona — a pair of 150-mile races (formerly called the Gatorade Twin 125s) to determine the starting field for the Daytona 500. Lineup procedures were modified to conform to the new rules, with those drivers

in even-numbered positions in the final 2004 point standings starting in the first Duel and drivers in the odd-numbered positions starting in the second. Those who were not among the top 35 at the end of last season were split between the two events, and all drivers were lined up based on their qualifying speeds.

(Above) Ken Schrader's crew tends to the No. 49 BAM Racing Dodge during the first Gatorade Duel at Daytona. Schrader finished the 60-lap contest on the lead lap to secure the 31st starting position for the Daytona 500.

(Left) Tony Stewart celebrates his win in the second Gatorade Duel. Stewart took the lead from Jeff Burton with 12 laps remaining and led from there to win the first Daytona qualifying race of his career.

(Below) Two-time Daytona 500 winner Michael Waltrip shone in the first Gatorade Duel, passing Mike Skinner on the final lap and barely beating teammate Dale Earnhardt Jr. in a side-by-side finish to score the win.

(Bottom) Dale Jarrett started on the pole for the Bud Shootout by the luck of the draw, but the next day he proved it was his for the taking by posting the fastest lap in qualifying and winning his third Daytona 500 Bud Pole.

In Duel No. 1, as in the Bud Shootout, Jarrett jumped to the early lead from the pole, an advantage that lasted but one lap. This time it was Jeff Gordon who shot past to lead the next 28 circuits. Michael Waltrip worked his way through the field from his 18th starting spot and arrived at the front on Lap 33, holding the point until pitting during the second caution of the race.

Mike Skinner, driving a Dodge for Bill Davis Racing, had been running among the lead pack and emerged at the point with 10 laps remaining and held that position through the third and final caution, which set up a four-lap sprint to the finish. Leading on the restart, Skinner tried his best but could not hold off the fleet-running Waltrip, who moved into the lead before taking the white flag and held on for the win ahead of Dale Earnhardt Jr., while Skinner fell to third.

Johnson led off Duel No. 2 and appeared strongest in the field, leading three times for 28 laps before becoming involved in a multi-car accident along the backstretch. That left Jeff Burton and Tony Stewart to battle it out between them, with Stewart taking the point from Burton with 12 laps to go and hanging on for the victory.

With the preliminaries out of the way, the Daytona 500 starting field was set behind Jarrett and Johnson. Duel winners Waltrip and Stewart filled the second row ahead of Earnhardt and Burton, while Skinner lined up alongside Kevin Lepage, who had a strong third-place showing in his Duel 150 driving a Dodge fielded by John Carter. Ryan Newman and reigning NASCAR Busch Series champion Martin Truex Jr. rounded out the top 10.

Fourteen drivers failed to make it into the Daytona 500, while Joe Nemechek, Dave Blaney, Rusty Wallace, Kasey Kahne and Kevin Harvick all moved to backup cars following accidents in their qualifying races and were forced to start at the rear of the field.

Defending Daytona 500 champ Dale Earnhardt Jr. climbs aboard the Budweiser Chevrolet during a practice session. Earnhardt nearly pulled off a back-to-back wins, but wound up a close third behind Jeff Gordon and Kurt Busch.

Sunny skies and mild Florida temperatures greeted the crowd of 200,000 fans on Sunday as engines roared to life to begin the official start of the 2005 NASCAR NEXTEL Cup Series season.

Johnson continued to demonstrate the power of his Hendrick Chevrolet by leading the first three laps before giving way to a hard-charging Stewart and his Home Depot Mote Carlo. Stewart then began a dominating run, leading seven times in large chucks for a total of 107 laps. Eleven other drivers took their turns at the front, but as the race wore on, it appeared more and more likely that Stewart had the winning mount.

While the battle ensued among the lead pack, defending race winner Earnhardt Jr. quietly toured the high-banked superspeedway, fighting an ill-handling Budweiser Chevrolet while avoiding trouble. Earnhardt had fallen back as far as 25th place after receiving an air-pressure adjustment that did not suit his car. Pete Rondeau, in his first official race as crew chief of the No. 8, discussed the problem with his driver over the radio and made corrections on the next stop.

With 48 laps to go and the Chevrolet's handling mended, Earnhardt began slicing through the field toward the leaders. With 15 circuits remaining, he had his sights firmly set on Stewart and closed in on his bumper before the caution flag appeared for the 10th time.

Stewart led the field through the first turn following the restart on Lap 195 with Earnhardt right behind. As they hit the backstretch, Earnhardt swept to the outside and eased into the lead for the first time in the race while the crowd roared its approval. Stewart charged right back, leading at the stripe on Lap 196, only to see Earnhardt pull away once again on the next lap.

Twice before, Jeff Gordon had conquered the biggest race of the year, and on both occasions he did it with daring, skillful moves in the closing laps of the race. Now, with three laps remaining of the scheduled 200, Gordon, who had followed Stewart closely for most of the race, knew it was now or never. With Earnhardt and Stewart glued nose-to-tail in the low groove, Gordon faded up the track with Johnson on his bumper and pulled alongside the defending Daytona 500 champion through the first turn and onto the backstretch.

"I had momentum," Gordon later said. "I went to the outside of the '20' car, and [Earnhardt] went with the '20' car. That was a risk that I was willing to take to try to win the race, even though I might end up finishing 10th."

Once again, it appeared that a restrictor-plate battle would come down to Gordon and Earnhardt, and as the two drivers charged to the line, Gordon eased ahead on the outside to lead Lap 198.

Ricky Rudd (21) fights to save the Motorcraft Ford after cutting a tire in turn four during the early going in the Daytona 500. Carl Edwards (99) squeezes past with Jamie McMurray on the high side.

What's left of Scott Wimmer's Caterpillar Dodge sits on the apron after tumbling out of the fourth turn in a late-race melee. Wimmer was uninjured in the incident.

"I got the lead, then Jeff got a run around the outside and got by me," Earnhardt said after the race. "I couldn't stop him, he was going too fast."

But with victory in sight, another car brushed the wall, sending debris onto the track. The yellow flag flew immediately, which set up the first green-white-checkered finish of the new season.

Sophomore drivers Scott Riggs (10) and Kasey Kahne (9) tackle Daytona's high banks. Riggs got his season off to a particularly fine start by following up a fifth-place effort in his Gatorade Duel with a career-best fourth-place finish in the Daytona 500.

GATORADE DUEL NO.1
Thursday, February 17, 2005

Fin.	St.	Driver	Laps	Led	Status
1	18	Michael Waltrip	60	13	Running
2	21	Dale Earnhardt Jr.	60		Running
3	8	Mike Skinner	60	9	Running
4	16	Ryan Newman	60		Running
5	5	Ricky Rudd	60		Running
6	4	Kurt Busch	60		Running
7	2	Jeff Gordon	60	28	Running
8	12	Jamie McMurray	60		Running
9	11	Kyle Busch	60		Running
10	22	Kenny Wallace	60		Running
11	17	Kerry Earnhardt	60		Running
12	3	Jason Leffler	60	2	Running
13	9	Greg Biffle	60		Running
14	25	Travis Kvapil	60		Running
15	14	Carl Edwards	60		Running
16	15	Mike Wallace	60		Running
17	19	Casey Mears	60		Running
18	26	Stanton Barrett	60		Running
19	20	Ken Schrader	60		Running
20	7	Kyle Petty	60		Running
21	1	Dale Jarrett	60	1	Running
22	13	Mike Bliss	60		Running
23	23	Johnny Sauter	54	6	Engine
24	10	Kasey Kahne	52	1	Accident
25	24	Hermie Sadler	46		Accident
26	6	Elliott Sadler	45		Trans.
27	28	Randy LaJoie	41		Engine
28	27	Morgan Shepherd	3		Accident

GATORADE DUEL NO.2
Thursday, February 17, 2005

Fin.	St.	Driver	Laps	Led	Status
1	13	Tony Stewart	60	12	Running
2	7	Jeff Burton	60	13	Running
3	20	Kevin Lepage	60		Running
4	15	Martin Truex Jr.	60		Running
5	4	Scott Riggs	60		Running
6	22	Matt Kenseth	60		Running
7	18	Robby Gordon	60		Running
8	12	Scott Wimmer	60	1	Running
9	16	Sterling Marlin	60		Running
10	5	Boris Said	60		Running
11	6	John Andretti	60		Running
12	11	Bobby Labonte	60	1	Running
13	24	Bobby Hamilton Jr.	60		Running
14	25	Derrike Cope	60		Running
15	9	Jeremy Mayfield	60		Running
16	28	Jeff Green	60		Running
17	21	Eric McClure	60		Running
18	26	Larry Gunselman	59		Running
19	17	Brian Vickers	39		Rear End
20	1	Jimmie Johnson	35	20	Accident
21	2	Kevin Harvick	35	13	Accident
22	10	Mark Martin	35		Accident
23	3	Joe Nemechek	35		Accident
24	8	Rusty Wallace	35		Accident
25	14	Dave Blaney	35		Accident
26	27	Andy Belmont	24		Accident
27	19	Kirk Shelmerdine	2		Accident
28	23	Greg Sacks	2		Accident

Jeff Gordon (24) heads for the checkers with Kurt Busch (97) in tow. While Jimmie Johnson (48) and Dale Earnhardt Jr. diced for position in the outside lane, Gordon scooted away to his third Daytona 500 victory.

DAYTONA 500

NASCAR NEXTEL Cup Series Race No. 1

Fin. Pos.	Start Pos.	Car No.	Driver	Team	Laps	Laps Led	Status
1	15	24	Jeff Gordon	DuPont Chevrolet	203	29	Running
2	13	97	Kurt Busch	Sharpie/IRWIN Industrial Tools Ford	203		Running
3	5	8	Dale Earnhardt Jr.	Budweiser Chevrolet	203	2	Running
4	12	10	Scott Riggs	Valvoline Chevrolet	203		Running
5	2	48	Jimmie Johnson	Lowe's Chevrolet	203	3	Running
6	32	6	Mark Martin	Viagra Ford	203		Running
7	4	20	Tony Stewart	The Home Depot Chevrolet	203	107	Running
8	10	40	Sterling Marlin	Coors Light Dodge	203		Running
9	8	37	Kevin Lepage	Patron Tequila Dodge	203		Running
10	36	2	Rusty Wallace	Miller Lite Dodge	203		Running
11	39	38	Elliott Sadler	M&M's Ford	203		Running
12	27	99	Carl Edwards	Office Depot Ford	203		Running
13	34	01	Joe Nemechek	U.S. Army Chevrolet	203	2	Running
14	38	07	Dave Blaney	Jack Daniel's Chevrolet	203		Running
15	1	88	Dale Jarrett	UPS Ford	203		Running
16	26	43	Jeff Green	Cheerios/Betty Crocker Dodge	203		Running
17	33	45	Kyle Petty	Georgia-Pacific/Brawny Dodge	203	1	Running
18	35	0	Mike Bliss	NetZero/Best Buy Chevrolet	203		Running
19	25	77 #	Travis Kvapil	Kodak/Jasper Eng. & Trans. Dodge	203		Running
20	9	12	Ryan Newman	ALLTEL Dodge	203	1	Running
21	28	25	Brian Vickers	GMAC/ditech.com Chevrolet	203		Running
22	37	9	Kasey Kahne	Dodge Dealers/UAW Dodge	203		Running
23	24	19	Jeremy Mayfield	Dodge Dealers/UAW Dodge	203	1	Running
24	11	21	Ricky Rudd	Motorcraft Quality Parts Ford	202		Running
25	23	16	Greg Biffle	National Guard Ford	201		Running
26	29	41	Casey Mears	Target Dodge	199		Running
27	41	36	Boris Said	Centrix Financial Chevrolet	198		Running
28	30	29	Kevin Harvick	GM Goodwrench Chevrolet	198	1	Running
29	6	31	Jeff Burton	Cingular Wireless Chevrolet	194	6	Running
30	7	23	Mike Skinner	Bill Davis Racing Dodge	187		Accident
31	42	14	John Andretti	VB/APlus at Sunoco Ford	187		Accident
32	17	42	Jamie McMurray	Texaco/Havoline Dodge	184		Accident
33	16	22	Scott Wimmer	Caterpillar Dodge	182	8	Accident
34	10	1	Martin Truex Jr.	Bass Pro Shops Chevrolet	178		Engine
35	22	32	Bobby Hamilton Jr.	Tide Coldwater Chevrolet	173		Running
36	40	11	Jason Leffler	FedEx Express Chevrolet	168		Accident
37	3	15	Michael Waltrip	NAPA Auto Parts Chevrolet	161	42	Engine
38	19	5 #	Kyle Busch	Kellogg's Chevrolet	148		Running
39	31	49	Ken Schrader	Schwan's Home Service Dodge	120		Engine
40	21	00	Kenny Wallace	Aaron's Chevrolet	39		Engine
41	43	4	Mike Wallace	Lucas Oil Chevrolet	35		Overheating
42	14	17	Matt Kenseth	DeWalt Power Tools Ford	34		Engine
43	20	18	Bobby Labonte	Interstate Batteries Chevrolet	14		Engine

Raybestos Rookie of the Year Contender.

Track crews were quickly disbursed and, on Lap 202, Gordon led the field onto the frontstretch ahead Earnhardt, Johnson, Kurt Busch, Scott Riggs and Stewart for the two-lap sprint to the finish.

As they came up to speed, it was clear that anyone with designs on passing Gordon would have to do it on the outside. Earnhardt moved up the track with Johnson right behind. Stewart made his attempt to go high but was blocked by Johnson in a move that allowed Kurt Busch to tuck in behind the leader.

While the challengers jostled for any advantage they could get, Gordon held firm on the inside and took the checkers with Busch still trailing in second. Earnhardt settled for third ahead of Riggs, who posted a very solid finish in the Valvoline Chevrolet. Johnson fell in line in fifth, while Stewart faded over the final lap-and-a-half to take seventh behind Mark Martin.

Reflecting on his accomplishment with reporters, Gordon said: "When I think of Daytona victories here, especially the two Daytona 500s (Gordon won in 1997 and 1999), they all came down to something that you had to do ... out of the ordinary, to make a risky move, to do something to get the victory. It was not given to us. It wasn't just something that was easy. It took hard work and it took risk taking."

Those risks now had paid off in winning the series' biggest race three times to join multiple winners Richard Petty (seven), Cale Yarborough (four) and Dale Jarrett (three) as the only drivers to win the Daytona 500 more than twice.

"To have three now is just incredible," Gordon mused. "That's some great company to be a part of."

AUTO CLUB 500

In the hyper-competitive world of the NASCAR NEXTEL Cup Series, predictions — particularly of winning — are seldom and bold. At California Speedway, Greg Biffle was not shy regarding his chances in the Auto Club 500, feeling so confident that, after qualifying fifth, he forecasted he would go to the front by Lap 5 and had a great shot at winning the event.

As it turned out, it took Biffle just four laps to reach the point and, indeed, he went on to post the win. It was, however, anything but easy.

Biffle's challenging weekend began much like everyone else's, with all competitors having to adjust to the new format of practice followed by qualifying, after which all cars would be impounded by NASCAR until race time.

Kyle Busch, in the CAR-QUEST Chevrolet, looks for an opening to the inside of Jeremy Mayfield (19) with a double-file pack bearing down from behind. Busch made history two days earlier when he became NASCAR's youngest-ever pole winner.

Perhaps that adjustment was felt least by rookie Kyle Busch who, in his eighth NASCAR NEX-TEL Cup Series event, blistered the two-mile oval at 188.245 mph and captured the first pole of his young career. Busch's track-record lap also distinguished him as the youngest pole winner in NASCAR NEXTEL Cup Series history at 19 years, 9 months and 24 days, supplanting a record set in 1952 by 20-year-old Donald Thomas at Georgia's Lakewood Speedway.

Sophomore driver Brian Vickers set the second-fastest time in qualifying and would line up to the outside of his young Hendrick teammate, while five drivers — John Andretti, Randy LaJoie, Kevin Lepage, Elliott Sadler and Jeff Green — were sent to the back of the field for impound violations, where they joined Tony Stewart (transmission change) and Dave Blaney (backup car) for the start of the race.

When the green flag dropped, Biffle watched as Busch and Vickers took turns leading the first three laps. With some heat in his tires, Biffle dropped the hammer and blew past the Hendrick duo and into the lead.

Once in clean air, however, Biffle suddenly found that his car was extremely loose and had to fight to keep the National Guard Ford in front. The day's first caution came at Lap 26 and provided a welcome opportunity for crew chief Doug Richert to begin adjusting the chassis on Biffle's Ford.

Greg Biffle brings the lead pack to pit road during the first of the event's seven cautions. Biffle, who needed adjustments at the time, would not return to the lead until the final stages of the race.

TOP 10 QUALIFIERS

Pos.	Driver	Seconds	mph
1	Kyle Busch	38.248	*188.245
2	Brian Vickers	38.351	187.740
3	Jeremy Mayfield	38.377	187.612
4	Joe Nemechek	38.392	187.539
5	Greg Biffle	38.502	187.003
6	Matt Kenseth	38.503	186.998
7	Dale Jarrett	38.580	186.625
8	Jimmie Johnson	38.610	186.480
9	Ryan Newman	38.614	186.461
10	Mike Bliss	38.626	186.403

* Track Record

Thus began a tumultuous afternoon for Biffle. Two times he was forced to fight his way through traffic from the back of the field — once following an extended pit stop to insert a spring rubber, and again when he was caught by a caution flag while pitting under green.

Ultimately, the outcome of the Auto Club 500 had as much to do with pit strategy as it did with who had the fastest car.

Jimmie Johnson, a California winner in 2002, had been running among the leaders when the day's fifth caution appeared with 90 laps remaining, and Johnson elected to take fuel only, trading fresh tires for track position. That gamble would prove to work against him as the Lowe's Chevrolet faded to 10th place by the time the next yellow appeared some 40 laps later.

Rusty Wallace (2) and Bobby Labonte (18) battle down the frontstretch while Jeff Green (43) makes it three wide on the outside. Wallace matched his 10th-place finish in the Daytona 500 to get his season off to a solid start, while Labonte completed the day in 13th, a much-needed effort after falling to last place at Daytona.

The day's seventh and final yellow flag appeared with 32 laps to go, and Johnson, along with Kevin Harvick and Jamie McMurray pitted for fresh tires. This time, Biffle made the quick decision to gamble and stayed on the track along with Roush teammates Kurt Busch, Mark Martin and Carl Edwards.

Busch paced the field on the final restart and managed to lead the next seven circuits before Biffle surged into the lead for only the second time in the race. With older tires, however, Biffle's car again became a handful, and he struggled mightily to keep it off the wall as he wrestled the Ford through the corners.

(Above) Greg Biffle (16) looks for room on the inside of Jimmie Johnson (48) in California's first turn. Later, Johnson would challenge Biffle for the win but fall just short as the laps ran out.

(Left) Dave Blaney's Jack Daniel's Chevrolet shows the aftermath of a practice crash that relegated Blaney to his backup car for the race. That one didn't fare much better as Blaney met the fourth-turn wall before the 150-lap mark.

(Opposing Page) Greg Biffle celebrates his triumph in the Auto Club 500. He took the lead with 23 laps remaining after gambling against a pit stop late in the race and held on to take his second win his last three starts, dating back to the 2004 season finale at Homestead-Miami.

AUTO CLUB 500

NASCAR NEXTEL Cup Series Race No. 2

Fin. Pos.	Start Pos.	Car No.	Driver	Team	Laps	Laps Led	Status
1	5	16	Greg Biffle	National Guard/Post-It Ford	250	46	Running
2	8	48	Jimmie Johnson	Lowe's Chevrolet	250	4	Running
3	20	97	Kurt Busch	Sharpie Ford	250	11	Running
4	15	42	Jamie McMurray	Texaco/Havoline Dodge	250		Running
5	19	99	Carl Edwards	Office Depot Ford	250	33	Running
6	31	29	Kevin Harvick	GM Goodwrench Chevrolet	250	23	Running
7	18	6	Mark Martin	Viagra Ford	250	4	Running
8	41	38	Elliott Sadler	Pedigree/M&M's Ford	250		Running
9	9	12	Ryan Newman	ALLTEL Dodge	250		Running
10	23	2	Rusty Wallace	Miller Lite Dodge	250		Running
11	7	88	Dale Jarrett	UPS Ford	250		Running
12	10	0	Mike Bliss	NetZero Best Buy Chevrolet	250		Running
13	14	18	Bobby Labonte	Interstate Batteries Chevrolet	250		Running
14	38	49	Ken Schrader	Schwan's Home Service Dodge	250		Running
15	13	40	Sterling Marlin	Coors Light Dodge	250		Running
16	27	22	Scott Wimmer	Caterpillar Dodge	250		Running
17	29	20	Tony Stewart	The Home Depot Chevrolet	250		Running
18	36	45	Kyle Petty	Georgia-Pacific/Brawny Dodge	250	2	Running
19	32	31	Jeff Burton	Cingular Wireless Chevrolet	250		Running
20	26	32	Bobby Hamilton Jr.	Tide/Give Kids the World Chevrolet	250		Running
21	2	25	Brian Vickers	GMAC Chevrolet	250	1	Running
22	16	41	Casey Mears	Target Dodge	249		Running
23	1	5 #	Kyle Busch	CARQUEST/Kellogg's Chevrolet	249	2	Running
24	35	77 #	Travis Kvapil	Kodak/Jasper Eng. & Trans. Dodge	249		Running
25	33	4	Mike Wallace	Lucas Oil Chevrolet	249		Running
26	6	17	Matt Kenseth	USG Sheetrock/DeWalt Ford	249	57	Running
27	37	43	Jeff Green	General Mills Whole Grain Dodge	249	1	Running
28	3	19	Jeremy Mayfield	Dodge Dealers/UAW Dodge	248	1	Running
29	24	14	John Andretti	VB/APlus at Sunoco Ford	248		Running
30	28	24	Jeff Gordon	DuPont Chevrolet	246		Engine
31	43	37	Kevin Lepage	R&J Racing Dodge	241		Running
32	40	8	Dale Earnhardt Jr.	Budweiser Chevrolet	237		Running
33	12	10	Scott Riggs	Valvoline Chevrolet	229		Engine
34	42	07	Dave Blaney	Jack Daniel's Chevrolet	224		Running
35	25	7	Robby Gordon	Harrah's Chevrolet	222		Engine
36	11	44	Terry Labonte	Kellogg's Chevrolet	216		Rear Gear
37	39	11	Jason Leffler	FedEx Express Chevrolet	215		Engine
38	30	15	Michael Waltrip	NAPA Auto Parts Chevrolet	203		Engine
39	4	01	Joe Nemechek	U.S. Army Chevrolet	180	63	Engine
40	17	9	Kasey Kahne	Dodge Dealers/UAW Dodge	167		Accident
41	21	21	Ricky Rudd	Motorcraft Genuine Parts Ford	145		Engine
42	34	34	Randy LaJoie	Mach 1 Racing Chevrolet	47	2	Transmission
43	22	91	Bill Elliott	Stanley Tools Dodge	23		Accident

Raybestos Rookie of the Year Contender.

NASCAR NEXTEL Cup Series Point Standings
(After 2 Races)

Pos.	Driver	Points	Behind	Change
1	**Kurt Busch**	**340**	—	+1
2	Jimmie Johnson	335	-5	+3
3	Mark Martin	301	-39	+4
4	Carl Edwards	287	-53	+9
5	Greg Biffle	273	-67	+20
6	Elliott Sadler	272	-68	+5
7	Tony Stewart	268	-72	-1
8	Rusty Wallace	268	-72	+2
9	Sterling Marlin	260	-80	-1
10	Jeff Gordon	258	-82	-9

Johnson, this time shod with four fresh tires, had restarted from 10th place and began to track down the leaders. One by one, the Lowe's driver picked off his competition, arriving on Busch's bumper with just three laps to go. Johnson dispatched of Busch and set his sights on Biffle, closing the gap in chunks as the final laps clicked by.

At the checkered flag, Biffle managed to outlast the Hendrick driver by just 0.231-second, while Busch trailed close behind in third.

"Coming through [traffic], I really thought I could get up to fourth," said Johnson. "And then before I knew it, I had caught [Biffle] and [Busch]. If we just had another corner, I think there would have been a different outcome to the race. ... But it was a great finish."

"Ninety percent of the time in our sport, the fastest car doesn't win the race," Biffle stated flatly after capturing his fourth career victory. "Today, the fastest car won."

Biffle also benefited when other contenders fell by the wayside. Joe Nemechek, who led 63 laps, suffered engine failure on Lap 178. Matt Kenseth led 57 laps but cut a tire in the late going and fell to 26th place. Defending Auto Club 500 champion and three-time California winner Jeff Gordon was running in the top five but had engine problems as well and finished 30th, while Kasey Kahne, who barely missed his first victory here last September, crashed on Lap 160 while running in the top 10.

UAW-DaimlerChrysler 400

Homecomings are supposed to be fun. So that's exactly how Las Vegas natives Kurt and Kyle Busch approached the UAW-DaimlerChrysler 400 at beautiful Las Vegas Motor Speedway.

Kurt Busch returned to his home track triumphantly as the defending NASCAR NEXTEL Cup Series champion, and although he had yet to crack the top five in his four previous starts there, he was well aware of the stranglehold Roush Racing had on the 1.5-mile tri-oval. In the previous seven events at Las Vegas, Roush drivers had accounted for five victories, including two straight by Matt Kenseth in the last two years. Given that, and how the Roush juggernaut had rolled to two straight series championships, Busch had plenty of reasons to be optimistic.

Matt Kenseth pits under green with a cut tire, a stop that cost him two laps to the leaders. The two-time defending event winner fought back onto the lead lap and was able finish in eighth place, his best result of the season so far.

The battered Budweiser Chevrolet limps toward the garage after Dale Earnhardt Jr. plowed into Brian Vickers on lap 12. The cars of Ricky Rudd and Bobby Labonte also sustained heavy damage as a result of the incident.

The younger Busch, Kyle, returned home riding an emotional wave after scoring his first Bud Pole two weeks ago at California Speedway in just his eighth series start. He knew that despite problems suffered at California by several teams running Hendrick-built engines — himself included — director of engine assembly Jeff Andrews and his team of more than 100 at Hendrick Motorsports had been burning the midnight oil over the two weeks between California and Las Vegas to correct any lingering issues.

The rookie driver also knew that his Hendrick teammate, Jeff Gordon, with a win in the Daytona 500, had officially broken DEI's domination of restrictor-plate races, and Kyle was determined to do the same to Roush Racing at Las Vegas.

The week off gave team members time to ponder some of the changes the new season had brought about. First, NASCAR had implemented an electronic timing system to clock the speeds of all cars over the entire length of pit road — largely in response to competitors' complaints about inconsistencies in the "manual" method used in the past.

At Daytona, 17 speeding penalties were handed out, a number that shrank significantly to just three at California. Although some drivers were still unhappy, all were necessarily coping as NASCAR NEXTEL Cup Series Director John Darby announced that the new system would become permanent — at least for now.

Fans were treated to a spectacular day in the picturesque southern Nevada desert.

TOP 10 QUALIFIERS

Pos.	Driver	Seconds	mph
1	Ryan Newman	31.080	173.745
2	Elliott Sadler	31.086	173.712
3	Greg Biffle	31.181	173.182
4	Scott Riggs	31.410	171.920
5	Kurt Busch	31.420	171.865
6	Travis Kvapil	31.447	171.717
7	Kasey Kahne	31.482	171.527
8	Matt Kenseth	31.589	170.946
9	Jimmie Johnson	31.607	170.848
10	Kyle Busch	31.610	170.832

(Top, Opposing page) Kevin Harvick (29) finds room to pass on the inside of Casey Mears (41), while Ryan Newman tries to make up ground on the outside. After starting at the rear under penalty, Harvick fought all the way to a fifth-place finish in a very strong effort.

(Above) One of Ken Schrader's crew members prepares tires prior to the 400-miler at Las Vegas. Newer, softer tires combined with shorter rear spoilers still had some teams flustered in trying to figure out their race-day setups.

(Right) NASCAR NEXTEL Cup Series officials check the wheelbase on Joe Nemechek's U.S. Army Chevrolet during inspection. Penalties for rules violations were handed out to several teams at Las Vegas, including those of race-winner Jimmie Johnson, runner-up Kyle Busch and Kevin Harvick.

The Auto Club 500 was the first event run using the new "aero" package with shorter rear spoilers and softer tires, and that also met with mixed reviews. The consensus was that the new rules favored those drivers who could more easily cope with a loose race car and who had formulated setups better suited to the softer tire compounds.

Again, NASCAR stated the rules would stay in effect, although they would keep a close eye on how competition was affected and continue to solicit feedback from teams and manufacturers as the season progressed.

Las Vegas was also the second event at which cars would be impounded immediately after qualifying and held until race time. Polemeister Ryan Newman (26 over the last three seasons) got back on track with his first of 2005, followed by Elliott Sadler, Greg Biffle and Kevin Harvick.

For Harvick, however, the fourth-fastest lap turned against him when an illegal fuel cell was discovered during post-qualifying inspection. In response to the violation, the GM Goodwrench Chevrolet was sent to the rear of the field for the start of the race.

A beautiful day in the Nevada desert greeted an estimated 156,000 fans, all on hand to witness a race that featured a record-tying 25 lead changes among 12 drivers and a record-setting 10 yellow flags.

As always, the cautions turned out to be bad news for some, a blessing for others. The first yellow appeared just 12 laps into the event when Dale Earnhardt Jr. ran into Brian Vickers, abruptly ending the day for both. Earnhardt took the blame, citing simple driver error, but the resulting 42nd-place finish combined with a 32nd place at California had the Budweiser Chevrolet driver mired at 27th in the early-season point standings.

Conversely, Jimmie Johnson found the cautions working to his benefit. Johnson began the event fighting a loose setup, but with each stop on pit road, crew chief Chad Knaus was able to make adjustments that continuously improved the handling of the Lowe's Chevrolet.

(Above) Jimmie Johnson (48) and pole-winner Ryan Newman (12) come to the stripe side by side while racing for the lead. The pair battled late in the race, trading the top position between them seven times over a 30-lap stretch before Johnson took over for good.

(Opposing Page) Jimmie Johnson gives the "thumbs up" after driving to his first win of the season, the 15th of his career. That, combined with a fifth at Daytona and a runner-up finish at California put him atop the points. Days later, a penalty for failing post-race inspection would drop him to second in points behind Kurt Busch.

UAW-DAIMLERCHRYSLER 400 — NASCAR NEXTEL Cup Series Race No. 3

Fin. Pos.	Start Pos.	Car No.	Driver	Team	Laps	Laps Led	Status
1	9	48	Jimmie Johnson	Lowe's Chevrolet	267	107	Running
2	10	5 #	Kyle Busch	Kellogg's Chevrolet	267		Running
3	5	97	Kurt Busch	Sharpie Ford	267	40	Running
4	11	24	Jeff Gordon	DuPont Chevrolet	267		Running
5	42	29	Kevin Harvick	GM Goodwrench Chevrolet	267		Running
6	3	16	Greg Biffle	National Guard Ford	267	52	Running
7	15	41	Casey Mears	Target/Energizer Dodge	267		Running
8	8	17	Matt Kenseth	DeWalt Power Tools Ford	267		Running
9	1	12	Ryan Newman	Mobil 1/ALLTEL Dodge	267	44	Running
10	23	20	Tony Stewart	The Home Depot Chevrolet	267		Running
11	16	32	Bobby Hamilton Jr.	Tide Chevrolet	267		Running
12	21	2	Rusty Wallace	Mobil 1/Miller Lite Dodge	267		Running
13	29	07	Dave Blaney	Jack Daniel's Chevrolet	267	7	Running
14	20	99	Carl Edwards	World Financial Group Ford	267		Running
15	22	42	Jamie McMurray	Texaco/Havoline Dodge	267		Running
16	18	0	Mike Bliss	NetZero Best Buy Chevrolet	267		Running
17	24	31	Jeff Burton	Cingular Wireless Chevrolet	267		Running
18	13	88	Dale Jarrett	UPS Ford	267		Running
19	12	01	Joe Nemechek	U.S. Army Chevrolet	267		Running
20	26	19	Jeremy Mayfield	Dodge Dealers/UAW Dodge	267		Running
21	36	15	Michael Waltrip	NAPA Auto Parts Chevrolet	266		Running
22	17	11	Jason Leffler	FedEx Express Chevrolet	266		Running
23	39	43	Jeff Green	Cheerios/Betty Crocker Dodge	266	1	Running
24	30	4	Mike Wallace	Lucas Oil Chevrolet	266	1	Running
25	35	45	Kyle Petty	Georgia-Pacific/Brawny Dodge	266	2	Running
26	6	77 #	Travis Kvapil	Kodak/Jasper Eng. & Trans. Dodge	266	9	Running
27	28	22	Scott Wimmer	Caterpillar Dodge	266		Running
28	37	14	John Andretti	VB/APlus at Sunoco Ford	265		Running
29	2	38	Elliott Sadler	M&M's Ford	265		Running
30	19	6	Mark Martin	Viagra Ford	243		Running
31	4	10	Scott Riggs	Valvoline Chevrolet	243		Running
32	41	73 #	Eric McClure	ARC Dehooker/RFA Chevrolet	237		Too Slow
33	40	66	Hermie Sadler	Peak Fitness/Stratosphere LV Ford	226		Accident
34	14	49	Ken Schrader	Schwan's Home Service Dodge	225		Running
35	25	40	Sterling Marlin	Coors Light Dodge	219	1	Running
36	38	34	Randy LaJoie	Mach 1 Inc. Chevrolet	182		Engine
37	33	21	Ricky Rudd	Motorcraft Quality Parts Ford	181		Running
38	7	9	Kasey Kahne	Dodge Dealers/UAW Dodge	154	1	Accident
39	27	7	Robby Gordon	Harrah's Chevrolet	57		Engine
40	43	89	Morgan Shepherd	Racing with Jesus/Red Line Oil Dodge	39	2	Too Slow
41	31	18	Bobby Labonte	Interstate Batteries Chevrolet	15		Accident
42	34	8	Dale Earnhardt Jr.	Budweiser Chevrolet	11		Accident
43	32	25	Brian Vickers	GMAC/ditech.com Chevrolet	11		Accident

Raybestos Rookie of the Year Contender.

NASCAR NEXTEL Cup Series Point Standings
(After 3 Races)

Pos.	Driver	Points	Behind	Change
1	**Kurt Busch**	**510**	—	—
2	Jimmie Johnson	*500	-10	—
3	Greg Biffle	428	-82	+2
4	Jeff Gordon	418	-92	+6
5	Carl Edwards	408	-102	-1
6	Tony Stewart	402	-108	+1
7	Rusty Wallace	395	-115	+1
8	Ryan Newman	389	-121	+4
9	Mark Martin	374	-136	-6
10	Kevin Harvick	*369	-141	+3

* Point Totals Reflect 25-Point Penalties for Rules Violations

By the 200-lap mark, Johnson had finally worked his way up to second place behind leader Newman and was able to make his first challenge for the lead. The Dodge and Chevrolet drivers dueled vigorously before Johnson was able to pull away with 55 laps remaining.

Like Johnson, the multiple interruptions allowed Kyle Busch and crew chief Alan Gustafson to correct an ill-handling Chevrolet that was far too tight in the center of the corners. Although he ran among the top 10 all day, Busch finally got the Kellogg's Monte Carlo freed up enough to make a charge at his Hendrick teammate.

"I saw him coming," said Johnson of Busch, "and I thought, 'Run. He's hungry, he's at home, and he's in the same equipment I'm in.'

"I worked hard to get a cushion so that if I had problems with lapped traffic, I had space to give up or play with."

That thinking ultimately made the difference, as lapped traffic allowed Busch to close the gap, but only enough to cross the finish line in second place, 1.661 seconds behind Johnson.

Kurt Busch trailed the Hendrick duo in third ahead of Jeff Gordon, who managed to salvage fourth after a late-race tussle with Newman that dropped the ALLTEL Dodge driver to ninth. Harvick drove a hard-fought race that included a penalty for speeding on pit road to rally to a fifth-place finish.

GOLDEN CORRAL 500

The excitement at Hendrick Motorsports surrounding the 1-2 finish by teammates Jimmie Johnson and Kyle Busch at Las Vegas was dampened somewhat following post-race inspection when both cars were found to be in violation of the rules. Johnson's Lowe's Chevrolet measured too low at the roofline, while Busch's Kellogg's Monte Carlo was too high at the rear quarter panel.

Subsequently, both teams were docked 25 driver and owner points — although their finishes were allowed to stand — while crew chiefs Chad Knaus and Alan Gustafson were ultimately put on probation by NASCAR. Johnson's loss of 25 points had a particular sting in that it dropped him out of first place in the standings, where he now sat second behind Kurt Busch.

Pit road was a busy place during the Golden Corral 500 at Atlanta Motor Speedway. There were eight cautions for 40 laps in the 325-lap contest.

(Above) Cars pile up literally seconds after the initial green flag fell, when Casey Mears spun mid-pack. The accident involved 10 drivers, two of whom, Shane Hmiel and Travis Kvapil, retired from the race without being credited with completing a single lap.

(Right) Ryan Newman (left) and crew chief Matt Borland share a laugh in the garage after Newman notched his second consecutive Bud Pole with a lap at nearly 195 miles per hour.

Kevin Harvick and team owner Richard Childress also lost 25 points each for the illegal fuel cell found after Harvick's fourth-fastest qualifying run at Las Vegas, and NASCAR considered the infraction egregious enough to suspend crew chief Todd Berrier for four races.

With three events in the books, the early-season notion that the combined teams fielded by Roush Racing and Hendrick Motorsports would prove their superiority rang true. Jeff Gordon and Johnson and sandwiched their wins for Hendrick around Greg Biffle's triumph at California for Roush. That left Johnson and Gordon second and fourth in the points,

respectively, and rookie Kyle Busch had already made noise with a pole-winning run at California followed by his runner-up finish at Las Vegas.

Roush had four drivers in the top 10 entering Atlanta, led by Kurt Busch in first, with Biffle third and Carl Edwards fifth. With a poor 30th-place finish at Las Vegas, Mark Martin fell six positions to ninth place, 136 points behind Busch.

Leading the way for the Dodge Boys were Penske Racing South teammates Rusty Wallace and Ryan Newman, seventh and eighth in points and each with two top 10s to their credit.

Entering last week's UAW-DaimlerChrysler 400, Newman had gone a full four races without winning a Bud Pole dating back to last season. So, the three-time winner of the annual Bud Pole Award quickly put an end to that at Las Vegas. And just to show he hadn't lost his touch for turning fast laps, Newman followed that effort at Atlanta by posting a lap at 194.690 to grab his second pole of 2005.

Newman's lap was nearly a full mile per hour faster than that of Bobby Hamilton Jr., who raised some eyebrows by placing his Tide Chevrolet beside Newman on the front row for the start of the Golden Corral 500.

(Above) Greg Biffle's crew did an outstanding job throughout most of the day, consistently putting their driver on the track in front for restarts. But a pair of slower stops near the end of the race dropped Biffle to third, where he remained until the finish.

(Right, Above) Teammates Kasey Kahne (9) and Jeremy Mayfield (19) run nose to tail with Jeff Burton coming from behind. Kahne's fifth-place finish was a welcome turnaround after doing no better than 22nd in the season's first three events.

(Right, Below) Mike Bliss (0) and Michael Waltrip (15) race for position on Atlanta's frontstretch. Waltrip, who started 37th, picked up 30 positions during the race and gained his first top-10 finish of the season.

TOP 10 QUALIFIERS

Pos.	Driver	Seconds	mph
1	Ryan Newman	28.476	194.690
2	Bobby Hamilton Jr.	28.609	193.785
3	Jimmie Johnson	28.698	193.184
4	Carl Edwards	28.729	192.976
5	Kasey Kahne	28.891	191.894
6	Greg Biffle	28.988	191.252
7	Joe Nemechek	28.997	191.192
8	Brian Vickers	29.007	191.126
9	Tony Stewart	29.016	191.067
10	Jason Leffler	29.036	190.935

(Above) Carl Edwards (99) and Jimmie Johnson (48) take the checkered flag side by side after a thrilling last-lap duel for the win. Edwards' first NASCAR NEXTEL Cup Series victory came in his 17th career start.

(Left) Although disappointed not to win, Jimmie Johnson showed there were no hard feelings when he showed up to congratulate Edwards in victory lane.

Newman jumped out front at the drop of the green flag, but as he came around to complete Lap 1, the first of eight yellow flags was flying. Casey Mears, who started 15th and was already battling a loose race car, had the air taken off his spoiler in traffic and spun in front of the field. When the smoke cleared, 12 cars had been involved, including former Atlanta winners Bobby Labonte and Jeff Gordon.

Newman again led on the Lap-5 restart but immediately gave way to Johnson, who motored past to assume the point until the first round of green-flag pit stops.

GOLDEN CORRAL 500

NASCAR NEXTEL Cup Series Race No. 4

Fin. Pos.	Start Pos.	Car No.	Driver	Team	Laps	Laps Led	Status
1	4	99	Carl Edwards	Scotts Ford	325	9	Running
2	3	48	Jimmie Johnson	Lowe's Chevrolet	325	156	Running
3	6	16	Greg Biffle	National Guard/Post-It Ford	325	151	Running
4	12	6	Mark Martin	Viagra Ford	325	2	Running
5	5	9	Kasey Kahne	Dodge Dealers/UAW Dodge	325		Running
6	8	25	Brian Vickers	GMAC Chevrolet	325		Running
7	37	15	Michael Waltrip	NAPA Auto Parts Chevrolet	325		Running
8	27	07	Dave Blaney	Snap-On Chevrolet	325	1	Running
9	17	10	Scott Riggs	Valvoline Chevrolet	325		Running
10	11	38	Elliott Sadler	Combos Ford	325		Running
11	13	42	Jamie McMurray	Texaco/Havoline Dodge	325		Running
12	42	5 #	Kyle Busch	Kellogg's Chevrolet	325		Running
13	14	19	Jeremy Mayfield	Dodge Dealers/UAW Dodge	325		Running
14	1	12	Ryan Newman	ALLTEL Dodge	325	5	Running
15	38	31	Jeff Burton	Cingular Wireless Chevrolet	325		Running
16	39	40	Sterling Marlin	Coors Light Dodge	325		Running
17	9	20	Tony Stewart	The Home Depot Chevrolet	325		Running
18	16	0	Mike Bliss	Net Zero Best Buy Chevrolet	324		Running
19	15	41	Casey Mears	Nicorette Dodge	324		Running
20	33	22	Scott Wimmer	Caterpillar Dodge	324		Running
21	36	29	Kevin Harvick	GM Goodwrench Chevrolet	324		Running
22	18	91	Bill Elliott	Visteon Dodge	324		Running
23	34	88	Dale Jarrett	UPS Ford	323	1	Running
24	35	8	Dale Earnhardt Jr.	Budweiser Chevrolet	323		Running
25	10	11	Jason Leffler	FedEx Express Chevrolet	323		Running
26	28	49	Ken Schrader	Red Baron Pizza Dodge	323		Running
27	32	2	Rusty Wallace	Miller Lite Dodge	322		Running
28	40	43	Jeff Green	Cheerios/Betty Crocker Dodge	321		Running
29	22	50	Jimmy Spencer	U.S. Micro Dodge	314		Running
30	29	37	Kevin Lepage	Newell Recycling Dodge	314		Running
31	23	17	Matt Kenseth	Trex USG Sheetrock Ford	311		Running
32	24	97	Kurt Busch	Sharpie Ford	304		Running
33	31	21	Ricky Rudd	Motorcraft Quality Parts Ford	300		Running
34	26	7	Robby Gordon	Harrah's Chevrolet	290		Engine
35	7	01	Joe Nemechek	CENTRIX Financial Chevrolet	280		Engine
36	41	45	Kyle Petty	Georgia-Pacific/Brawny Dodge	271		Engine
37	19	18	Bobby Labonte	Interstate Batteries Chevrolet	266		Accident
38	2	32	Bobby Hamilton Jr.	Tide Chevrolet	245		Running
39	25	24	Jeff Gordon	DuPont Chevrolet	214		Accident
40	30	4	Mike Wallace	Lucas Oil Chevrolet	113		Engine
41	43	75	Mike Garvey	Jani-King/KGB Swimwear Dodge	15		Vibration
42	20	77 #	Travis Kvapil	Kodak/Jasper Eng. & Trans. Dodge	0		Accident
43	21	08	Shane Hmiel	WIN Fuel Chevrolet	0		Accident

Raybestos Rookie of the Year Contender.

NASCAR NEXTEL Cup Series Point Standings

(After 4 Races)

Pos.	Driver	Points	Behind	Change
1	**Jimmie Johnson**	680	—	+1
2	Greg Biffle	598	-82	+1
3	Carl Edwards	593	-87	+2
4	Kurt Busch	577	-103	-3
5	Mark Martin	539	-141	+4
6	Ryan Newman	515	-165	+2
7	Tony Stewart	514	-166	-1
8	Elliott Sadler	482	-198	+5
9	Rusty Wallace	477	-203	-2
10	Jamie McMurray	475	-205	+4

When all the leaders had cycled through, Biffle emerged at the point and from then on, the Golden Corral 500 turned into the Johnson & Biffle Show. Eight times the two swapped the lead between them, with Biffle leading on nine occasions for 151 laps, while Johnson led eight times for a race-high 156 circuits.

Biffle seemed to have the advantage on pit road as outstanding work by his crew put him out in front of Johnson time and again. Then, on the day's final stop, the National Guard crew faltered slightly, which sent Biffle out in third behind Johnson and Edwards with 28 laps remaining.

With two cars in front of him, Biffle's Ford developed the dreaded "aero push," challenging him to make up ground on the leaders.

Edwards, who had driven to his first NASCAR Busch Series victory less than 24 hours earlier, diligently searched the Atlanta asphalt for a line well suited to his car. Finally finding traction high in Turns 3 and 4, the 25-year-old began his pursuit of leader Johnson.

"I looked up, and all I saw was windshield," Johnson said of the charging Edwards, "so I knew he was coming."

Bit by bit, Edwards closed the gap, and by the time Johnson took the white flag, Edwards was in position to challenge. Entering the final turns, Edwards found his line on the high side and managed to pull alongside the Lowe's Chevrolet.

Johnson faded up the track, ever higher in his attempt to stave off Edwards' charge and perhaps find some traction of his own. The two roared off the fourth turn door to door as they headed toward the checkered flag, neither driver willing to lift or give.

As they crossed the line, Edwards managed to eek ahead by a fender to take the win by 0.028-second, earning his first NASCAR NEXTEL Cup Series victory in his 17th career start.

"I could tell that I was giving him a little bit of pressure," Edwards said of the final laps, "but man, it just all came together there on that last lap. It was pretty neat."

A very disappointed Biffle hung on to take third place ahead of teammate Mark Martin, while Kasey Kahne was able to break an early-season slump by finishing fifth.

FOOD CITY 500

L ook up perseverance in the dictionary and you will find something similar to: "Persisting in a purpose or a task in the face of obstacles or discouragement." After the Food City 500 at Bristol Motor Speedway, the fifth event on the 2005 NASCAR NEXTEL Cup Series schedule, one might find an additional footnote: "See KEVIN HARVICK."

Harvick must have arrived at Bristol feeling somewhat discouraged, mired in the throws of a 55-race winless streak dating back to his triumph at Indianapolis Motor Speedway in 2003. That year, his third full season of NASCAR NEXTEL Cup Series competition, Harvick finished fifth in points and was looking forward to making a strong run at a championship in 2004. That didn't happen, however, as the native of Bakersfield, Calif., gathered only five top-five finishes and was listed 14th in the final standings.

So far this season, everything was going the way of Roush Racing and Hendrick Motorsports, with their drivers gathering up wins and top fives like squirrels at an acorn festival, leaving Harvick and others to scrape for mere leftovers.

Ricky Rudd (21) gets crunched between Mark Martin (6) and Rusty Wallace (2) in a lap-332 accident that began when Bobby Hamilton Jr. (32) collided with Ken Schrader. In all, 14 cars were involved, including Kurt Busch (97) and several other frontrunners.

Add to that, the fact that Harvick faced Bristol without longtime crew chief and very close friend Todd Berrier, who remained at home to serve the second week of a four-race suspension following the discovery of an illegal fuel cell at California.

If Harvick could take some solace in turning a decent lap to be the 13th-fastest qualifier at Bristol, a track on which he has run well in the past, it quickly evaporated when his crew discovered a problem with the steering box in the GM Goodwrench Chevrolet prior to the race. The necessary repairs were deemed unapproved under the impound rule, which forced Harvick to the back of the field for the start of the race.

Further discouragement came from Harvick's knowledge that, at Bristol, only seven times in the track's 88 NASCAR NEXTEL Cup Series events had a winner come from outside the top 15, with Elliott Sadler's drive from 38th to first in 2001 being the farthest back any Bristol

Rusty Wallace takes the green flag for the lap-143 restart ahead of Kevin Harvick (29), Matt Kenseth (17) and Jamie McMurray (42), with Jeff Gordon (24) leading the lap-down cars on the inside. On the next lap Gordon bumped Wallace, giving Harvick room to take the lead for the second time in the race.

TOP 10 QUALIFIERS

Pos.	Driver	Seconds	mph
1	Elliott Sadler	15.022	127.733
2	Dave Blaney	15.056	127.444
3	Rusty Wallace	15.103	127.048
4	Jeff Gordon	15.113	126.964
5	Travis Kvapil	15.114	126.955
6	Jeff Green	15.156	126.603
7	Ryan Newman	15.164	126.537
8	Jeremy Mayfield	15.164	126.537
9	Kasey Kahne	15.168	126.503
10	Greg Biffle	15.168	126.503

Elliott Sadler, winner of this event in 2001, was feeling good about his chances at Bristol after winning the Bud Pole, the third of his career. Sadler led the first 35 laps and stayed among the leaders all day, but he was no match for Harvick at the end.

victor had ever started. As if discouragement wasn't enough for Harvick to overcome, he now had obstacles — 42 of them to be exact — to overtake if he were to return to victory lane this weekend.

As the field flashed under the green flag to begin the Food City 500, Harvick began his task, deliberately and cautiously picking his way through the treacherous minefield the high-banked bullring traditionally becomes. Avoiding two multi-car accidents early in the race and Stanton Barrett's spin at the 50-lap mark, Harvick soldiered on, careful to take care of his Monte Carlo while working in mid-pack traffic.

Then, on the day's fourth (of 14) caution for an accident involving Mike Bliss and Kyle Busch, Harvick and interim crew chief Scott Miller opted for track position over fresh tires and remained on the track while most of the leaders pitted. By the time the field lined up for the Lap-75 restart, Harvick sat fourth behind Michael Waltrip, Mark Martin and Jamie McMurray.

Dare he consider it would be that easy?

Although Harvick found he could run among the leaders, even fronting the field at times, one more obstacle still lay in his path. On the 11th caution of the race, loose lug nuts required a return trip to pit road, which put the GM Goodwrench driver at the back of the lead-lap pack with 125 circuits remaining.

(Above) Joe Nemechek (01) and Casey Mears (41) bring out the second caution of the day. The accident began when Nemechek and Kyle Busch spun, leaving Mears with no place to go but into the U.S. Army Chevrolet.

(Right) Tony Stewart's Chevrolet shows damage from debris, but it had a minimal effect as Stewart drove to a solid third-place finish, his best result of the season so far.

Once again, Harvick began working through traffic, and 50 laps later only Greg Biffle stood in his way. Biffle, however, was on worn tires after staying on the track under a previous caution and was no match for the charging Harvick, who easily picked off the National Guard Ford and set sail over the final 66 laps to gain his fifth career NASCAR NEXTEL Cup Series victory by a whopping 4.652-second margin of victory.

Sadler, who scored his third career Bud Pole with a lap at 127.733 mph, finished second ahead of Tony Stewart and Dale Earnhardt Jr., while Dale Jarrett rounded out the top five.

Although Harvick clearly had one of the best cars on the track, his quest for victory was aided by the misfortune of others. Nine-time Bristol winner Rusty Wallace led four times for a race-high 157 laps and appeared to be a winning contender before tire problems dropped him two laps off the pace.

(Above) The GM Goodwrench team had their work cut out for them at Bristol. Once Harvick reached the leaders, strong performances on pit road helped keep him in the top three and put him in position to run away with the win.

(Left) Kyle Petty (45) gets some heat from Dale Earnhardt Jr. and the Budweiser Chevrolet. Earnhardt hit the top 10 before the 100-lap mark and came away with fourth place after a three-race slump, while Petty came on strong over the last 150 laps to gain his first top-10 finish in more than two years.

(Opposing Page) Kevin Harvick lets his emotions go after a worst-to-first drive for his fifth career win.

FOOD CITY 500

NASCAR NEXTEL Cup Series Race No. 5

Fin. Pos.	Start Pos.	Car No.	Driver	Team	Laps	Laps Led	Status
1	13	29	Kevin Harvick	GM Goodwrench Chevrolet	500	109	Running
2	1	38	Elliott Sadler	M&M's Ford	500	35	Running
3	11	20	Tony Stewart	The Home Depot Chevrolet	500		Running
4	19	8	Dale Earnhardt Jr.	Budweiser Chevrolet	500		Running
5	21	88	Dale Jarrett	UPS Ford	500		Running
6	14	48	Jimmie Johnson	Lowe's Chevrolet	500	1	Running
7	5	77 #	Travis Kvapil	Kodak/Jasper Eng. & Trans. Dodge	500		Running
8	37	45	Kyle Petty	Georgia-Pacific/Brawny Dodge	500		Running
9	10	16	Greg Biffle	Charter Communications Ford	500	91	Running
10	28	10	Scott Riggs	Valvoline Chevrolet	500		Running
11	15	40	Sterling Marlin	Coors Light Dodge	499		Running
12	12	25	Brian Vickers	GMAC/ditech.com Chevrolet	498		Running
13	3	2	Rusty Wallace	Miller Lite Dodge	498	157	Running
14	9	9	Kasey Kahne	Dodge Dealers/UAW Dodge	498		Running
15	4	24	Jeff Gordon	DuPont Chevrolet	498	38	Running
16	25	17	Matt Kenseth	DeWalt Power Tools Ford	497	50	Running
17	8	19	Jeremy Mayfield	Dodge Dealers/UAW Dodge	497		Running
18	16	44	Terry Labonte	Kellogg's Chevrolet	496	10	Running
19	27	15	Michael Waltrip	NAPA Auto Parts Chevrolet	496	19	Running
20	2	07	Dave Blaney	Jack Daniel's Chevrolet	495		Running
21	29	50	Jimmy Spencer	US Micro Dodge	492		Running
22	38	18	Bobby Labonte	Interstate Batteries Chevrolet	468		Running
23	30	49	Ken Schrader	Schwan's Home Service Dodge	467		Running
24	17	42	Jamie McMurray	Texaco-Havoline/Autism Society Dodge	456		Running
25	20	21	Ricky Rudd	Motorcraft Quality Parts Ford	452		Running
26	42	99	Carl Edwards	Office Depot Ford	447		Running
27	32	22	Scott Wimmer	Caterpillar Dodge	437		Running
28	39	5 #	Kyle Busch	Carquest Chevrolet	428		Running
29	6	43	Jeff Green	Cheerios/Betty Crocker Dodge	427		Running
30	7	12	Ryan Newman	ALLTEL Dodge	418		Running
31	34	6	Mark Martin	Viagra Ford	406		Running
32	35	66	Hermie Sadler	East Tennessee Trailers Ford	395		Running
33	40	01	Joe Nemechek	U.S. Army Chevrolet	393		Running
34	22	4	Mike Wallace	Food City/Lucas Oil Chevrolet	379		Accident
35	26	97	Kurt Busch	Sharpie Ford	360		Accident
36	24	31	Jeff Burton	Cingular Wireless Chevrolet	358		Accident
37	41	0	Mike Bliss	Net Zero Best Buy Chevrolet	351		Running
38	36	11	Jason Leffler	FedEx Express Chevrolet	342		Running
39	18	32	Bobby Hamilton Jr.	Tide Chevrolet	330		Accident
40	33	08	Shane Hmiel	WINFuel Chevrolet	305		Overheating
41	23	92 #	Stanton Barrett	USMilitary.com Chevrolet	83		Oil Pressure
42	43	00	Carl Long	Buyer's Choice Auto Warranty Chevrolet	37		Overheating
43	31	41	Casey Mears	Target Dodge	20		Accident

Raybestos Rookie of the Year Contender.

NASCAR NEXTEL Cup Series Point Standings
(After 5 Races)

Pos.	Driver	Points	Behind	Change
1	**Jimmie Johnson**	**835**	—	—
2	Greg Biffle	741	-94	—
3	Tony Stewart	679	-156	+4
4	Carl Edwards	670	-157	-1
5	Elliott Sadler	657	-178	+3
6	Kevin Harvick	654	-181	+5
7	Kurt Busch	635	-200	-3
8	Dale Jarrett	611	-224	+7
9	Rusty Wallace	611	-224	—
10	Mark Martin	609	-226	-5

Matt Kenseth led 50 laps before being bumped around in traffic and spun later by Ricky Rudd. He made it back into the top five but suffered a flat tire with 15 laps to go and fell to 16th place. Jeff Gordon led 28 circuits but, like Wallace and Kenseth, dropped off the pace with tire problems in the final laps.

Others, including Kurt Busch, winner of the last three spring events and four of the last six races at Bristol, became involved in accidents and fell from contention as well.

"It's big," Harvick exclaimed after capturing the emotional win. "Todd [Berrier] put so much hard work into this thing and to be home watching this on TV, it's pretty awesome. We fought a lot of adversity."

And adversity's antidote for Harvick and the GM Goodwrench team? Plain old perseverance.

ADVANCE AUTO PARTS 500

As NASCAR NEXTEL Cup Series team members viewed the point standings heading into the Advance Auto Parts 500 at beautiful Martinsville Speedway, some were considering their strategies to reach or maintain positions among the top 10, eyeing a chance to compete for the championship in the Chase for the NASCAR NEXTEL Cup, which would begin after 21 more events.

Other competitors, however, had their attention focused much further down the points list. In this, the sixth event on the schedule, 2005 owner points would begin being used to determine who would have "guaranteed" spots in the starting lineups for subsequent events. Only those listed among the top 35 in owner points would be assured of a starting position each week, while those listed 36th or lower would be forced to gain one of only eight remaining spots in the field based on their qualifying speeds.

Jeff Gordon lights 'em up after a hard-fought and emotional win in his first visit to Martinsville since the Hendrick Motorsports airplane tragedy last October. Gordon had to come from two laps down to earn his sixth Martinsville win.

TOP 10 QUALIFIERS

Pos.	Driver	Seconds	mph
1	Scott Riggs	19.588	96.671
2	Ryan Newman	19.591	96.657
3	Jeremy Mayfield	19.606	96.583
4	Rusty Wallace	19.611	96.558
5	Kevin Harvick	19.648	96.376
6	Bobby Labonte	19.672	96.259
7	Tony Stewart	19.685	96.195
8	Greg Biffle	19.699	96.127
9	Kurt Busch	19.712	96.063
10	Joe Nemechek	19.722	96.015

(Above) Kurt Busch nurses his battered Ford around the Martinsville half mile after he and Jeff Gordon tangled late in the race. Busch was less than happy about the incident and showed his frustration later by running Gordon up the track when he came by to put Busch a lap down.

(Right) Greg Biffle checks out the cockpit of his Roush Racing Ford before 500 laps around the Virginia bullring.

Heading into Martinsville, Joe Gibbs Racing teammates Jason Leffler and Bobby Labonte were keeping an extra-sharp eye on the point totals. Leffler's No. 11 Chevrolet currently held down the 35th position in owner points, while Labonte's No. 18 was listed 34th, just six points ahead of Leffler. Above them in the standings, but with only a slight cushion, sat Bobby Hamilton's No. 32 Tide machine, Ken Schrader's BAM Racing Dodge and Joe Nemechek's No. 01 Chevrolet.

A wheel from Tony Stewart's The Home Depot Chevrolet wanders aimlessly down the track after falling completely off the car. Stewart spent a good portion of the day in front of Jeff Gordon (inset), who had wheel problems of his own but was able to recover for the win. Stewart wound up 26th, four laps off Gordon's pace.

Among those outside the top 35 sat Ricky Rudd and the Wood Brothers' famed No. 21 Ford. All drivers hovering near the 35th spot would have to focus on staying out of trouble at Martinsville and come away with solid finishes to avoid the weekly challenge of needing a strong qualifying run just to make the field for upcoming events.

One driver feeling pretty good about things so far in 2005 was Scott Riggs. Riggs, in his second full season, had posted a fourth place in the Daytona 500, stumbled a bit at California and Las Vegas with finishes of 33rd and 31st, but roared back with a ninth-place effort at Atlanta followed by another top 10 at Bristol.

Riggs currently sat 14th in the standings but was just 43 points behind 10th-place Mark Martin. Now, Riggs arrived at Martinsville, the track where he campaigned Late Models earlier in his career and posted his first NASCAR Craftsman Truck Series victory almost exactly four years ago. And the driver of the Valvoline Chevrolet made it a homecoming of sorts by circling the flat half-mile at 96.671 mph in qualifying and beating Ryan Newman by three one-thousandths of a second to grab his first career NASCAR NEXTEL Cup Series Bud Pole.

Jeff Gordon started Sunday's 500-lapper from the 16th staring position but quickly found himself at the back of the field after a loose wheel forced him to pit under green. The unscheduled stop cost Gordon two laps — a deficit worsened by another lap when additional repairs were needed.

(Above) Front-row starters Scott Riggs (10) and Ryan Newman (12) get together in the opening laps in front of third-fastest qualifier Jeremy Mayfield (19). Riggs scored the Bud Pole for the event, the first of his career coming at the track he calls home.

(Left) Kasey Kahne's Dodge shows the scars of a tough day on the short track, but that didn't bother him much. Kahne brought the battered Charger home in second after a late-race pass on Mark Martin and Sterling Marlin.

ADVANCE AUTO PARTS 500 — NASCAR NEXTEL Cup Series Race No. 6

Fin. Pos.	Start Pos.	Car No.	Driver	Team	Laps	Laps Led	Status
1	16	24	Jeff Gordon	DuPont Chevrolet	500	36	Running
2	35	9	Kasey Kahne	Dodge Dealers/UAW Dodge	500		Running
3	22	6	Mark Martin	Viagra Ford	500	1	Running
4	2	12	Ryan Newman	ALLTEL Dodge	500	25	Running
5	4	2	Rusty Wallace	Miller Lite Dodge	500	47	Running
6	20	40	Sterling Marlin	Coors Light Dodge	500	6	Running
7	13	21	Ricky Rudd	Motorcraft Quality Parts Ford	500		Running
8	37	48	Jimmie Johnson	Lowe's Chevrolet	500		Running
9	25	38	Elliott Sadler	M&M's Ford	500		Running
10	10	01	Joe Nemechek	U.S. Army Chevrolet	500		Running
11	18	17	Matt Kenseth	DeWalt Power Tools Ford	500	1	Running
12	12	11	Jason Leffler	FedEx Express Chevrolet	500		Running
13	26	8	Dale Earnhardt Jr.	Budweiser Chevrolet	500		Running
14	32	88	Dale Jarrett	UPS Ford	500		Running
15	3	19	Jeremy Mayfield	Dodge Dealers/UAW Dodge	499	68	Running
16	30	31	Jeff Burton	Cingular Wireless Chevrolet	499		Running
17	24	41	Casey Mears	Target Dodge	499		Running
18	19	45	Kyle Petty	Georgia-Pacific/Brawny Dodge	498		Running
19	9	97	Kurt Busch	Crown Royal Ford	498	33	Running
20	43	7	Robby Gordon	Harrah's Chevrolet	498	4	Running
21	1	10	Scott Riggs	Valvoline Chevrolet	498		Running
22	14	43	Jeff Green	Cheerios/Betty Crocker Dodge	497		Running
23	23	4	Mike Wallace	Lucas Oil Chevrolet	497		Running
24	11	49	Ken Schrader	Schwan's Home Service Dodge	497		Running
25	29	42	Jamie McMurray	Texaco/Havoline Dodge	496		Running
26	7	20	Tony Stewart	The Home Depot Chevrolet	493	247	Running
27	17	77 #	Travis Kvapil	Kodak/Jasper Eng. & Trans. Dodge	490		Engine
28	41	37	Kevin Lepage	R&J Racing Dodge	489		Running
29	8	16	Greg Biffle	National Guard/Jackson Hewitt Ford	487		Running
30	31	15	Michael Waltrip	NAPA Auto Parts Chevrolet	477		Running
31	33	22	Scott Wimmer	Caterpillar Dodge	466		Running
32	5	29	Kevin Harvick	GM Goodwrench Chevrolet	436		Running
33	6	18	Bobby Labonte	Interstate Batteries Chevrolet	435	32	Engine
34	42	07	Dave Blaney	Jack Daniel's Chevrolet	416		Running
35	27	25	Brian Vickers	GMAC/ditech Chevrolet	412		Running
36	15	0	Mike Bliss	Net Zero Best Buy Chevrolet	410		Overheating
37	38	66	Hermie Sadler	Peak Fitness Ford	340		Accident
38	36	99	Carl Edwards	Office Depot Ford	321		Running
39	21	5 #	Kyle Busch	Kellogg's Chevrolet	304		Overheating
40	28	32	Bobby Hamilton Jr.	Tide Chevrolet	151		Overheating
41	40	09	Johnny Sauter	Miccosukee Resorts Dodge	55		Brakes
42	39	34	Randy LaJoie	Mach 1 Inc. Chevrolet	26		Engine
43	34	75	Mike Garvey	Jani-King/Rinaldi Air Conditioning Dodge	18		Brakes

Raybestos Rookie of the Year Contender.

NASCAR NEXTEL Cup Series Point Standings
(After 6 Races)

Pos.	Driver	Points	Behind	Change
1.	Jimmie Johnson	977	—	—
2.	Greg Biffle	817	-160	—
3.	Elliott Sadler	795	-182	+2
4.	Mark Martin	779	-198	+6
5.	Tony Stewart	774	-203	-2
6.	Jeff Gordon	772	-205	+6
7.	Rusty Wallace	771	-206	+2
8.	Ryan Newman	753	-224	+3
9.	Kurt Busch	746	-231	-2
10.	Dale Jarrett	732	-245	-2

Running as low as 40th place at one point, Gordon began the long, arduous climb back through the field. Aided by the yellow flag — there were 16 cautions during the race — the five-time Martinsville winner methodically worked his way back onto the lead lap, and with 150 laps to go, Gordon finally had reached the top 10.

When the field lined up for a restart following the day's 14th caution on Lap 438, Gordon found himself in fourth place behind Newman, Sterling Marlin and Elliott Sadler, all of whom had decided not to pit in favor of track position.

By Lap 461, Gordon had moved to third. Three laps later, he took second and, on the following lap, Gordon passed Marlin to take the point for the first time in the race. From there, the four-time champion set sail, leading the final 36 circuits on the way to his sixth Martinsville win.

Kasey Kahne celebrated his 25th birthday by finishing second after getting past Marlin and Martin while they battled each other for position. Kahne, who started 35th, gained 33 positions during the event to lead all drivers.

Of the other contenders, Tony Stewart assumed the point for the first time at Lap 117 and began a dominating run, leading 247 of the next 273 laps and looking very much like the man to beat. That, however, was not to be. With less than 70 laps remaining, a wheel fell completely off The Home Depot Chevrolet, effectively ending any chance Stewart might have had to win the race.

Jeremy Mayfield led twice for 68 laps but suffered a cut tire and later was assessed a penalty for speeding on pit road, which dropped him to 15th. Rusty Wallace got caught speeding as well, but was able to battle back to a fifth place finish, while Labonte retired with 65 laps remaining after his engine failed.

Kurt Busch took the lead for the first time at the 400-lap mark and appeared to be a contender until he and Gordon tangled while fighting for fourth place in an incident that sent Busch backing into the outside wall. Later, Busch showed what he termed his "displeasure" with the incident by laying a heavy fender on Gordon's Chevrolet as he lapped the ailing Ford on the way to the win.

SAMSUNG/RADIOSHACK 500

It's not surprising that for Jack Roush, engineer and mathematician, making something work often boils down to an equation. When it comes to making race teams work, it takes, according to Roush, three things: "a driver that can do it, technology that's competitive and a team that can do it."

Judging by the results of the Samsung/RadioShack 500, it seems Roush's No. 16 National Guard team is working just fine.

As far as having a "driver that can do it," Greg Biffle came to the NASCAR NEXTEL Cup Series with more than adequate credentials, listing rookie honors and series championships in both the NASCAR Craftsman Truck Series and the NASCAR Busch Series, all within a five-year stretch.

In terms of "technology that's competitive," all Roush teams have at their disposal some of the very best available in motorsports, period. Roush would have it no other way, and his race-shop complex in Concord, N.C., has become a virtual factory of championship-caliber equipment.

(Right) Greg Biffle flashes under the flagstand at Texas Motor Speedway on the way to his fifth victory in the 85th start of his career. The win, his second of the season, came in convincing fashion as he led nearly two-thirds of the 500-mile distance.

(Below) Jamie McMurray's Havoline crew hustles into action on pit road. McMurray fell a lap down after an accident in the opening laps, but was able to make up the distance — much of it with outstanding pit stops — and brought his Ganassi Dodge home in second.

TOP 10 QUALIFIERS

Pos.	Driver	Seconds	mph
1	Ryan Newman	28.040	192.582
2	Jeremy Mayfield	28.062	192.431
3	Kasey Kahne	28.164	191.734
4	Ricky Rudd	28.190	191.557
5	Greg Biffle	28.208	191.435
6	Rusty Wallace	28.230	191.286
7	Jeff Gordon	28.266	191.042
8	Elliott Sadler	28.327	190.631
9	Joe Nemechek	28.330	190.611
10	Tony Stewart	28.333	190.590

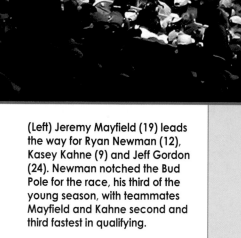

(Left) Jeremy Mayfield (19) leads the way for Ryan Newman (12), Kasey Kahne (9) and Jeff Gordon (24). Newman notched the Bud Pole for the race, his third of the young season, with teammates Mayfield and Kahne second and third fastest in qualifying.

A Texas-sized crowd estimated at 211,000 lines the double-dog-leg frontstretch at Texas Motor Speedway. This was the ninth NASCAR NEXTEL Cup Series event at the track in Fort Worth, with Biffle becoming the ninth different winner.

So the X-factor for Biffle seemed to lie in having the "team that can do it." Read: chemistry.

After Biffle's seven-race foray into the series in 2002 teamed with longtime crew chief Randy Goss, Roush installed Doug Richert — the same Doug Richert who helped lead Dale Earnhardt to his first championship in 1980 — as crew chief of the "16" team. In their first season together, Biffle and Richert managed six top-10 finishes, including a win in the Pepsi 400 at Daytona, and finished 20th in points.

Last year, they went 19 races into the season with just one top-10 finish, an eighth place at Atlanta. Then something clicked. In the final 17 events of 2004, Biffle and company scored seven more top 10s, won at Michigan, climbed eight positions in the point standings and capped off the season with another win at Homestead-Miami, gathering momentum for 2005.

Biffle started this season with a disappointing 25th place in the Daytona 500, but roared back with a win at California followed by three straight top 10s. A 29th place at Martinsville was viewed as a brief setback, and Biffle rolled into Texas Motor Speedway second in points to Jimmie Johnson and prepared to challenge on a track where Roush drivers had already scored three wins since the speedway opened in 1997.

If team chemistry was still in doubt, it was put to the test at Texas. Biffle ripped off the fifth-fastest lap in qualifying in a car that delighted him, but a blown right-front tire in practice sent the primary car hard into the wall. The National Guard crew unloaded their backup machine and they, along with members of other Roush teams, immediately began the transition of parts and pieces.

"I was over there watching them get the car ready," Biffle said. "There were probably five or six different colored uniforms working on pulling the fuel cell out of my backup car, taking the shocks and springs and putting them in the new car. I mean they were all just in there digging, and that really makes me feel proud to know I've got supporters like that in our organization."

When the green flag flew on Sunday, Biffle went to work from the back of the field. Over the first 20 laps, he gained 25 positions. Eighteen laps later he reached the top 10, and on Lap 87 he passed Tony Stewart to take the lead for the first time. From that point on, Biffle simply dominated. He led 219 of the remaining 247 laps, giving up the lead only briefly

(Above) Michael Waltrip pits his NAPA Chevrolet ahead of Casey Mears (41) and Jimmie Johnson (48) during one of the day's 11 caution periods. Mears started in a backup car after crashing his primary in practice and drove a fine race to fourth place, matching his career best.

(Opposite Page) Team owner Jack Roush is one happy cowboy at Texas, where Biffle scored the organization's third win of the season. Roush left the Lone Star State with three drivers among the top 10 in points.

SAMSUNG/RADIOSHACK 500 NASCAR NEXTEL Cup Series Race No. 7

Fin. Pos.	Start Pos.	Car No.	Driver	Team	Laps	Laps Led	Status
1	5	16	Greg Biffle	National Guard/Post-it Ford	334	219	Running
2	31	42	Jamie McMurray	Texaco/Havoline Dodge	334		Running
3	18	48	Jimmie Johnson	Lowe's Chevrolet	334		Running
4	32	41	Casey Mears	FujiFilm/Target Dodge	334	15	Running
5	13	40	Sterling Marlin	Coors Light Dodge	334	3	Running
6	21	15	Michael Waltrip	NAPA Auto Parts Chevrolet	334	7	Running
7	19	97	Kurt Busch	IRWIN Industrial Tools Ford	334	2	Running
8	4	21	Ricky Rudd	Rent-A-Center/Motorcraft Ford	334		Running
9	11	8	Dale Earnhardt Jr.	Budweiser Chevrolet	334		Running
10	6	2	Rusty Wallace	Kodak/Miller Lite Dodge	334		Running
11	2	19	Jeremy Mayfield	Dodge Dealers/UAW Dodge	334	34	Running
12	41	31	Jeff Burton	Cingular Wireless Chevrolet	334		Running
13	17	29	Kevin Harvick	GM Goodwrench Chevrolet	334		Running
14	27	88	Dale Jarrett	UPS Ford	334		Running
15	7	24	Jeff Gordon	DuPont Chevrolet	334	1	Running
16	1	12	Ryan Newman	ALLTEL Dodge	334	1	Running
17	9	01	Joe Nemechek	U.S. Army Chevrolet	334		Running
18	39	17	Matt Kenseth	DeWalt Power Tools Ford	334	1	Running
19	20	99	Carl Edwards	Scotts Ford	334		Running
20	16	6	Mark Martin	Viagra Ford	334		Running
21	35	5 #	Kyle Busch	Kellogg's/Delphi Chevrolet	334		Running
22	42	0	Mike Bliss	Coast Guard Chevrolet	333		Running
23	30	49	Ken Schrader	Schwan's Home Service Dodge	333	3	Running
24	28	45	Kyle Petty	Brawny/Georgia-Pacific Dodge	333	1	Running
25	26	4	Mike Wallace	Lucas Oil Chevrolet	333	1	Running
26	12	07	Dave Blaney	Jack Daniel's Chevrolet	332		Running
27	40	36	Boris Said	CENTRIX Financial Chevrolet	327		Running
28	8	38	Elliott Sadler	M&M's Ford	324	1	Engine
29	37	66	Hermie Sadler	Peak Fitness Ford	319		Running
30	25	77 #	Travis Kvapil	Jasper Engines & Transmissions Dodge	297		Running
31	10	20	Tony Stewart	The Home Depot Chevrolet	296	45	Engine
32	14	10	Scott Riggs	Valvoline Chevrolet	288		Running
33	15	91	Bill Elliott	Stanley Tools Dodge	286		Engine
34	24	25	Brian Vickers	GMAC/Garnier Fructis Chevrolet	278		Running
35	3	9	Kasey Kahne	Dodge Dealers/UAW Dodge	269		Engine
36	29	11	Jason Leffler	FedEx Express Chevrolet	250		Running
37	33	7	Robby Gordon	Jim Beam Chevrolet	238		Accident
38	22	18	Bobby Labonte	Interstate Batteries Chevrolet	232		Running
39	38	32	Bobby Hamilton Jr.	Tide Chevrolet	219		Running
40	43	44	Terry Labonte	GMAC Chevrolet	202		Engine
41	34	09	Johnny Sauter	Miccosukee Resorts Dodge	98		Handling
42	36	22	Scott Wimmer	Caterpillar Dodge	39		Accident
43	23	43	Jeff Green	Pillsbury Bake Off Dodge	31		Accident

Raybestos Rookie of the Year Contender.

NASCAR NEXTEL Cup Series Point Standings
(After 7 Races)

Pos.	Driver	Points	Behind	Change
1	**Jimmie Johnson**	**1142**	—	—
2	Greg Biffle	1007	-135	—
3	Rusty Wallace	905	-237	+4
4	Kurt Busch	897	-245	+5
5	Jeff Gordon	895	-247	+1
6	Sterling Marlin	883	-259	+6
7	Mark Martin	882	-260	-3
8	Elliott Sadler	879	-263	-5
9	Ryan Newman	873	-269	-1
10	Dale Jarrett	853	-289	—

during pit sequences and driving to a 3.244-second margin of victory for his second win of the year, his third in his last eight starts.

Realizing that track position might be their only hope of beating Biffle to the checkered flag, Casey Mears and Sterling Marlin, who were running among the leaders, opted for two-tire stops on the day's final caution. It took, however, just two laps under green for Biffle to retake the lead and, from there, he never faced a challenge.

Mears and Marlin fell to fourth and fifth, respectively, while teammate Jamie McMurray drove to second place ahead of Jimmie Johnson in a banner day for Chip Ganassi Racing that saw all three teams finish in the top five.

Although Biffle made it look easy, it was anything but that. "If there was an in-car camera that could have watched me saw on that wheel for 500 [miles] — I worked my butt off today," Biffle quipped. "There wasn't one time where I could relax inside that race car because you've got to keep digging all day, and that's what I did."

It appears then, that Roush Racing's No. 16 team has come of age. "I hate to admit it, but it took me three years to get this team where it could do for Greg what we've been able to do with Mark, Matt and Kurt," Roush explained after the race. "They had confidence in the backup car and in themselves ... they pulled it off.

"It just takes awhile to get people assembled who work together and have the right chemistry."

Driver, technology and now, team: Equation complete.

SUBWAY FRESH 500

The NASCAR NEXTEL Cup Series made the trip to Arizona for the eighth race of the 2005 season and, in retrospect, one would have to say the weekend produced some unusual results.

The Subway Fresh 500, new to the schedule this year, would be the first springtime visit to Phoenix International Raceway since the track began hosting series events in 1988. Also, the timing of the event was a departure from the norm at PIR, with the race starting in the late afternoon and continuing into the evening under the lights.

How those factors, when compared to the usual late-season, early-afternoon contest, would affect the outcome had yet to be seen.

The weekend began hot and sunny for Thursday afternoon practice, followed 24 hours later by qualifying under cloudy skies that caused the mercury to plummet. As if that weren't enough to confound crew chiefs and drivers attempting to derive their race-day setups, sweltering heat on Saturday eventually gave way to heavy rains, leaving a cool, green track for the start of the event.

(Below) The lights at Phoenix International Raceway begin to glow as the sun fades behind late-afternoon clouds. The Subway Fresh 500 was the NASCAR NEXTEL Cup Series' first springtime visit to the Arizona desert.

(Opposite Page) Tony Stewart (left) gladly signs an autograph for one of the many soldiers in attendance at Phoenix. Stewart had a great run going in the race until an accident dropped him from contention, while his Joe Gibbs Racing teammate, Bobby Labonte (right), had a strong outing to gain a much-needed top-10 finish.

TOP 10 QUALIFIERS

Pos.	Driver	Seconds	mph
1	Jeff Gordon	26.931	133.675
2	Kurt Busch	27.016	133.254
3	Greg Biffle	27.035	133.161
4	Bobby Labonte	27.069	132.993
5	Brian Vickers	27.075	132.964
6	Tony Stewart	27.078	132.949
7	Ryan Newman	27.085	132.915
8	Jeremy Mayfield	27.144	132.626
9	Rusty Wallace	27.151	132.592
10	Kevin Harvick	27.164	132.528

Jeff Gordon led the field under the green flag, having won his first Bud Pole of the year, but immediately gave way to second-place starter Kurt Busch.

Busch, longing to join teammates Greg Biffle and Carl Edwards in the race-winners' column, broke out of a three-race slump last week at Texas Motor Speedway with a seventh-place effort. Still riding that momentum, the defending series champion drove away, leading the field six times for 219 of 312 laps, including 132 of the first 133 as well as the final 44 on the way to victory.

That Busch took the win was not that unusual, especially considering Roush drivers had enjoyed success at Phoenix over the years, and Busch had posted finishes of 10th, fourth and sixth in his last three Phoenix starts.

But one need only look at the rest of the top 10 to see vast departures from the ordinary.

Second place went to Michael Waltrip, who tied his best finish since winning at Talladega in 2003, 50 races ago. Waltrip, who started 28th after a sub-par qualifying effort, did it his way — alone in the high groove, rolling past car after car, all of them glued to the yellow line on the inside of the track. It took the NAPA driver just 60 laps to join the top five, and as the race began winding down, Waltrip drove like a man possessed, slapping the wall on several occasions in his pursuit of Busch. With the white flag in sight, the blue-and-yellow Chevrolet became more than a handful, and one last crack against the fence ended Waltrip's challenge 2.315 seconds behind the victor.

Jeff Burton returned to Phoenix, site of his last win in 2001, feeling as though he and crew chief Kevin Hamlin were finally beginning to click. Having scored no better than 12th so far in 2005, Burton brought the Cingular Chevrolet home in third, tying his best finish since the 2002 season finale, 79 races ago.

Despite a third place in the Daytona 500, Dale Earnhardt Jr.'s season had gotten off to a rocky start. Finishes of 32nd, 42nd and 24th in the next three events dropped the Budweiser driver all the way to 27th in the standings. Other than a fourth place at Bristol, there wasn't much to crow about, but the winner of the last two Phoenix events kept the nose of his Monte Carlo clean and notched a fourth-place finish behind Burton. Not what he had hoped for to be sure, but as Earnhardt headed home, he was listed in 12th place in the standings, just 13 points out of 10th.

Teammates Jeff Gordon and Jimmie Johnson had been hogging the headlines at Hendrick Motorsports this season, with Kyle Busch showing occasional flashes of rookie greatness.

Brian Vickers keeps his ditech.com Chevrolet ahead of Michael Waltrip's NAPA machine. Vickers had a career day, leading 50 laps on the way to his first top five, while Waltrip's challenge for the win fell just short but left him with his best finish in more than a year.

(Opposite Page) Joe Nemechek (01) charges into the first turn with rookie Kyle Busch peeking to the inside. Both drivers came on strong over the final third of the race and each scored their second top 10 of the season, with Busch finishing eighth ahead of Nemechek in 10th.

At Phoenix, however, sophomore driver Brian Vickers carried the Hendrick banner. Vickers took the lead on Lap 179 after a decision to forego new tires under caution and led twice for 50 laps before finishing in fifth — a career best. Although the call on pit road put him in position to take the point, savvy driving kept him among the leaders as his tires began to give up. Like Burton, Vickers was feeling his team come together behind crew chief Lance McGrew, who coached the young driver to the NASCAR Busch Series championship in 2003.

The desert air proved to be good medicine for Bobby Labonte as well. Other than a 13th place at California, the 2000 series champ had so far scored no better than 22nd, failed to finish four times in seven events as was mired in 37th place in the points. After qualifying with the fourth-fastest lap, Labonte drove a smart, yeoman-like race and was quite satisfied to leave Phoenix with a sixth-place result.

Seventh place went to Carl Edwards, who broke a three-race skid that followed his Atlanta win, with Kyle Busch in eighth after four straight finishes of 12th or worse.

This was Johnny Sauter's third start of the year, the first two resulting in 41st-place DNFs, at Martinsville and Texas. Driving a Dodge fielded by Phoenix Racing, Sauter put together a splendid career-best, ninth-place effort to his delight, and that of team owner James Finch.

Joe Nemechek rounded out the rather unlikely top 10 to match his season best. After sputtering through the first five events of the year, Nemechek and his U.S. Army team were beginning to make the long journey up the point ladder toward the coveted top 10 and a shot at the Chase for the NASCAR NEXTEL Cup.

(Above) Jeff Burton brings his Cingular Chevrolet into turn 1 ahead of Sterling Marlin (40) and Jeff Gordon (24). Burton, a two-time Phoenix winner, climbed steadily through the field from his 20th-place start to get as high as third for his best finish in more than two full seasons.

(Opposite Page) The Irwin Tools team was as flawless on pit road as their driver, Kurt Busch, was on the one-mile oval. That proved to be an unbeatable combination as Busch ruled the competition on the way to his first victory of 2005.

SUBWAY FRESH 500

NASCAR NEXTEL Cup Series Race No. 8

Fin. Pos.	Start Pos.	Car No.	Driver	Team	Laps	Laps Led	Status
1	2	97	Kurt Busch	IRWIN Industrial Tools Ford	312	219	Running
2	28	15	Michael Waltrip	NAPA Auto Parts Chevrolet	312	23	Running
3	20	31	Jeff Burton	Cingular Wireless Chevrolet	312		Running
4	15	8	Dale Earnhardt Jr.	Budweiser Chevrolet	312		Running
5	5	25	Brian Vickers	ditech.com/GMAC Chevrolet	312	50	Running
6	4	18	Bobby Labonte	Interstate Batteries Chevrolet	312		Running
7	11	99	Carl Edwards	Scotts Ford	312		Running
8	27	5 #	Kyle Busch	Kellogg's Chevrolet	312	8	Running
9	26	09	Johnny Sauter	Miccosukee Resort Dodge	312		Running
10	13	01	Joe Nemechek	U.S. Army Chevrolet	312		Running
11	33	38	Elliott Sadler	M&M's Ford	312		Running
12	1	24	Jeff Gordon	DuPont Chevrolet	312	4	Running
13	8	19	Jeremy Mayfield	Dodge Dealers/UAW Dodge	312		Running
14	7	12	Ryan Newman	ALLTEL Dodge	312		Running
15	12	48	Jimmie Johnson	Lowe's Chevrolet	312		Running
16	22	6	Mark Martin	Viagra Ford	312		Running
17	14	9	Kasey Kahne	Dodge Dealers/UAW Dodge	312		Running
18	16	10	Scott Riggs	CENTRIX Financial Chevrolet	312	1	Running
19	10	29	Kevin Harvick	GM Goodwrench Chevrolet	312		Running
20	23	0	Mike Bliss	Net Zero Best Buy Chevrolet	311		Running
21	37	43	Jeff Green	Cheerios/Betty Crocker Dodge	311		Running
22	25	33	Clint Bowyer	Sylvania Chevrolet	311		Running
23	35	88	Dale Jarrett	M&Ms/UPS Ford	311		Running
24	21	07	Dave Blaney	Jack Daniel's Chevrolet	311		Running
25	34	42	Jamie McMurray	Home123 Dodge	311		Running
26	31	40	Sterling Marlin	Coors Light Dodge	311		Running
27	42	4	Mike Wallace	Lucas Oil Chevrolet	310		Running
28	29	37	Kevin Lepage	R&J Racing Dodge	310		Running
29	18	11	Jason Leffler	FedEx Express Chevrolet	309		Running
30	40	92 #	Stanton Barrett	Front Row Motorsports Chevrolet	309		Running
31	39	45	Kyle Petty	Georgia-Pacific/Brawny Dodge	306		Running
32	36	22	Scott Wimmer	Caterpillar Dodge	305	1	Running
33	6	20	Tony Stewart	The Home Depot Chevrolet	305		Running
34	38	21	Ricky Rudd	U.S. Air Force/Motorcraft Ford	293		Running
35	19	32	Bobby Hamilton Jr.	Tide Chevrolet	283		Running
36	9	2	Rusty Wallace	Miller Lite Dodge	272		Running
37	43	7	Robby Gordon	Harrah's Chevrolet	262		Running
38	30	49	Ken Schrader	Schwan's Home Service Dodge	255	4	Accident
39	32	41	Casey Mears	Target Dodge	243		Running
40	24	77 #	Travis Kvapil	Kodak/Jasper Eng. & Trans. Dodge	237		Accident
41	3	16	Greg Biffle	National Guard/Subway Ford	172	2	Overheat.
42	17	17	Matt Kenseth	DeWalt Power Tools Ford	164		Accident
43	41	00	Carl Long	Buyer's Choice Auto Warranty Chevrolet	52		Engine

Raybestos Rookie of the Year Contender.

NASCAR NEXTEL Cup Series Point Standings

(After 8 Races)

Pos.	Driver	Points	Behind	Change
1	**Jimmie Johnson**	**1260**	—	—
2	Kurt Busch	1087	-173	+2
3	Greg Biffle	1052	-208	-1
4	Jeff Gordon	1027	-233	+1
5	Elliott Sadler	1009	-251	+3
6	Mark Martin	997	-263	+1
7	Ryan Newman	994	-266	+2
8	Carl Edwards	979	281	+5
9	Sterling Marlin	968	-292	-3
10	Rusty Wallace	960	-300	-7

AARON'S 499

On a beautiful day for racing in central Alabama, fans at Talladega stand as the field thunders past in the opening laps of the Aaron's 499.

If Jeff Gordon made the statement at Daytona Beach, Fla., earlier in the year that Dale Earnhardt, Inc.'s, reign over restrictor-plate racing was ending, he put a huge exclamation point on it at Talladega, Ala.

At Daytona, Gordon seemed content to drive a conservative race, leading once in the first half for 23 laps, and then falling in line among the lead pack for much of the remaining distance. With just three of the scheduled 200 laps to go, Gordon moved to the outside and simply powered past Dale Earnhardt Jr. and Tony Stewart, who appeared to have had the strongest cars, and drove away to the win.

That victory to start the 2005 NASCAR NEXTEL Cup Series season was Gordon's third in the last four restrictor-plate events, thus ending the domination by DEI that saw Michael Waltrip and Earnhardt Jr. combine to win 11 of the previous 15 events run on the two giant superspeedways.

Elliott Sadler (38) uses the center lane to inch ahead of Martin Truex Jr. (1) and Jimmie Johnson (48). Truex had a strong run in his second start of the season, but got together with Dale Earnhardt Jr. in the closing laps, while Sadler managed a sixth-place finish.

If any doubt lingered about Gordon's rise to supremacy at Daytona and Talladega, it was officially put to rest in the Aaron's 499. It wasn't just that Gordon won the race; it was *how* he won it.

Gordon led 12 times for 139 laps and all but 43 under the green flag, with most of those due to pit sequencing. He led on five of the eight restarts, and on the other three it took the DuPont driver two laps, one lap and five laps, respectively, to regain the point once the field got back underway.

TOP 10 QUALIFIERS

Pos.	Driver	Seconds	mph
1	Kevin Harvick	50.452	189.804
2	Jeff Gordon	50.670	188.988
3	Elliott Sadler	50.788	188.548
4	Scott Riggs	50.808	188.474
5	Ryan Newman	50.872	188.237
6	Jimmie Johnson	50.875	188.226
7	Ricky Rudd	50.894	188.156
8	Dave Blaney	50.958	187.919
9	Travis Kvapil	50.975	187.857
10	Kurt Busch	50.982	187.831

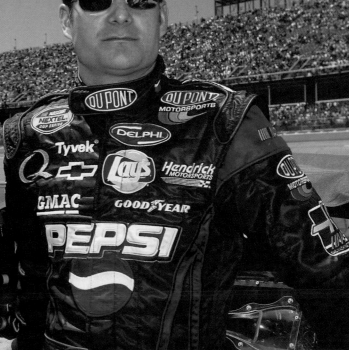

Jeff Gordon wears a look of confidence while waiting for the start of the race. Once underway, he jumped straight into the lead and remained there for most of the day in a dominant performance.

(Far Left) Kevin Harvick won his first Bud Pole of the season and led 12 laps in the race, second to Gordon's 139. Unfortunately, he got tangled up with Dale Earnhardt Jr. in the closing laps and fell to 12th at the finish.

(Left) Team member Gene Pasquale brings the GM Goodwrench Chevrolet to the line after it turned a qualifying lap nearly a full mile per hour faster than second-quickest Jeff Gordon.

(Right) Dale Jarrett (88), Jamie McMurray (42) and Jeremy Mayfield (19) ride in formation through Talladega's frontstretch. All three drivers picked up top 10s in the race, allowing Jarrett and McMurray to join the top 10 in points, while Mayfield moved up four spots to 12th in the standings.

Most impressive, however, was that in this form of racing where partnerships are king, Gordon could do it all on his own. That fact was most evident after the last caution for a six-car accident on the backstretch that set up a green-white-checkered dash to the finish.

Gordon led on the final restart followed by Jamie McMurray, Elliott Sadler, Stewart and Waltrip. With Gordon guarding his position on the bottom, McMurray and Sadler fell in line

Scott Riggs tries to keep pace with Jeff Gordon (24) on the inside, while Tony Stewart (20) looks for help from Matt Kenseth (17) in his challenge for the lead. Stewart got past Gordon only once in the race but managed to take second at the finish.

behind him. Stewart and Waltrip, however, hooked up in a draft of their own and went after the leader.

"Michael and I got a great run out of [Turns] 3 and 4," Stewart explained of the final laps, "and really caught [Sadler] and Jamie [McMurray] off guard and got by them."

Now running second and third, they made their last-lap attempt on Gordon.

"Michael pushed me all the way down the backstretch," Stewart continued, "and we still

(Above) Ken Schrader stops under green for fresh tires and fuel. Schrader, who started 42nd, arrived at the top 10 with 20 laps remaining and brought the BAM Racing Dodge home in eighth place.

(Left) Greg Biffle's Ford limps to the pits after being caught in a late-race accident on the backstretch. Biffle was able to remain on the lead lap and salvage a 13th-place finish, falling one spot to fourth in the standings.

AARON'S 499

NASCAR NEXTEL Cup Series Race No. 9

Fin. Pos.	Start Pos.	Car No.	Driver	Team	Laps	Laps Led	Status
1	2	24	Jeff Gordon	DuPont Chevrolet	194	139	Running
2	11	20	Tony Stewart	The Home Depot Chevrolet	194	2	Running
3	38	15	Michael Waltrip	NAPA Auto Parts Chevrolet	194	2	Running
4	22	19	Jeremy Mayfield	Dodge Dealers/UAW Dodge	194		Running
5	13	42	Jamie McMurray	Texaco/Havoline Dodge	194		Running
6	3	38	Elliott Sadler	M&M's Ford	194	9	Running
7	10	97	Kurt Busch	IRWIN Industrial Tools Ford	194	1	Running
8	42	49	Ken Schrader	Schwan's Home Service Dodge	194	1	Running
9	14	88	Dale Jarrett	UPS Ford	194		Running
10	27	31	Jeff Burton	Cingular Wireless Chevrolet	194		Running
11	23	17	Matt Kenseth	DeWalt Power Tools Ford	194		Running
12	1	29	Kevin Harvick	GM Goodwrench Chevrolet	194	12	Running
13	29	16	Greg Biffle	National Guard/Charter Ford	194	2	Running
14	26	41	Casey Mears	Target Dodge	193		Running
15	36	8	Dale Earnhardt Jr.	Budweiser Chevrolet	193	3	Running
16	43	09	Johnny Sauter	Miccosukee Resort Dodge	192		Running
17	31	33	Kerry Earnhardt	Bass Pro Shops Chevrolet	190		Running
18	9	77 #	Travis Kvapil	Kodak/Jasper Eng. & Trans. Dodge	188		Accident
19	8	07	Dave Blaney	Jack Daniel's Chevrolet	187		Running
20	6	48	Jimmie Johnson	Lowe's Chevrolet	186	8	Accident
21	32	1	Martin Truex Jr.	Bass Pro Shops/Tracker Chevrolet	186		Accident
22	20	2	Rusty Wallace	Miller Lite Dodge	180		Running
23	15	18	Bobby Labonte	Interstate Batteries Chevrolet	174	1	Engine
24	19	9	Kasey Kahne	Dodge Dealers/UAW Dodge	172		Running
25	39	43	Jeff Green	Cheerios/Betty Crocker Dodge	172		Running
26	18	11	Jason Leffler	FedEx Express Chevrolet	171		Running
27	4	10	Scott Riggs	Valvoline Chevrolet	171	4	Running
28	33	4	Mike Wallace	Lucas Oil Chevrolet	171	1	Running
29	30	66	Hermie Sadler	Peak Fitness Ford	170		Rear End
30	7	21	Ricky Rudd	Motorcraft Quality Parts Ford	170		Running
31	24	01	Joe Nemechek	U.S. Army Chevrolet	169	1	Running
32	21	99	Carl Edwards	Scotts/Ortho Ford	166		Running
33	16	6	Mark Martin	Viagra Ford	166	3	Running
34	25	40	Sterling Marlin	Coors Light Dodge	162		Running
35	12	36	Boris Said	CENTRIX Financial Chevrolet	146		Accident
36	28	0	Mike Bliss	Net Zero Best Buy Chevrolet	141		Accident
37	37	25	Brian Vickers	GMAC/ditech.com Chevrolet	139		Accident
38	17	22	Scott Wimmer	Caterpillar Dodge	139		Accident
39	5	12	Ryan Newman	ALLTEL Dodge	135	5	Accident
40	40	32	Bobby Hamilton Jr.	Tide Chevrolet	132		Accident
41	35	5 #	Kyle Busch	Kellogg's Chevrolet	132		Accident
42	34	23	Mike Skinner	Bad Boy Mowers Dodge	132		Accident
43	41	45	Kyle Petty	Georgia-Pacific/Brawny Dodge	106		Running

Raybestos Rookie of the Year Contender.

NASCAR NEXTEL Cup Series Point Standings
(After 9 Races)

Pos.	Driver	Points	Behind	Change
1	**Jimmie Johnson**	1368	—	—
2	Kurt Busch	1238	-130	—
3	Jeff Gordon	1217	-151	+1
4	Greg Biffle	1181	-187	-1
5	Elliott Sadler	1164	-204	—
6	Tony Stewart	1088	-280	+8
7	Dale Jarrett	1085	-283	+6
8	Kevin Harvick	1083	-285	+3
9	Dale Earnhardt Jr.	1070	-298	+3
10	Jamie McMurray	1067	-301	+5

couldn't catch him. They (Gordon) just had a better car than we did."

Effectively unchallenged, Gordon drove to a 0.193-second margin of victory over Stewart and Waltrip, while Jeremy Mayfield moved up to fourth ahead of McMurray and Sadler.

"This was the best [restrictor] plate car I've ever had," Gordon told reporters after the race. "I'll tell you how good it was: I got up behind Junior one time and pushed him to the front. Just pushed him past people and into the lead for a few laps. Then I pulled out and drove right by him. Man, I'd never been able to do that before. This car did everything I asked of it. It was just awesome."

With that, Gordon staked his claim to being the new king of the superspeedways.

And what of Earnhardt? After starting 36th, Junior drove into the top 10, fell back to 35th, found the top five and even led near the halfway point, dropped to 15th and finally fought back to as high as third place before he and Martin Truex Jr. tangled in the closing laps in an accident that also collected Johnson, Greg Biffle, Kevin Harvick and Travis Kvapil, setting up the final three-lap dash.

That however, wasn't The Big One — the seemingly inevitable that occurs when 43 drivers race inches apart at 190 miles per hour. This time Johnson and Mike Wallace touched while running side by side, with Earnhardt and Scott Riggs right behind. The contact triggered a pileup entering the first turn that ultimately involved 25 drivers. Four cars — those of Mike Skinner, Kyle Busch, Bobby Hamilton Jr. and Ryan Newman — were unable to continue as a result of the accident that left just 16 cars on the lead lap.

Other notables in the race included Ken Schrader, who started 42nd and picked up 34 positions to finish eighth in his best performance in more than a year, Dale Jarrett, who finished in ninth for his second top 10 of the season, and Jeff Burton, who took the 10th position on the heels of his third-place finish the week before at Phoenix.

Gordon's win, his 10th with restrictor plates in 50 career starts and overall the 72nd of his career, brought him to within four victories of sixth place on the all-time wins list, currently held by the acknowledged master of the superspeedways, the late Dale Earnhardt.

DODGE CHARGER 500

There were a few new twists to this season's NASCAR NEXTEL Cup Series visit to South Carolina's venerable Darlington Raceway. For the first time in the history of NASCAR's original superspeedway, the event would be run under the lights on Mother's Day weekend. The race would also cover 500 miles for the first time since the spring race was shortened to 400 miles 12 years ago.

The changes were apparently well received, as fans gathered up the last remaining tickets six days before the event. By the time the engines fired on Saturday night, a sellout crowd was on hand to witness all the action. They wouldn't be disappointed.

For the first 433 miles of the Dodge Charger 500, Greg Biffle had things pretty much going his way. By then, he had already led eight times for 170 laps, nearly tripling the number of laps led by each of his closest competitors: Jeff Gordon, Jimmie Johnson and pole-winner Kasey Kahne.

Kyle Petty's Dodge was one of several race cars at Darlington painted in recognition of Mother's Day weekend. Kyle's wife, Pattie, also had the honor of throwing the green flag to begin the Dodge Charger 500.

The sun begins to fade behind the Turn 4 grandstand as twilight descends on the event. To the delight of track officials, tickets sold out days before the race, prompting optimism regarding the raceway's future.

Then, with the race entering its final stages, here came Ryan Newman. After starting second, Newman had fallen through the top 10 over the first 80 laps, but he and crew chief Matt Borland had consistently improved their car over the course of the evening, and with 50 laps to go, the ALLTEL Dodge moved to the point for the first time in the race.

Biffle could only watch as Newman increased his advantage, eventually opening a convincing four-second lead and appearing to be a lock to win his first race of the season. This, however, is Darlington. And the "Lady in Black," who has so often waved her cruel hand of fate over those vying for victory, struck once again.

With only two of the slated 367 laps remaining, Newman's hopes went up in smoke, literally, as Mark Martin went sliding down the frontstretch after an aggressive attempt to take third place away from Kahne, which brought out the 12th and final caution of the night.

Now facing a green-white-checkered finish, Newman had a choice to make: stay out on the track and in the lead, or pit to replace his worn, hot tires. In reality, it wasn't much of a choice at all. With 19 drivers on the lead lap, enough of them would surely remain on the track to drop Newman back into traffic if he pitted. Stay out, and his competition would seize the opportunity to get fresh rubber for a shot at the win.

Newman elected to stay put, while Biffle, the memory of his costly decision to forego tires late in a race weeks earlier at Bristol, peeled onto pit road. Newman's heart sank as he watched in his mirror while all of the lead-lap cars except Ken Schrader followed Biffle into their pits.

Carl Edwards returned to the track first, ahead of Biffle, Gordon and Kahne, and as they lined up behind second-place Schrader, Newman knew his only remaining chance to win would be a caution on the restart, which would end the race immediately.

Newman brought the field around slowly, if not a bit erratically, and when the green flag fell the leaders bunched together but somehow managed to avoid any serious mishaps.

"I gave them too clean of a restart," Newman said when asked about the final green flag. "I was just hoping they would crash right away at the start."

Kurt Busch's battered Ford gets extended service during one of 12 cautions in the race. Busch brought out the first yellow flag when he spun and hit the inside wall just two laps after the initial green flag.

Biffle dove straight to the inside in Turns 1 and 2, dispatching Schrader and Edwards, who fought to keep his car off the wall after a bump from behind by Gordon. Down the backstretch Biffle closed in on Newman, dropping to the inside of the ALLTEL Dodge at the entrance to Turn 3 and completing the pass with relative ease. Biffle then dropped the hammer on the National Guard Ford and turned his fastest lap of the entire race on the way to the checkered flag.

Gordon followed to take second place ahead of Kahne, while Martin, eighth on the restart, charged to fourth over the final two laps. Newman was able to hang on to finish fifth, Edwards gathered up his Ford in time to fall in line in ninth place, while Schrader dropped all the way back to 18th over the final two trips around the track.

TOP 10 QUALIFIERS

Pos.	Driver	Seconds	mph
1	Kasey Kahne	28.923	170.024
2	Ryan Newman	29.003	169.555
3	Greg Biffle	29.060	169.222
4	Elliott Sadler	29.156	168.665
5	Brian Vickers	29.166	168.607
6	Kyle Busch #	29.256	168.089
7	Sterling Marlin	29.311	167.773
8	Jeremy Mayfield	29.325	167.693
9	Jimmie Johnson	29.328	167.676
10	Carl Edwards	29.334	167.642

(Above) Bud Pole-winner Kasey Kahne (9) sets up the starting field with Ryan Newman (12) on his right. Kahne led three times for 60 laps, second only to Biffle's 176, and scored his third top-five finish of the season.

(Left) Greg Biffle gets four new Goodyears for the final two laps of the race. With fresh tires, it took him less than a lap to pass Ken Schrader and Ryan Newman on the way to his third win of the year.

(Opposite Page) Fans and media members keep an eye on early-race action from the packed grandstand and press box along Darlington's backstretch.

DODGE CHARGER 500

NASCAR NEXTEL Cup Series Race No. 10

Fin. Pos.	Start Pos.	Car No.	Driver	Team	Laps	Laps Led	Status
1	3	16	Greg Biffle	National Guard/Travelodge Ford	370	176	Running
2	14	24	Jeff Gordon	DuPont Chevrolet	370	20	Running
3	1	9	Kasey Kahne	Dodge Dealers/UAW Dodge	370	60	Running
4	20	6	Mark Martin	Viagra Ford	370		Running
5	2	12	Ryan Newman	ALLTEL Dodge	370	47	Running
6	13	42	Jamie McMurray	Texaco/Havoline Dodge	370		Running
7	9	48	Jimmie Johnson	Lowe's Chevrolet	370	55	Running
8	39	8	Dale Earnhardt Jr.	Budweiser Chevrolet	370		Running
9	10	99	Carl Edwards	Office Depot Ford	370	4	Running
10	15	20	Tony Stewart	The Home Depot Chevrolet	370		Running
11	27	01	Joe Nemechek	U.S. Army Chevrolet	370	2	Running
12	12	2	Rusty Wallace	Miller Lite Dodge	370		Running
13	35	21	Ricky Rudd	Motorcraft Quality Parts Ford	370		Running
14	24	29	Kevin Harvick	GM Goodwrench Chevrolet	370		Running
15	22	88	Dale Jarrett	UPS Ford	370		Running
16	5	25	Brian Vickers	GMAC/ditech.com Chevrolet	370	1	Running
17	36	18	Bobby Labonte	Interstate Batteries Chevrolet	370		Running
18	28	49	Ken Schrader	Schwan's Home Service Dodge	370		Running
19	29	0	Mike Bliss	Net Zero Best Buy Chevrolet	370		Running
20	4	38	Elliott Sadler	M&M's Ford	369		Running
21	34	31	Jeff Burton	Cingular Wireless Chevrolet	369		Running
22	23	43	Jeff Green	Cheerios/Betty Crocker Dodge	369		Running
23	6	5 #	Kyle Busch	Kellogg's Chevrolet	369		Running
24	42	4	Mike Wallace	Lucas Oil Chevrolet	369	1	Running
25	33	22	Scott Wimmer	Caterpillar Dodge	368		Running
26	31	17	Matt Kenseth	Carhartt Ford	367	1	Running
27	32	00	Kenny Wallace	Bryan Meats Chevrolet	367		Running
28	37	45	Kyle Petty	Georgia-Pacific/Brawny/Dodge	366		Running
29	30	07	Dave Blaney	Jack Daniel's Chevrolet	366		Running
30	26	32	Bobby Hamilton Jr.	Tide Chevrolet	365		Running
31	43	92 #	Stanton Barrett	Front Row Motorsports Chevrolet	365		Running
32	38	37	Kevin Lepage	R&J Racing Dodge	363	1	Running
33	8	19	Jeremy Mayfield	Dodge Dealers/UAW Dodge	333	1	Accident
34	19	15	Michael Waltrip	NAPA Auto Parts Chevrolet	330		Running
35	17	77 #	Travis Kvapil	Kodak/Jasper Eng. & Trans. Dodge	323		Running
36	18	10	Scott Riggs	Valvoline Chevrolet	311		Running
37	11	97	Kurt Busch	IRWIN Industrial Tools Ford	306		Running
38	25	11	Jason Leffler	FedEx Express-St Jude Classic Chevrolet	285		Running
39	16	41	Casey Mears	Target Dodge	285		Running
40	41	66	Hermie Sadler	East Tennessee Trailers/Peak Fitness Ford	234		Pwr. Steering
41	7	40	Sterling Marlin	Coors Light Dodge	221	1	Engine
42	21	80	Carl Long	Buyer's Choice Auto Warranty Chevrolet	69		Rear End
43	40	34	Jeff Fuller	Mach 1 Inc. Chevrolet	24		Transmission

Raybestos Rookie of the Year Contender.

NASCAR NEXTEL Cup Series Point Standings
(After 10 Races)

Pos.	Driver	Points	Behind	Change
1	**Jimmie Johnson**	**1519**	—	–
2	Jeff Gordon	1392	-127	+1
3	Greg Biffle	1371	-148	+1
4	Kurt Busch	1290	-229	-2
5	Elliott Sadler	1267	-252	—
6	Mark Martin	1226	-293	+5
7	Tony Stewart	1222	-297	-1
8	Jamie McMurray	1217	-302	+2
9	Dale Earnhardt Jr.	1212	-307	—
10	Ryan Newman	1205	-314	+5

When questioned about his decision regarding whether or not to pit before the final restart, Biffle responded: "There was no question in my mind that we were coming in for tires, no matter what."

"I wouldn't do it the same way as Bristol again," said crew chief Doug Richert, recalling that the decision not to pit had cost them the win. "Believe me, I thought about the same thing when it was coming down to the end. ... I know exactly what [Newman] feels like because we did that to ourselves [at Bristol]."

CHEVY AMERICAN REVOLUTION 400

For Kasey Kahne, it was a long time coming — inevitable to be sure after six second-place showings, five Bud Poles and 16 top-five finishes over his first 45 career starts — but a long time nonetheless.

The fact is, however, Kasey Kahne's first career NASCAR NEXTEL Cup Series victory probably couldn't have come at a much better place or in a much better way.

Eight months ago, in the midst of a brilliant rookie season, Kahne came to Richmond International Raceway ninth in the point standings and with every intention of making it into the Chase for the NASCAR NEXTEL Cup. But a rough night on the track led to a 24th-place finish and dropped Kahne to 12th in points, knocking him out of championship contention

Kasey Kahne (left) gets a chuckle out of younger brother Kale as they wait for the start of the race at Richmond. Kahne would start the race from first place after winning his second Bud Pole in as many weeks.

TOP 10 QUALIFIERS

Pos.	Driver	Seconds	mph
1	Kasey Kahne	20.775	129.964
2	Ryan Newman	20.801	129.801
3	Tony Stewart	20.842	129.546
4	Kurt Busch	20.857	129.453
5	Elliott Sadler	20.920	129.063
6	Ricky Rudd	20.932	128.989
7	Kevin Harvick	20.942	128.928
8	Rusty Wallace	20.948	128.891
9	Greg Biffle	20.952	128.866
10	Kyle Busch	20.955	128.848

Elliott Sadler's M&M's mates fly through a four-tire stop during a caution, one of nine yellow-flag periods during the evening. Sadler fell back from his fifth-place starting spot in the early laps, but recovered to finish seventh for his sixth top 10 of the year.

— a bitter pill to swallow while watching teammate Jeremy Mayfield drive into the championship field with his first win of the season.

That finish, combined with a 28th place in his first attempt at the three-quarter-mile oval one year ago, prompted Kahne, crew chief Tommy Baldwin and the Evernham Motorsports team to schedule a test session there to see if they could solve the tricky short track. Apparently they did.

In Bud Pole qualifying, Kahne took to the track 41st in the field of 47 drivers with Tony Stewart atop the leader board, and posted a lap more than four-tenths of a second faster than his friendly rival. Ryan Newman, the last driver to make an attempt, gave it all he had but fell just short and joined Kahne on the front row for the start of the race with Stewart right behind in third.

Kyle Busch (5) looks to the inside of Johnny Sauter (09) as they head into the first turn. Busch hung around the top 10 for the entire race before finishing fourth for his third top-10 finish of the season.

Kahne, Newman and Stewart all share similar backgrounds, having cut their racing teeth in the open-wheel divisions of the Midwest driving Midgets and Sprint Cars. In fact, Stewart and Kahne had sometimes raced together as teammates and had developed a friendly and mutually-respectful relationship.

"We started there (in open wheel) and he helped me there," Kahne said of Stewart, "and once I got in the NASCAR Busch Series car he helped me. We've been friends since then."

So when asked in a pre-race interview for TV who he would most like to beat in his first NASCAR NEXTEL Cup Series victory, Kahne naturally cited Stewart.

As it turned out, this would be his opportunity. Together, Kahne and Stewart thoroughly dominated the Chevy American Revolution 400. Between them, they led all but 15 of the 400 laps; they fronted the field on 15 occasions and swapped the lead between them six times. Neither driver was listed lower than fourth at any of the 20-lap scoring intervals during the entire contest and, over the final 140 laps, Kahne, Stewart and Newman were shown 1-2-3 at every scoring segment.

Woes beset the Hendrick teams of Jimmie Johnson and Jeff Gordon at Richmond. Johnson's car (right) was heavily damaged in an accident at the 80-lap mark. The Lowe's team made repairs, but a broken steering box later in the race sidelined them for good. Gordon's DuPont Monte Carlo (below) suffered various mechanical woes that eventually led Gordon to park it for good.

(Top) Kasey Kahne's crew was flawless at Richmond, not giving up a single position on pit road. Kahne did his part as well, with superb restarts that kept him at the front.

Tony Stewart (20) tries to chase down Kasey Kahne (9) in the final laps, but the second-year driver placed every wheel right and eased away to the win, while Stewart was left to defend second place.

CHEVY AMERICAN REVOLUTION 400

**NASCAR NEXTEL Cup Series
Race No. 11**

Fin. Pos.	Start Pos.	Car No.	Driver	Team	Laps	Laps Led	Status
1	1	9	Kasey Kahne	Dodge Dealers/UAW Dodge	400	242	Running
2	3	20	Tony Stewart	The Home Depot Chevrolet	400	143	Running
3	2	12	Ryan Newman	ALLTEL Dodge	400		Running
4	10	5 #	Kyle Busch	Kellogg's/Star Wars Episode III Chevrolet	400		Running
5	7	29	Kevin Harvick	GM Goodwrench Chevrolet	400	1	Running
6	9	16	Greg Biffle	National Guard Ford	400		Running
7	5	38	Elliott Sadler	M&M's Ford	400		Running
8	39	18	Bobby Labonte	Boniva Chevrolet	400		Running
9	23	15	Michael Waltrip	NAPA Auto Parts Chevrolet	400		Running
10	17	42	Jamie McMurray	Texaco/Havoline Dodge	400		Running
11	6	21	Ricky Rudd	Motorcraft Quality Parts Ford	400		Running
12	26	17	Matt Kenseth	DeWalt Power Tools Ford	400	2	Running
13	15	19	Jeremy Mayfield	Dodge Dealers/UAW Dodge	400		Running
14	27	8	Dale Earnhardt Jr.	Budweiser Chevrolet	400		Running
15	14	6	Mark Martin	Viagra Ford	400		Running
16	12	31	Jeff Burton	Cingular Wireless Chevrolet	400		Running
17	4	97	Kurt Busch	IRWIN Industrial Tools Ford	400	11	Running
18	25	01	Joe Nemechek	U.S. Army Chevrolet	399		Running
19	8	2	Rusty Wallace	Miller Lite Dodge	399		Running
20	34	22	Scott Wimmer	Caterpillar Dodge	399		Running
21	11	99	Carl Edwards	RoundUp Ford	399		Running
22	21	77 #	Travis Kvapil	Kodak/Jasper Eng. & Trans. Dodge	399		Running
23	22	40	Sterling Marlin	Coors Light Dodge	399		Running
24	18	43	Jeff Green	Cheerios/Betty Crocker Dodge	399		Running
25	38	11	Jason Leffler	FedEx Ground Chevrolet	399		Running
26	36	10	Scott Riggs	Arometrics Chevrolet	399		Running
27	19	07	Dave Blaney	Bass Pro Shops Chevrolet	398		Running
28	16	41	Casey Mears	Target Dodge	398		Running
29	30	4	Mike Wallace	Lucas Oil Chevrolet	398		Running
30	40	49	Ken Schrader	Schwan's Home Service Dodge	398		Running
31	33	7	Robby Gordon	Jim Beam Chevrolet	398		Running
32	29	25	Brian Vickers	GMAC/ditech.com Chevrolet	397		Running
33	41	45	Kyle Petty	Georgia-Pacific/Brawny Dodge	397	1	Running
34	35	88	Dale Jarrett	UPS Ford	396		Running
35	31	92	Tony Raines	Front Row Motorsports Chevrolet	392		Running
36	32	32	Bobby Hamilton Jr.	Tide Chevrolet	387		Running
37	24	0	Mike Bliss	Net Zero Best Buy Chevrolet	375		Accident
38	43	66	Hermie Sadler	Peak Fitness Ford	367		Engine
39	20	24	Jeff Gordon	DuPont Chevrolet	252		Accident
40	28	48	Jimmie Johnson	Lowe's Chevrolet	80		Accident
41	13	09	Johnny Sauter	Miccosukee Resort Dodge	64		Accident
42	42	89	Morgan Shepherd	Racing with Jesus/Red Line Oil Dodge	36		Brakes
43	37	75	Mike Garvey	Jani-King/Rinaldi AC Service Dodge	23		Brakes

NASCAR NEXTEL Cup Series Point Standings
(After 11 Races)

Pos.	Driver	Points	Behind	Change
1	**Jimmie Johnson**	**1562**	—	—
2	Greg Biffle	1521	-41	+1
3	Jeff Gordon	1438	-124	-1
4	Elliott Sadler	1413	-149	+1
5	Kurt Busch	1407	-155	-1
6	Tony Stewart	1397	-165	+1
7	Ryan Newman	1370	-192	+3
8	Kevin Harvick	1364	-198	+3
9	Jamie McMurray	1351	-211	-1
10	Mark Martin	1344	-218	-4

Kahne led a total of 242 laps, taking the lead from Stewart for the last time with 106 circuits remaining. Holding that position, however, would not be easy, as there were four cautions over the final 68 laps.

Assisted by his crew, which did not give up a single position on pit road during the race that included nine yellow flags, Kahne was rock solid, calculating each restart with expert precision.

His final test came when the caution flew on Lap 390, which set up a seven-lap sprint to the finish and provided Stewart one last shot at the win.

"I kept him honest on the restart, that's for sure," Stewart said. "He was not going to make it easy, I promise you that. He did everything right. ... When it came time at the end to go, he was the fastest car on the track and he made zero mistakes. He didn't give anybody an opportunity to get to him."

As the green flag dropped, Stewart took one last shot at Kahne, pulling alongside the Dodge's rear quarter panel as the pair attacked the first turn. But Kahne held firm on the inside and began to pull away, leaving Stewart to battle with Newman for second place while opening a 1.674-second margin to score the long-awaited and well-deserved victory.

Kahne arrived in Victory Lane to the cheers of his crew, including Kale Kahne, who greeted his older brother by shouting, "Dude, we finally did it! We finally got it!"

Not one to relish in finishing second, Stewart had an uncharacteristic smile on his face as he climbed from The Home Depot Chevrolet and rushed to Victory Lane to be one of the first to congratulate Kahne.

"It was just like when I won here in '99 and got that first win," Stewart recalled, "and Dale Earnhardt was the first guy to come congratulate me.

"I just remember what that feeling was like, and I guess it's bringing me back to '99 to a certain degree."

"Tony Stewart has helped me as much as any driver to get where I am right now," Kahne responded. "It was awesome to be able to race with him. ... To beat him was even better."

NASCAR NEXTEL All-Star Challenge

In the style of a classic racer, he pulled up to start-finish line and stopped, took the checkered flag in hand and then quietly motored around Lowe's Motor Speedway on a simple, dignified victory lap that defined the man, the driver, the true professional that Mark Martin is, and has always been. This was an all-star moment featuring one of the greatest drivers the sport has known.

Mark Martin circles Lowe's Motor Speedway with checkered flag in hand following a popular win in the NASCAR NEXTEL All-Star Challenge, his second career triumph in the special non-points event.

Mike Bliss (0) slides toward the finish line while Brian Vickers (25) snatches the checkered flag in the NEXTEL Open. Vickers had just come from behind to make a last-lap pass that sent Bliss spinning.

There were no donuts on the grass, no burnouts to entice the crowd. Yet every fan in attendance, regardless of their allegiance to any particular driver or team, stood and cheered enthusiastically as the retro-painted No. 6 Ford toured the 1.5-mile oval.

Martin's victory celebration was a fitting end to an all-star celebration that spanned several days in and around Charlotte, N.C., home to many NASCAR NEXTEL Cup Series teams.

The events began on Thursday evening with the first ever NASCAR NEXTEL Pit Crew Challenge Presented by Motorola, held inside the Charlotte Coliseum. The unique format pitted over-the-wall crews from 24 eligible teams against each other in a multi-round elimination that tested the skills of crewmen at their individual positions and as a team.

The final round came down to Jamie McMurray's No. 42 crew against the No. 9 team for driver Kasey Kahne. Perhaps still riding momentum from their first win only days earlier at Richmond, the group from Evernham Motorsports performed a four-tire stop in 16.14 seconds to win the fist event of its kind, with each of the seven crew members taking home $10,000 in prize money.

Back at the Speedway, Friday night's activities featured qualifying for the NEXTEL Open, won by Mike Bliss with Kyle Busch, Casey Mears, Travis Kvapil and Brian Vickers filling out the top five starting positions.

Time trials for the NASCAR NEXTEL All-Star Challenge followed, using the three-lap format that includes a mandatory pit stop for four tires and fuel. Ryan Newman and his ALLTEL mates clicked off a great stop and three fast laps in just over two minutes to beat Martin by just three-quarters of a second in the ultra-competitive competition to win the pole for the all-star race.

At stake in the NEXTEL Open on Saturday night was one transfer position into the main event for the winner of the 30-lap sprint. Bliss and Kvapil swapped the lead between them six times over the first 29 laps in their battle for top honors. On the lap that counted, however, Vickers pulled up on Bliss' bumper through the final turns and, as the pair peeled onto the frontstretch for the final time, Vickers tapped the NetZero Chevrolet from behind and sent it

QUALIFYING RESULTS
NASCAR NEXTEL All-Star Challenge

Pos.	Team	Seconds	mph
1	Ryan Newman	122.443	132.306
2	Mark Martin	123.192	131.502
3	Rusty Wallace	123.227	131.465
4	Elliott Sadler	123.414	131.265
5	Kasey Kahne	124.197	130.438
6	Jimmie Johnson	124.625	129.990
7	Carl Edwards	124.887	129.717
8	Kurt Busch	125.171	129.423
9	Joe Nemechek	125.271	129.320
10	Matt Kenseth	125.896	128.678
11	Greg Biffle	126.725	127.836
12	Bobby Labonte	127.116	127.443
13	Terry Labonte	128.399	126.169
14	Jeff Gordon	128.673	125.901
15	Jeremy Mayfield	129.691	124.912
16	Michael Waltrip	134.626	120.333
17	Tony Stewart	137.820	117.545
18	Kevin Harvick	144.000	112.500
19	Dale Jarrett	145.571	111.286
20	Dale Earnhardt Jr.	146.022	110.942

spinning. Sliding sideways through the tri-oval grass, Bliss crossed the finish line just 0.114-second behind, and while Bliss expressed his disappointment to reporters after the race, the ditech.com crew busily prepared their Chevrolet for the feature event.

Twenty-two drivers made up the field for the NASCAR NEXTEL All-Star Challenge, including Vickers and Martin Truex Jr., who won the popular vote by the fans and lined up last on the grid in his DEI-owned Chevrolet.

Like last year, the event was split into segments of 40, 30 and 20 laps, with an undetermined number of positions to be inverted at the start of the second segment.

Two cautions flew over the opening round, the most significant for a 10-car accident on Lap 35 that began when Tony Stewart tagged Joe Nemechek from behind, turning the U.S. Army Chevrolet into Kevin Harvick on the frontstretch. When the smoke cleared, the cars of Stewart, Nemechek and Harvick were unable to continue, as were those of Kahne, Terry Labonte, Michael Waltrip and Truex Jr.

A random draw inverted the top six finishers from the first segment and put Vickers and Newman on the front row for the start of Segment 2. Newman took over immediately and led flag to flag in the caution-free, 30-lap run, followed across the line by Elliott Sadler and Vickers.

(Opposing Page) Ryan Newman tries to poke the nose of his ALLTEL Dodge between Kurt Busch and Jeff Gordon. Newman won the pole for the NASCAR NEXTEL All-Star Challenge and led 45 of the first 70 laps before spinning and hitting the wall.

(Below) Teammates and former winners of the special event, Dale Earnhardt Jr. (8) and Michael Waltrip (15) pace each other in the first segment. Waltrip retired from the race after both drivers were involved in the multi-car accident on Lap 35, while Earnhardt nursed his Chevrolet to a lead-lap finish in 10th.

Martin finished fourth in the second segment and pitted during the break with a decision to make: four tires or two? Confident with the car on fresh rubber, he and crew chief Pat Tryson made the call to take a full set of new Goodyears, and Martin returned to the track behind Sadler and Jeff Gordon, both of whom elected to move up in the running order with two-tire stops.

(Above) Mark Martin (6) engages Elliott Sadler (38) door to door immediately following the final restart. The two touched in Turns 1 and 2, allowing Martin to take the lead he held over the last 19 laps.

(Left) Joe Nemechek (01) hits Kevin Harvick (29) after being tapped from behind by Tony Stewart (20). The contact touched off the Lap-35 incident that involved 10 cars, seven of which could not continue in the race.

(Opposing Page) With fans roaring their approval, Mark Martin salutes the crowd from Victory Lane to touch off the post-race celebration.

When the green flag flew for the final restart, Martin charged into the first turn on Sadler's outside and the two touched, knocking the right-front fender in just a bit on Sadler's M&M's Ford. Martin took full advantage and moved into the lead with Sadler in tow. Once out front, the 46-year-old from Batesville, Ark., put his years of experience to work, driving with perfection over the final 19 laps on the way to his second career all-star triumph.

With victory laps completed, Martin pulled into the Winner's Circle, climbed out of the car and onto its window ledge, faced the main grandstand and saluted the fans. The roar of the crowd swelled disproportionately as fans expressed their approval of the wildly popular win.

At that moment, as thousands cheered in admiration for the man they had watched race over the past two decades, one had to consider the sweet irony of the name Martin had chosen to mark his final full season of competition: "A Salute to You."

NASCAR NEXTEL ALL-STAR CHALLENGE

Fin. Pos.	Start Pos.	Car No.	Driver	Team	Laps	Laps Led	Status
1	2	6	Mark Martin	Viagra Ford	90	24	Running
2	4	38	Elliott Sadler	Pedigree/M&M's Ford	90	21	Running
3	21	25	Brian Vickers	GMAC/ditech.com Chevrolet	90		Running
4	14	24	Jeff Gordon	DuPont Chevrolet	90		Running
5	6	48	Jimmie Johnson	Lowe's Chevrolet	90		Running
6	19	00	Dale Jarrett	UPS Ford	90		Running
7	8	97	Kurt Busch	IRWIN Industrial Tools Ford	90		Running
8	15	19	Jeremy Mayfield	Dodge Dealers/UAW Dodge	90		Running
9	12	18	Bobby Labonte	Interstate Batteries Chevrolet	90		Running
10	20	8	Dale Earnhardt Jr.	Budweiser Chevrolet	90		Running
11	10	17	Matt Kenseth	DeWalt Power Tools Ford	89		Couldn't Improve
12	1	12	Ryan Newman	ALLTEL Dodge	71	45	Accident
13	3	2	Rusty Wallace	Miller Lite Dodge	71		Accident
14	11	16	Greg Biffle	Charter/National Guard Ford	69		Suspension
15	7	99	Carl Edwards	Scotts/Miracle-Gro Ford	57		Accident
16	5	9	Kasey Kahne	Dodge Dealers/UAW Dodge	35		Accident
17	17	20	Tony Stewart	The Home Depot/Madagascar Chevrolet	35		Accident
18	18	29	Kevin Harvick	GM Goodwrench Chevrolet	35		Accident
19	13	44	Terry Labonte	Pizza Hut Chevrolet	35		Accident
20	16	15	Michael Waltrip	NAPA Auto Parts Chevrolet	35		Accident
21	9	01	Joe Nemechek	U.S. Army Chevrolet	35		Accident
22	22	1	Martin Truex Jr.	Bass Pro Shops/Tracker Chevrolet	35		Accident

SEGMENT 1
(40 LAPS)

Fin.	Driver
1	Mark Martin
2	Elliott Sadler
3	Greg Biffle
4	Kurt Busch
5	Ryan Newman
6	Brian Vickers
7	Jimmie Johnson
8	Jeff Gordon
9	Rusty Wallace
10	Dale Jarrett
11	Carl Edwards
12	Matt Kenseth
13	Bobby Labonte
14	Jeremy Mayfield
15	Dale Earnhardt Jr.
16	Kasey Kahne
17	Tony Stewart
18	Kevin Harvick
19	Terry Labonte
20	Joe Nemechek
21	Martin Truex Jr.
22	Michael Waltrip

SEGMENT 2
(30 LAPS)

Fin.	Driver
1	Ryan Newman
2	Elliott Sadler
3	Brian Vickers
4	Mark Martin
5	Kurt Busch
6	Rusty Wallace
7	Jimmie Johnson
8	Jeff Gordon
9	Dale Jarrett
10	Matt Kenseth
11	Bobby Labonte
12	Jeremy Mayfield
13	Dale Earnhardt Jr.
14	Greg Biffle
15	Carl Edwards
16	Kasey Kahne
17	Tony Stewart
18	Kevin Harvick
19	Terry Labonte
20	Joe Nemechek
21	Martin Truex Jr.
22	Michael Waltrip

Coca-Cola 600

Records, it's said, are made to be broken. That certainly was true in a wild and wooly affair at Lowe's Motor Speedway with the 46th running of the Coca-Cola 600, NASCAR's longest race.

And long, it was. It took 5 hours, 13 minutes and 52 seconds to cover the prescribed 600-mile distance, and although that of itself is not a record (it was the third-longest Coca-Cola 600) it felt like it was to some.

Jimmie Johnson (48) and Bobby Labonte (18) race door-to-door toward the checkered flag. Labonte, who had to start at the rear of the field due to a transmission change, was inched out at the finish line as Johnson took his third straight Coca-Cola 600 win.

TOP 10 QUALIFIERS

Pos.	Driver	Seconds	mph
1	Ryan Newman	27.981	192.988
2	Jeff Gordon	28.136	191.925
3	Matt Kenseth	28.234	191.259
4	Kasey Kahne	28.305	190.779
5	Jimmie Johnson	28.311	190.739
6	Kyle Busch #	28.319	190.685
7	Dale Jarrett	28.348	190.490
8	Mike Bliss	28.368	190.355
9	Tony Stewart	28.404	190.114
10	Elliott Sadler	28.424	189.980

Pit road is packed as the field takes advantage of an early-race caution, one of 22 yellow-flag periods during the evening, which set a NASCAR record.

By the end of the race, 13 cars sat idle in the garage, 11 of those too heavily damaged to have continued. Three of the crumpled race cars belonged to Jack Roush (those of Mark Martin, Matt Kenseth and Kurt Busch) and three belonged to Rick Hendrick (the cars of Jeff Gordon, Brian Vickers and Terry Labonte).

Numbers like that would indicate a plethora of yellow flags, which indeed was the case. The caution flew 22 times, which broke two records: the previous mark of 14 in any event at Lowe's Motor Speedway, and the all-time high of 20 in any NASCAR NEXTEL Cup event dating back to the series' inception in 1949.

Throughout the night, drivers seemed to have problems negotiating the newly levigated surface after track officials "smoothed out" some of the bumps with the diamond-grinding process. Some drivers said the revamped asphalt curtailed passing, especially in Turns 1 and 2, but that didn't stop a total of 21 competitors from leading the race at some point, which broke the old track record of 18 different leaders set in 1988.

One thing the new surface did do was provide was plenty of speed, allowing Ryan Newman to get the record breaking started early by shattering the track-record speed of 186.657 mph in qualifying with a blazingly-fast lap at 192.988 mph, the fastest of 18 drivers to eclipse the old mark.

Martin Truex Jr. got Sunday evening's wreckfest going when he spun and slapped the barrier just seven laps into the event. He was followed by Kurt Busch, who went around and met the Turn-2 wall less than two laps after the Lap-10 restart. Busch returned to action after lengthy repairs but was involved in another incident and finished last after completing a total of just 26 laps.

Dale Earnhardt Jr., in his first race with Steve Hmiel as crew chief, started 15th in a car that was not handling well. Using frequent pit stops under caution, driver and crew chief got

(Top) Michael Waltrip (15) gets a nudge from teammate Dale Earnhardt Jr. Moments later, Watlrip's NAPA Chevrolet went spinning down the frontstretch and into the wall, ending his night as well as those of Matt Kenseth and Terry Labonte.

(Above) Sterling Marlin (40) and Kyle Petty (45) roll off the fourth turn together ahead of Elliott Sadler (38), whose spinning Ford brought out the seventh caution at the 150-lap mark.

Excess fuel from Johnny Sauter's Miccosukee Dodge ignites after Sauter smacked the Turn-3 wall, the result of a cut tire at the 140-lap mark.

Jeremy Mayfield gets fresh rubber and fuel from his Dodge Dealers/UAW crewmates, while the Chevrolets of Jimmie Johnson (49) and Brian Vickers (25) flash past. Mayfield put together a strong run to match his season-best fourth place for his second top 10 of the year.

the Budweiser Chevrolet fixed, and Earnhardt began slicing through the field toward the front. His car was so good in fact, when he came up on teammate Michael Waltrip he drove straight into the back of the NAPA Monte Carlo, triggering an accident that not only ended the race for Waltrip, but for Terry Labonte and Kenseth as well.

Like Earnhardt, traffic also got the best of Vickers. After starting 14th, Vickers drove straight into the top 10 in the opening laps and firmly into the lead before the halfway point. Fronting the field five times for 98 laps to lead all drivers, Vickers appeared a strong winning contender until he pitted under green with fewer than 50 laps remaining.

Jeff Gordon, Elliott Sadler, Rusty Wallace, Kevin Harvick and Jimmie Johnson followed one lap later, but before the round of green-flag stops was completed, tire problems on Kasey Kahne's Dodge left debris on the track, brining out the 19th caution in what would become a turning point in the race.

COCA-COLA 600

NASCAR NEXTEL Cup Series Race No. 12

Fin. Pos.	Start Pos.	Car No.	Driver	Team	Laps	Laps Led	Status
1	5	48	Jimmie Johnson	Lowe's Chevrolet	400	11	Running
2	34	18	Bobby Labonte	FedEx Freight Chevrolet	400	10	Running
3	12	99	Carl Edwards	RoundUp Ford	400	10	Running
4	36	19	Jeremy Mayfield	Dodge Dealers/UAW Dodge	400		Running
5	1	12	Ryan Newman	Alltel Dodge	400	43	Running
6	29	16	Greg Biffle	National Guard/Charter Ford	400	1	Running
7	30	1	Martin Truex Jr.	Bass Pro Shops/Tracker Chevrolet	400	4	Running
8	7	88	Dale Jarrett	UPS Ford	400		Running
9	21	49	Ken Schrader	Schwan's Home Service Dodge	400	6	Running
10	20	2	Rusty Wallace	Miller Lite Dodge	400	15	Running
11	39	43	Jeff Green	Bugles/Cheerios Dodge	400		Running
12	43	37	Kevin Lepage	Underdog Dodge	400		Running
13	10	38	Elliott Sadler	Pedigree Ford	400	4	Running
14	33	29	Kevin Harvick	GM Goodwrench Chevrolet	400		Running
15	8	0	Mike Bliss	Net Zero Best Buy Chevrolet	400		Running
16	42	4	Mike Wallace	Lucas Oil Chevrolet	400		Running
17	37	45	Kyle Petty	Georgia-Pacific/Brawny Dodge	400	1	Running
18	38	01	Joe Nemechek	U.S. Army Chevrolet	400	26	Running
19	28	10	Scott Riggs	Valvoline Chevrolet	400		Running
20	27	91	Bill Elliott	Stanley Tools Dodge	400	13	Running
21	11	42	Jamie McMurray	Texaco/Havoline Dodge	399		Running
22	40	31	Jeff Burton	Cingular Wireless go phone Chevrolet	399		Running
23	32	22	Scott Wimmer	Caterpillar Dodge	399		Running
24	9	20	Tony Stewart	The Home Depot Chevrolet	398		Running
25	6	5 #	Kyle Busch	CARQUEST Chevrolet	398	55	Running
26	4	9	Kasey Kahne	Dodge Dealers/UAW Dodge	396	11	Running
27	25	7	Robby Gordon	Fruit of the Loom Chevrolet	393		Accident
28	13	6	Mark Martin	Viagra Ford	390		Accident
29	31	07	Dave Blaney	Jack Daniel's Country Cocktail Chevrolet	385		Running
30	2	24	Jeff Gordon	DuPont Chevrolet	382	49	Accident
31	14	25	Brian Vickers	GMAC/ditech.com Chevrolet	379	98	Accident
32	18	77 #	Travis Kvapil	Kodak/Jasper Eng. & Trans. Dodge	376	23	Running
33	15	8	Dale Earnhardt Jr.	Budweiser Chevrolet	373		Running
34	24	41	Casey Mears	Target Dodge	338	1	Running
35	16	21	Ricky Rudd	US Air Force/Motorcraft Ford	305	1	Engine
36	23	15	Michael Waltrip	NAPA Auto Parts Chevrolet	245	1	Accident
37	3	17	Matt Kenseth	DeWalt Power Tools Ford	245		Accident
38	26	44	Terry Labonte	Kellogg's Chevrolet	245	17	Accident
39	41	40	Sterling Marlin	Coors Light Dodge	215		Accident
40	19	09	Johnny Sauter	Miccosukee Resort Dodge	137		Accident
41	22	23	Mike Skinner	AutoManiac Dodge	99		Engine
42	17	50	Jimmy Spencer	Arnold Development Co. Dodge	98		Accident
43	35	97	Kurt Busch	Smirnoff Ice Ford	26		Accident

Raybestos Rookie of the Year Contender.

NASCAR NEXTEL Cup Series Point Standings
(After 12 Races)

Pos.	Driver	Points	Behind	Change
1	Jimmie Johnson	1747	—	—
2	Greg Biffle	1676	-71	—
3	Elliott Sadler	1542	-205	+1
4	Ryan Newman	1530	-217	+3
5	Jeff Gordon	1516	-231	-2
6	Tony Stewart	1488	-259	—
7	Kevin Harvick	1485	-262	+1
8	Carl Edwards	1459	-288	+5
9	Jamie McMurray	1451	-296	—
10	Kurt Busch	1441	-306	-5

Those who had pitted under green stayed on the track and lined up as cars on the tail end of the lead lap ahead of race leader Carl Edwards, Scott Riggs, Joe Nemechek, Tony Stewart and Bobby Labonte.

Vickers began his charge to make up ground but suddenly found himself in heavy traffic and ran into Bill Elliott in the first turn. The incident also involved Harvick and Mark Martin, as well as Gordon, who could not steer clear of Elliott's Dodge as it slid off the banking.

Johnson was able to avoid the mishap and lined up 11th for the Lap-387 restart, with Nemechek in front followed by Bobby Labonte, Edwards and Newman. Nemechek charged away at the drop of the green flag, but with victory in sight, a cut tire sent him spinning.

The race came down to a five-lap shootout led by Labonte, with Edwards and Newman right behind. Johnson, able to use late-race cautions to improve both car and track position, lined up fourth and immediately went to work on the leaders.

Johnson passed Newman in Turn 3 before circling the track once under green, overtook Edwards entering the next corner and, with three laps to go, pulled up on Labonte's bumper and weighed his options.

Knowing his Lowe's Chevrolet was strong in Turn 4, Johnson used his advantage to get a good run on Labonte as they headed for the white flag. Into Turn 1 for the last time, Johnson dove to the bottom of the track but bobbled slightly, allowing Labonte to pull ahead and to the inside on the back-stretch. Johnson charged aggressively into the third turn and pulled alongside Labonte on the outside, and the pair rocketed off the fourth corner side by side. As they raced to the stripe, Johnson barely inched ahead to take his second win of the year by a margin of just 0.027-second.

For Johnson, the win completed a string of three straight victories at Lowe's Motor Speedway, tying Fred Lorenzen's record set in 1964-65. It was also an unprecedented third consecutive Coca-Cola 600 win for Johnson, and it padded Rick Hendrick's total as the track's winningest car owner.

When the newspapers hit the streets the next morning, the headlines read: "Johnson Wins at Charlotte." For the rest of the NASCAR NEXTEL Cup Series competitors, that sounded like, well, a broken record.

MBNA RACEPOINTS 400

G reg Biffle and crew chief Doug Richert put on a racing clinic at Dover International Speedway in the MBNA RacePoints 400. And when they had finished, another tick mark in the "win" column had raised their total to a series-leading four, a point gain had moved them to within 46 of leader Jimmie Johnson, and a winner's check in the amount of $282,800 had boosted their total winnings for the first third of the NASCAR NEXTEL Cup Series season up and over the $2 million mark.

The "48" crew from Hendrick Motorsports swarms the Lowe's Chevrolet for driver Jimmie Johnson. With a fourth-place finish at Dover, Johnson hung on to the top spot in the points for the 10th straight event.

Four-time Dover winner Mark Martin is a picture of intensity before 400 grueling miles on the one-mile oval. Although he could not add to his victory total, his sixth top 10 of the season vaulted him back among point leaders after falling to 12th a week ago in Charlotte.

If the National Guard team began the day with an advantage in starting the race on the outside of the front row next to Johnson after Bud Pole qualifying was rained out, that advantage quickly disappeared when, upon attacking the Monster Mile in anger, Biffle immediately discovered he was battling a race car that was far too tight on a track that rewards the opposite — on the Dover concrete, loose is fast.

So the stage was set. If Biffle and Co. were going to go anywhere, they would have to adjust. And that, they did.

Aided by six caution flags neatly spread over the first 211 laps, Biffle and Richert orchestrated drastic changes to the car's setup, using various combinations of chassis adjustments and tire pressures until, with 160 laps to go, they finally had it right.

"I just couldn't believe that it could take that much adjustment," said Biffle. "So I just kept going and going and going and kept adjusting on it. We made some big changes. I raised the track bar probably and inch. We usually move it an eighth or three-sixteenths of an inch. I took all the [spring] rubbers out of the left rear and put rubbers in the right rear. I took wedge out of it. Finally, the thing was so loose I almost crashed."

(Left) Carl Long (00) makes room on the inside for race-leader Elliott Sadler (38), who's being chased by Kurt Busch (97) and Jimmie Johnson (48). Sadler led most of the first 240 laps but faded to 10th at the finish, one spot ahead of Busch.

(Below) Mark Martin (6) waits for tires while Scott Riggs (10) slips past on Dover's cramped pit road. Riggs had a solid run to an 11th-place finish, the final car on the lead lap.

Instead of crashing, however, Biffle consistently worked through the field until, on Lap 241, he passed Elliott Sadler to take his first lead of the day. Sadler, who started third by virtue of his position in the point standings, took the lead for the first of three times on Lap 23 and remained there for 128 of the next 218 trips around the one-mile speedbowl. But while Biffle's car was getting better and better, Sadler's M&M's Ford was, little by little, getting worse.

Once in front, Biffle held his position for the next 134 consecutive laps with the aid of his National Guard crewmates, who kept him in the lead during the seventh and final caution period with slightly more than 100 laps remaining.

(Above) Greg Biffle (16) challenges Elliott Sadler (38) for the lead with 160 laps to go. Once in front, Biffle led all but 10 of the remaining trips around the high-banked oval, giving up the point only for his final stop for fuel.

(Below) Rookie Kyle Busch uses the low groove to hold off veteran Rusty Wallace, a two-time victor at Dover. Busch, in his first NASCAR NEXTEL Cup Series start on the Monster Mile, performed admirably in a runner-up effort, his second of the season.

MBNA RacePoints 400

NASCAR NEXTEL Cup Series Race No. 13

Fin. Pos.	Start Pos.	Car No.	Driver	Team	Laps	Laps Led	Status
1	2	16	Greg Biffle	National Guard Ford	400	150	Running
2	22	5 #	Kyle Busch	Kellogg's Chevrolet	400	90	Running
3	12	6	Mark Martin	Viagra Ford	400		Running
4	1	48	Jimmie Johnson	Lowe's Chevrolet	400	24	Running
5	11	2	Rusty Wallace	Miller Lite Dodge	400		Running
6	27	25	Brian Vickers	GMAC/ditech.com Chevrolet	400		Running
7	23	17	Matt Kenseth	DeWalt Power Tools Ford	400		Running
8	4	12	Ryan Newman	Alltel Dodge	400		Running
9	10	97	Kurt Busch	Sharpie Ford	400		Running
10	3	38	Elliott Sadler	M&M's Ford	400	128	Running
11	21	10	Scott Riggs	Valvoline Chevrolet	400		Running
12	17	31	Jeff Burton	Cingular Wireless go phone Chevrolet	399		Running
13	18	15	Michael Waltrip	NAPA Auto Parts Chevrolet	399		Running
14	13	19	Jeremy Mayfield	Dodge Dealers/UAW Dodge	399		Running
15	6	20	Tony Stewart	The Home Depot Chevrolet	399		Running
16	8	99	Carl Edwards	Office Depot Ford	398		Running
17	33	77 #	Travis Kvapil	Jasper Eng. & Trans./Kodak Dodge	398		Running
18	29	0	Mike Bliss	Net Zero Best Buy Chevrolet	398		Running
19	30	45	Kyle Petty	Georgia-Pacific/Brawny Dodge	398		Running
20	36	11	Jason Leffler	FedEx Freight Chevrolet	398		Running
21	38	32	Bobby Hamilton Jr.	Tide to go Chevrolet	398		Running
22	15	8	Dale Earnhardt Jr.	Budweiser Chevrolet	397		Running
23	14	88	Dale Jarrett	UPS Ford	397		Running
24	28	41	Casey Mears	Target Dodge	397		Running
25	7	29	Kevin Harvick	GM Goodwrench Chevrolet	396		Running
26	9	42	Jamie McMurray	Texaco/Havoline Dodge	395		Running
27	19	01	Joe Nemechek	U.S. Army Chevrolet	395		Running
28	34	4	Mike Wallace	Wide Open Energy Drink/Lucas Oil Chev.	394		Running
29	39	7	Robby Gordon	Harrah's Chevrolet	394	8	Running
30	31	43	Jeff Green	Cheerios/Betty Crocker Dodge	390		Running
31	35	22	Scott Wimmer	Caterpillar Dodge	390		Running
32	20	40	Sterling Marlin	Coors Light Dodge	388		Running
33	37	37	Kevin Lepage	R&J Racing Dodge	382		Running
34	41	92 #	Stanton Barrett	Front Row Motorsports Chevrolet	377		Running
35	16	9	Kasey Kahne	Dodge Dealers/UAW Dodge	283		Accident
36	25	07	Dave Blaney	Jack Daniel's Chevrolet	135		Accident
37	26	49	Ken Schrader	Schwan's Home Service Dodge	135		Accident
38	24	18	Bobby Labonte	Interstate Batteries Chevrolet	51		Engine
39	5	24	Jeff Gordon	DuPont Chevrolet	41		Accident
40	32	21	Ricky Rudd	Motorcraft Genuine Parts Ford	41		Accident
41	40	66	Hermie Sadler	Peak Fitness Ford	37		Suspension
42	43	00	Carl Long	Buyer's Choice Auto Warranty Chevrolet	26		Overheating
43	42	34	Jeff Fuller	Revi Pit Crew Wear Chevrolet	15		Vibration

Raybestos Rookie of the Year Contender.

NASCAR NEXTEL Cup Series Point Standings
(After 13 Races)

Pos.	Driver	Points	Behind	Change
1	Jimmie Johnson	1912	—	—
2	Greg Biffle	1866	-46	—
3	Elliott Sadler	1681	-231	—
4	Ryan Newman	1672	-240	—
5	Tony Stewart	1606	-306	+1
6	Mark Martin	1588	-324	+6
7	Rusty Wallace	1584	-328	+4
8	Kurt Busch	1579	-333	+2
9	Carl Edwards	1574	-338	-1
10	Kevin Harvick	1573	-339	-3

While the rest of the teams planned their strategies for the final pit stops of the day, Biffle methodically stretched his advantage to a healthy five seconds over second-place Johnson, with Kyle Busch, Mark Martin and Rusty Wallace all figuring into the top-five mix.

Then, with 26 miles remaining, Biffle played his hand by peeling onto pit road, one of the first lead-pack cars to make a move. "I want four tires," he had told his crew in anticipation of his final stop of the day. "I wanted some bullets in the gun," Biffle later told reporters. "I wanted to be prepared with four [new tires] to race for the win."

One by one, the rest of the lead-lap cars pitted until only Johnson remained. "We wanted to stay out to see if we could catch a caution," Johnson's crew chief, Chad Knaus, explained. "If a caution would fall, then we would be sitting in the catbird seat."

It almost worked, too. With Johnson having lapped the field, Sadler's Ford began trailing smoke. But he was able to limp back around to pit road, and, seeing no oil on the track, NASCAR allowed the race to continue under green. With 15 laps to go and running nearly on fumes, Johnson pulled the Lowe's Chevrolet into the pits for a quick stop for two tires and a splash of fuel.

With the round of stops complete, Biffle emerged at the point once again, this time with a three-second advantage over Kyle Busch, who had elected to take two tires in favor of track position. Johnson fell back in line in third place ahead of Martin in fourth and Wallace in fifth.

"Once I got out into the clean air, the [car] was just smoking fast," Biffle said of the final laps. "Once I got out front running like that, it was a pretty uneventful day." Indeed, Biffle motored off to a comfortable 4.281-second margin of victory over Busch, who led twice for 90 laps in the first half of the race and then remained among the top five in a very impressive outing.

Martin, whose car came into its own over the latter half of the race, overtook Johnson with just a handful of laps remaining and finished third, which allowed him to jump six positions in the point standings, where he was now listed sixth. Wallace also cracked the top 10 in points by gaining four positions on the strength of his solid fifth-place finish in the race.

POCONO 500

Last week's MBNA RacePoints 400 at Dover International Speedway, the 13th race on the NASCAR NEXTEL Cup Series schedule, marked the halfway point of the 26 events that would determine the field of drivers to compete for the championship in the Chase for the NASCAR NEXTEL Cup.

With each passing week, competitors were paying more and more attention to the point standings, evaluating where they stood and what they needed to do to make it into the elite field of drivers who would have a chance to capture the year-end title.

At the top of the standings, Jimmie Johnson and Greg Biffle had run off and hid from everyone else. Separated by only 46 points, the pair accounted for six wins, with Biffle ahead of Johnson four wins to two. Johnson, however, had been more consistent, gathering seven top fives and 10 top 10s compared to five and nine, respectively, for Biffle.

Carl Edwards (left) listens intently to Rusty Wallace before making his first career start at Pocono. Wallace, a four-time winner on the odd-shaped track, must have had some great advice, as Edwards drove to his second career win.

Joe Nemechek (01) helped the Army celebrate 230 years of duty by placing third in the Pocono 500, by far his best finish of the season.

Some 200 points behind the leaders sat Elliott Sadler and Ryan Newman, the two separated by just nine points. Sadler, now in third, was displaying the consistency he showed throughout much of last season and had been listed among the top five in points following eight of the last nine events.

Newman, on the other hand, had bounced in and out of the top 10 until a recent surge of strong performances boosted him into fourth place.

The rest of the current top 10 — Tony Stewart, Mark Martin, Rusty Wallace, Kurt Busch, Carl Edwards and Kevin Harvick — were 300-plus points behind Johnson, but a mere 33 points separated fifth-place Stewart from Harvick in 10th. For this cluster of drivers, solid finishes would certainly be required each and every week to keep from being knocked out of the top 10 altogether.

A group of five drivers sat outside the top 10 but could still consider themselves contenders to make the Chase for the NASCAR NEXTEL Cup. Jeff Gordon had captured three wins already, but they were offset by five DNFs, including three straight in his last three starts. Although he sat 11th in points, 350 back of teammate Johnson, Gordon's ability coupled with the strength and experience of the DuPont team could be expected to keep Gordon's "Drive for Five" alive.

Jeff Burton (31), Kyle Busch (5), Robby Gordon (7), Jimmie Johnson (48) and Scott Wimmer (22) tackle Pocono's sweeping third turn in single-file formation. Busch had another impressive day with his second straight top-five finish, two spots ahead of point leader Johnson.

TOP 10 QUALIFIERS

Pos.	Driver	Seconds	mph
1	Michael Waltrip	53.238	169.052
2	Kurt Busch	53.356	168.678
3	Brian Vickers	53.465	168.334
4	Jamie McMurray	53.622	167.842
5	Scott Riggs	53.711	167.563
6	Jeremy Mayfield	53.873	167.060
7	Bobby Labonte	53.881	167.035
8	Kevin Harvick	53.896	166.988
9	Mike Bliss	53.905	166.960
10	Matt Kenseth	53.945	166.837

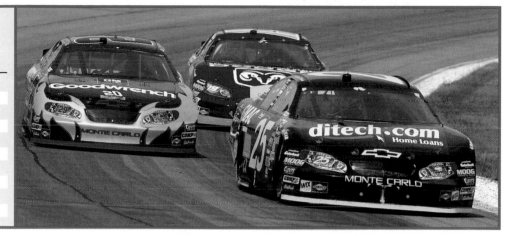

(Above) Brian Vickers (25) leads the way for Kevin Harvick (29) and Jeremy Mayfield (19). Vickers qualified third and led 121 of the first 171 laps in a strong, runner-up effort, the best finish of his young career.

(Below) A cut tire on the Budweiser Chevrolet, one of two during the race, ignites on the way to pit road, leading to a 33rd-place finish and a further drop in the points for Dale Earnhardt Jr.

Jeremy Mayfield and Jamie McMurray were next in line, listed 12th and 13th, respectively, with only two points separating the two. They, however, were within the magical 400-point window behind the leader and would, if the championship field were determined now, still qualify. But keeping the torrid pace set by Johnson and Biffle would not be easy, and a bad race or two for either driver would seriously diminish their chances.

Of those on the outside looking in, Dale Jarrett (14th in points and down 412 to Johnson) and Dale Earnhardt Jr. (15th, 418 back) still held out hope that a turnaround to their seasons would vault them back into the mix. Both drivers had already changed crew chiefs, and a string of good, strong finishes — along with a little luck — could restore their chances for a shot at the title.

Conventional wisdom would have dictated that Carl Edwards had little going for him when he arrived at Pennsylvania's Pocono Raceway two days before the Pocono 500. After all, when he rolled through the tunnel and into the infield, he cast his eyes upon the triangular-shaped

superspeedway for the very first time. Given the totally unique characteristics of Pocono's lay-out, with its three completely different turns connected by three straightaways of varying lengths, no one could expect a first-timer to hit it big on his initial crack at the track.

Add to that, the fact that — amazingly — Roush Racing had yet to post a single win at Pocono since Jack Roush began fielding cars back in the late 1980s, while drivers from Hendrick Motorsports had visited Victory Lane 10 different times, doubling the total of any other car owner over the track's 32-year history.

Conventional wisdom, however, can sometimes muddy the waters. In Edwards' case, he held no preconceived notions about the track's quirky nature. He had never tasted the wall after rounding the infamous Tunnel Turn. And he didn't have to worry about not having to shift (something on the minds of many veteran competitors), a practice used for a number of years but now obsolete given the newly-adopted gear rule.

So Edwards rolled off the staring grid on Sunday equipped with a few practice laps, the experience of turning the 29th fastest qualifying speed and knowledge gained from count-less hours of Pocono track time behind the wheel of his NASCAR computer game.

Michael Waltrip jumped to the early lead after posting the third Bud Pole of his career, his first in nearly 14 years. The NAPA driver led the first 29 laps before giving way to Brian Vickers, who then began a dominating stretch that had him at the point six times for 121 of the next 142 laps. Vickers was so strong that only one driver was able to pass him on the track — Carl Edwards.

Driving a car that excelled on long runs, Edwards took the lead for the first time just past the midpoint of the race and, for the next 170 miles, he and Vickers swapped the top spot

Carl Edwards (99) uses the out-side to ease past Michael Waltrip's NAPA Chevrolet in Pocono's flat, nine-degree-banked Turn 3. Waltrip broke a long dry spell by winning the Bud Pole and led the first 29 laps on the way to his third top five of the season.

(Opposing Page) Carl Edwards displays his back flip for the sec-ond time this year after taking the Pocono win.

POCONO 500

NASCAR NEXTEL Cup Series Race No. 14

Fin. Pos.	Start Pos.	Car No.	Driver	Team	Laps	Laps Led	Status
1	29	99	Carl Edwards	Stonebridge Life/Scott's Ford	201	46	Running
2	3	25	Brian Vickers	GMAC/ditech.com Chevrolet	201	121	Running
3	18	01	Joe Nemechek	U.S. Army Chevrolet	201		Running
4	38	5 #	Kyle Busch	Kellogg's Chevrolet	201		Running
5	1	15	Michael Waltrip	NAPA Auto Parts Chevrolet	201	29	Running
6	21	48	Jimmie Johnson	Lowe's Chevrolet	201		Running
7	13	6	Mark Martin	Viagra Ford	201		Running
8	8	29	Kevin Harvick	GM Goodwrench Chevrolet	201		Running
9	31	24	Jeff Gordon	DuPont Chevrolet	201		Running
10	4	42	Jamie McMurray	Texaco/Havoline Dodge	201		Running
11	12	2	Rusty Wallace	Miller Lite Dodge	201		Running
12	28	44	Terry Labonte	Pizza Hut Chevrolet	201		Running
13	16	88	Dale Jarrett	UPS Ford	201		Running
14	6	19	Jeremy Mayfield	Dodge Dealers/UAW Dodge	201		Running
15	35	43	Jeff Green	Cheerios/Betty Crocker Dodge	201		Running
16	14	40	Sterling Marlin	Coors Light Dodge	201		Running
17	33	77 #	Travis Kvapil	Kodak/Jasper Eng. & Trans. Dodge	201		Running
18	20	41	Casey Mears	Target Dodge	201		Running
19	22	31	Jeff Burton	Cingular Wireless Chevrolet	201		Running
20	19	49	Ken Schrader	Schwan's Home Service Dodge	201	1	Running
21	25	38	Elliott Sadler	M&M's Ford	201		Running
22	2	97	Kurt Busch	Sharpie Ford	200	2	Running
23	24	32	Bobby Hamilton Jr.	Tide to go Chevrolet	200		Running
24	37	07	Dave Blaney	Jack Daniel's Chevrolet	200		Running
25	36	66	Mike Garvey	Jani-King Ford	200	1	Running
26	7	18	Bobby Labonte	Interstate Batteries/Madagascar Chev.	199		Accident
27	15	9	Kasey Kahne	Dodge Dealers/UAW Dodge	199		Running
28	32	21	Ricky Rudd	Motorcraft Genuine Parts Ford	199		Running
29	26	20	Tony Stewart	The Home Depot Chevrolet	199		Running
30	23	16	Greg Biffle	National Guard/Post-It Ford	198		Running
31	42	4	Mike Wallace	Lucas Oil Products Chevrolet	198	1	Running
32	10	17	Matt Kenseth	DeWalt Power Tools Ford	197		Running
33	34	8	Dale Earnhardt Jr.	Budweiser Chevrolet	195		Running
34	17	12	Ryan Newman	Alltel Dodge	194		Accident
35	9	0	Mike Bliss	Net Zero Best Buy Chevrolet	194		Running
36	11	22	Scott Wimmer	Caterpillar Dodge	170		Suspension
37	5	10	Scott Riggs	Valvoline Chevrolet	165		Running
38	39	37	Kevin Lepage	R&J Racing Dodge	141		Accident
39	27	7	Robby Gordon	Harrah's Chevrolet	124		Engine
40	30	11	Jason Leffler	FedEx Kinko's Chevrolet	43		Accident
41	40	45	Kyle Petty	Georgia-Pacific/Brawny Dodge	43		Accident
42	43	89	Morgan Shepherd	Racing with Jesus/Red Line Oil Dodge	13		Brakes
43	41	13	Greg Sacks	Sacks Motorsports Dodge	12		Overheating

Raybestos Rookie of the Year Contender.

NASCAR NEXTEL Cup Series Point Standings
(After 14 Races)

Pos.	Driver	Points	Behind	Change
1	**Jimmie Johnson**	2062	—	—
2	Greg Biffle	1939	-123	—
3	Elliott Sadler	1781	-281	—
4	Carl Edwards	1759	-303	+5
5	Mark Martin	1734	-328	+1
6	Ryan Newman	1733	-329	-2
7	Kevin Harvick	1715	-347	+3
8	Rusty Wallace	1714	-348	-1
9	Jeff Gordon	1700	-362	+2
10	Tony Stewart	1682	-380	-5

between them until, with 28 laps remaining, Edwards was able to secure a distinct advantage. From that point on, he relinquished the lead only briefly during a late-race stop for fuel, and went on to take his second career victory.

Vickers did get one final shot at the win when the caution flew with less than five laps to go, setting up a green-white-checkered finish. That ended quickly, however, as the eighth and final yellow flag appeared on Lap 201, ending the event immediately.

Joe Nemechek followed Edwards and Vickers across the line to gain his first top five of the season — a fitting finish on the 230th birthday of his team's sponsor, the U.S. Army — while Kyle Busch posted yet another strong rookie performance for fourth place, his third top-four finish in the last four races.

BATMAN BEGINS 400

When it comes to driving race cars, no one questions Tony Stewart's toughness or resolve. But even a fierce competitor like Stewart had to be wondering how he — or anyone else for that matter — could beat the odds presented when the Roush juggernaut rumbled into Brooklyn, Mich., for the Batman Begins 400.

Roush Racing was on a roll, having won half of the season's first 14 events, including the last two, at Dover and Pocono. As if that kind of momentum wasn't formidable enough to overcome, one need only consider Roush's record at Michigan International Speedway and its "sister" track, California Speedway, to send shivers up the spine of any driver who felt he had a shot at victory this weekend.

At Michigan, Roush drivers had captured wins in three of the last six events, spread nicely amongst Matt Kenseth (June 2002), Kurt Busch (June 2003) and Greg Biffle (August 2004). Moreover, in Biffle's triumph, the other four Roush drivers followed him across the finish line all within the top 10, with Mark Martin second, Busch sixth, Kenseth eighth and Carl Edwards 10th in his NASCAR NEXTEL Cup Series debut.

The field spreads out around Michael Waltrip's NAPA Chevrolet on Michigan's roomy frontstretch as the Batman Begins 400 gets underway. Waltrip picked up a seventh place in the race and moved to within striking distance of the top 10 in points.

(Above) Five-time Michigan winner Rusty Wallace contemplates what's ahead before attacking the two-mile oval for 200 laps. At the end, his fifth 10th-place finish of the season kept him squarely in the fight among drivers competing for sixth through 10th in the standings.

(Right) Fan favorite Bill Elliott climbs aboard the McDonald's Dodge to make his fifth start of the season. Elliot leads all active drivers by far with seven career wins at Michigan, trailing only David Pearson (9) and Cale Yarborough (8) on the all-time list.

Back in February at California Speedway, a track sharing numerous characteristics with Michigan's D-shaped oval, Biffle grabbed the first of his series-leading four wins so far in 2005 and was followed by teammates Busch in third, Edwards in fifth and Martin in seventh.

Clearly, the teams employed by the man whose core automotive business resides in nearby Lavonia, Mich., had things figured out on these two-mile, low-banked super speedways, and

TOP 10 QUALIFIERS

Pos.	Driver	Seconds	mph
1	Ryan Newman	37.069	*194.232
2	Casey Mears	37.160	193.757
3	Tony Stewart	37.207	193.512
4	Kasey Kahne	37.282	193.123
5	Jeremy Mayfield	37.289	193.086
6	Bobby Labonte	37.295	193.055
7	Brian Vickers	37.341	192.818
8	Robby Gordon	37.350	192.771
9	Jeff Gordon	37.372	192.658
10	Bill Elliott	37.372	192.658

* Track Record

(Left) Ryan Newman streaks down Michigan's sweeping frontstretch. His blazingly fast lap at 194.232 miles per hour in qualifying set the new track record.

(Right) Joe Nemechek (01) surges through the middle of outside pole-winner Casey Mears (41) and Sterling Marlin (40), with Rusty Wallace in pursuit. Nemechek had a stout U.S. Army Chevrolet, finishing sixth in his second straight top-10 run.

(Below) Tony Stewart launches back into action after a critical late-race stop for fresh tires. Fast on new rubber, Stewart made it up to second place but couldn't overtake Greg Biffle for the win.

of the five drivers bearing the Roush Racing badge, Biffle had to be the most anxious to get things rolling.

A victory two weeks prior had closed the gap between Biffle and perennial point leader Jimmie Johnson to a mere 46 markers. A misstep at Pocono the next weekend, however, resulted in a 30th-place finish, widening the margin to 123. But here, this weekend, Biffle knew he had a chance to close in on Johnson once again, and he planned to take full advantage of his and his team's expertise at this track to put pressure on the Lowe's effort from Hendrick Motorsports.

As for Stewart, the 2005 season had so far been, well, less than satisfying. He dominated the season-opener at Daytona, only to see Jeff Gordon cruise past in the closing laps to take the win. At Martinsville in April, he led 247 laps in what appeared to be a rout until a wheel fell off his car with 70 laps to go. He ran well at Talladega in May, but no one could match what Gordon had in store that day and Stewart finished second. And at Richmond, he battled brilliantly with Kasey Kahne but was the runner-up in what became the young Dodge driver's first NASCAR NEXTEL Cup Series victory. Sitting 10th in points and winless for the season, The Home Depot driver felt parched and very much in need of some victory champagne.

Defending event champion Ryan Newman led the field on Sunday after crushing the track record in qualifying with a lap at 194.232 miles per hour. In all, 26 drivers broke Dale Earnhardt Jr.'s previous mark of 191.149 mph, but many found their setups for qualifying, held in cooler temperatures under cloudy skies, were not well suited for the hot, sunny conditions in effect when the green flag waved.

Stewart, who qualified third, was not among them and took the lead from second-fastest qualifier Casey Mears before 10 laps had passed. Behind him, however, the Roush contingent

The checkered flag falls for Greg Biffle to complete his series-leading fifth victory of the 2005 NASCAR NEXTEL Cup Series season. With the win, Biffle once again moved to within 50 points of leader Jimmie Johnson in the standings.

BATMAN BEGINS 400

NASCAR NEXTEL Cup Series Race No. 15

Fin. Pos.	Start Pos.	Car No.	Driver	Team	Laps	Laps Led	Status
1	25	16	Greg Biffle	Charter-National Guard Ford	200	63	Running
2	3	20	Tony Stewart	The Home Depot Chevrolet	200	97	Running
3	15	6	Mark Martin	Batman Begins/Pfizer Ford	200	10	Running
4	21	17	Matt Kenseth	Carhartt/DeWalt Ford	200		Running
5	23	99	Carl Edwards	AAA/Office Depot Ford	200		Running
6	11	01	Joe Nemechek	U.S. Army Chevrolet	200	1	Running
7	30	15	Michael Waltrip	NAPA Auto Parts Chevrolet	200	3	Running
8	18	38	Elliott Sadler	M&M's Ford	200		Running
9	17	5 #	Kyle Busch	Kellogg's Chevrolet	200		Running
10	12	2	Rusty Wallace	Miller Lite Dodge	200		Running
11	33	31	Jeff Burton	Beneficial/Cingular Chevrolet	200		Running
12	13	97	Kurt Busch	Sharpie Ford	200	12	Running
13	24	42	Jamie McMurray	Home123/Havoline Dodge	200	1	Running
14	6	18	Bobby Labonte	Interstate Batteries Chevrolet	200		Running
15	1	12	Ryan Newman	Alltel Dodge	200	3	Running
16	22	22	Scott Wimmer	Caterpillar Dodge	200		Running
17	41	8	Dale Earnhardt Jr.	Budweiser Chevrolet	200		Running
18	4	9	Kasey Kahne	Dodge Dealers/UAW Dodge	200		Running
19	16	48	Jimmie Johnson	Lowe's Chevrolet	200	2	Running
20	26	11	Jason Leffler	FedEx Kinko's Chevrolet	200		Running
21	2	41	Casey Mears	Target Dodge	199	7	Running
22	5	19	Jeremy Mayfield	Dodge Dealers/UAW Dodge	199		Running
23	29	10	Scott Riggs	Valvoline Chevrolet	199		Running
24	14	88	Dale Jarrett	UPS Ford	199		Running
25	28	29	Kevin Harvick	GM Goodwrench Chevrolet	199		Running
26	37	77 #	Travis Kvapil	Kodak/Jasper Eng. & Trans. Dodge	199		Running
27	20	0	Mike Bliss	Net Zero Best Buy Chevrolet	198		Running
28	38	49	Ken Schrader	Schwan's Home Service Dodge	198		Running
29	36	07	Dave Blaney	Jack Daniel's Country Cocktail Chevrolet	198		Running
30	32	45	Kyle Petty	Georgia-Pacific/Brawny Dodge	198		Running
31	27	32	Bobby Hamilton Jr.	Tide Chevrolet	198		Running
32	9	24	Jeff Gordon	DuPont Chevrolet	197		Running
33	34	21	Ricky Rudd	Rent-A-Center/Motorcraft Ford	197		Running
34	31	23	Mike Skinner	History Channel/AutoManiac Dodge	197		Running
35	10	91	Bill Elliott	McDonald's Dodge	196		Running
36	35	66	Mike Garvey	Jani-King/Peak Fitness Ford	196		Running
37	39	37	Kevin Lepage	Patron Tequila Dodge	195		Running
38	19	43	Jeff Green	Cheerios/Betty Crocker Dodge	184		Running
39	8	7	Robby Gordon	Menard's Chevrolet	182	1	Running
40	40	40	Sterling Marlin	Coors Light Dodge	167		Engine
41	7	25	Brian Vickers	GMAC/ditech.com Chevrolet	154		Running
42	43	51	Stuart Kirby	Marathon Multipower-3 HD Motor Oil Chev.	91		Accident
43	42	4	Mike Wallace	Lucas Oil Chevrolet	50		Engine

Raybestos Rookie of the Year Contender.

NASCAR NEXTEL Cup Series Point Standings
(After 15 Races)

Pos.	Driver	Points	Behind	Change
1	**Jimmie Johnson**	**2173**	—	—
2	Greg Biffle	2124	-49	—
3	Elliott Sadler	1923	-250	—
4	Carl Edwards	1914	-259	—
5	Mark Martin	1904	-269	—
6	Tony Stewart	1862	-311	+4
7	Ryan Newman	1856	-317	-1
8	Rusty Wallace	1848	-325	—
9	Kurt Busch	1813	-360	+2
10	Kevin Harvick	1803	-370	-3

seemed to have things going their way. Busch started 13th, the best of the five, with Martin (15th), Kenseth (21st), Edwards (23rd) and Biffle (25th) following along. By the time 80 laps had passed, all five Roush drivers were lined up directly behind race leader Stewart, with Biffle second followed by Busch, Kenseth, Martin and Edwards.

Of the fleet running Fords, Biffle emerged the strongest, and over the second half of the race, he and Stewart waged a battle between them that had one or the other at the point for all but three of the final 100 laps.

As they raced, a pattern materialized: Stewart clearly was quicker on fresh tires, while Biffle got stronger over long runs, able to overtake Stewart as tire wear took its toll.

That fact would ultimately dictate strategy as the race neared its conclusion. Both drivers pitted presumably for the last time when the caution flew on Lap 157 for debris. Stewart got off pit road first and was still holding the top position when Sterling Marlin's engine let go with 31 laps remaining.

Knowing that Biffle had steadily been closing the gap between them, Stewart and crew chief Greg Zipadelli decided that their hopes for winning rested with new tires. Biffle remained on the track and assumed the point followed by Kenseth, Edwards, Busch and Elliott Sadler.

Stewart sat eighth for the Lap-174 restart and immediately went to work, charging all the way to third place before five laps had passed. But reaching second-place Kenseth and passing him were different stories, and while the Home Depot driver fought for second, Biffle stretched his lead.

Finally, on Lap 198, Stewart managed to dispatch of Kenseth, but by then it was too late to catch Biffle, who cruised to his fifth win of the year with a 1.657-second margin of victory.

"It's like, what do we need to do to catch these guys?" a frustrated Stewart questioned after the finish. "We made a huge step and we're still not where we need to be."

Still, Stewart was the only driver able to break up the Roush party, as Martin moved ahead of Kenseth in the closing laps for third place, while Edwards finished fifth, giving the Ford team four of the top five positions in an overwhelming performance.

DODGE/SAVE MART 350

There's nothing like a road course to shake things up a bit, and for many NASCAR NEXTEL Cup Series competitors, Infineon Raceway, the twisty track nestled in the California wine country, seemed like a good place to loosen the grip that the drivers from Roush Racing and Hendrick Motorsports had on the season thus far.

Last week at Michigan, Roush Racing had solidified its position as the dominant force in the series, taking four of the top five positions. Although Jimmie Johnson remained atop the point standings, Greg Biffle was able to narrow the gap between himself and the Hendrick driver to a thin 49 points with his series-leading fifth win of the year. Elliott Sadler remained third in the points, but he was feeling the heat from Roush drivers Carl Edwards and Mark Martin, who both closed to within 19 points of the driver of the M&M's Ford based on their strong finishes at Michigan.

California's beautiful Sonoma Valley provides a picturesque setting as the field chases pole-winner Jeff Gordon through Infineon Raceway's second turn. Gordon won the Bud Pole with a record-setting lap over the 11-turn road course.

(Right) Boris Said (36), making his fourth start of the season for MB/Sutton Motorsports, holds the outside line against Scott Pruett (39), on board Ganassi Racing's Dodge for the first time this year.

(Below) Crewmen work feverishly from inside and underneath the DuPont Chevrolet, trying to correct transmission problems that beset Jeff Gordon. The four-time winner at Sonoma was firmly in front over the first 32 laps until mechanical woes took him from contention.

TOP 10 QUALIFIERS

Pos.	Driver	Seconds	mph
1	Jeff Gordon	75.950	*94.325
2	Jimmie Johnson	76.079	94.165
3	Mark Martin	76.203	94.012
4	Boris Said	76.233	93.975
5	Robby Gordon	76.306	93.885
6	Kurt Busch	76.465	93.690
7	Tony Stewart	76.560	93.574
8	Terry Labonte	76.788	93.296
9	Scott Pruett	76.810	93.269
10	Dale Earnhardt Jr.	76.880	93.184

* Track Record

After starting deep in the field, teammates Elliott Sadler (38) and Dale Jarrett (88) found each other among the top 10 and finished together (Jarrett in fifth, Sadler sixth) in a very respectable outing for Robert Yates Racing.

Although the contingent of teams fielded by Hendrick Motorsports had not quite kept pace with the Roush brigade, they clearly were the series' other main attraction. Johnson, leading all drivers with seven top-five and 11 top-10 finishes, continued to show the consistency necessary to remain the point leader, a position he had now held since the fourth race of the season. Teammate Jeff Gordon had the second-highest win total with three, but a recent slump consisting of four finishes of 30th or worse over the last five events had dropped him out of the top 10 in points.

Frustration had begun to set in with the four-time series champion, and Gordon was looking forward to righting his ship this week. Gordon was, after all, the reigning king of the road courses, boasting an unprecedented eight wins, four each at Sonoma, Calif., and Watkins Glen, N.Y. In the last five events here at Infineon, Gordon had four top-three finishes including two victories, and if ever there was a place to get things going in the right direction, this was it.

Like Gordon, Tony Stewart was also growing impatient. His Home Depot team had been inconsistent over the last 10 races, interspersing a few near wins with mid-pack runs that had Stewart bouncing around the bottom half of the top 10 in points. A strong, runner-up finish last week helped, but the driver from Rushville, Ind., covets winning — nothing less — and 15 races into the 2005 NASCAR NEXTEL Cup Series season, he had yet to visit Victory Lane. With a record of success on road courses — three wins in the last four seasons — Stewart felt like his chances to break into the win column this week were good.

(Above) Tony Stewart (20) makes the race's decisive move on Ricky Rudd (21), wresting the lead on the inside of Turn 11 with 11 laps remaining. Stewart held the point from there on to pick up his first win of the season.

(Left) After leading a 12-lap stretch, Rusty Wallace settled in to a fourth-place finish, which moved him up two spots to sixth in the points and continued a recent string of good, consistent performances.

DODGE / SAVE MART 350

NASCAR NEXTEL Cup Series Race No. 16

Fin. Pos.	Start Pos.	Car No.	Driver	Team	Laps	Laps Led	Status
1	7	20	Tony Stewart	The Home Depot Chevrolet	110	39	Running
2	20	21	Ricky Rudd	U.S. Air Force/Motorcraft Ford	110	18	Running
3	6	97	Kurt Busch	Crown Royal Ford	110		Running
4	14	2	Rusty Wallace	Snap-On/Miller Lite Dodge	110	12	Running
5	30	88	Dale Jarrett	UPS/"Herbie Fully Loaded" Ford	110		Running
6	42	38	Elliott Sadler	M&M's Ford	110		Running
7	32	19	Jeremy Mayfield	Dodge Dealers/UAW Dodge	110		Running
8	43	32	Ron Fellows	Tide Chevrolet	110		Running
9	11	12	Ryan Newman	Alltel Dodge	110		Running
10	22	33	Brian Simo	Korbel Chevrolet	110		Running
11	24	17	Matt Kenseth	DeWalt Power Tools Ford	110		Running
12	8	11	Terry Labonte	FedEx Freight Chevrolet	110		Running
13	17	42	Jamie McMurray	Texaco/Havoline Dodge	110		Running
14	41	16	Greg Biffle	National Guard/Post-It Ford	110	8	Running
15	3	6	Mark Martin	Viagra Ford	110		Running
16	5	7	Robby Gordon	Harrah's Chevrolet	110		Running
17	4	36	Boris Said	CENTRIX Financial Chevrolet	110		Running
18	33	18	Bobby Labonte	Interstate Batteries Chevrolet	110		Running
19	29	07	Dave Blaney	Jack Daniel's Chevrolet	110		Running
20	36	41	Casey Mears	Target Dodge	110		Running
21	39	77 #	Travis Kvapil	Kodak/Jasper Eng. & Trans. Dodge	110		Running
22	34	15	Michael Waltrip	NAPA Auto Parts Chevrolet	110		Running
23	12	01	Joe Nemechek	U.S. Army Chevrolet	110		Running
24	16	10	Scott Riggs	Valvoline Chevrolet	110		Running
25	27	22	Scott Wimmer	Caterpillar Dodge	110		Running
26	37	40	Sterling Marlin	Coors Light Dodge	110		Running
27	25	45	Kyle Petty	Georgia-Pacific/Brawny Dodge	110	1	Running
28	28	87	Chris Cook	Nemco/Christine Marie Mtrspts Chevrolet	110		Running
29	38	43	Jeff Green	Cheerios/Betty Crocker Dodge	110		Running
30	15	31	Jeff Burton	Cingular Chevrolet	110		Running
31	9	39	Scott Pruett	Texaco/Havoline Dodge	110		Running
32	40	4	P.J. Jones	Lucas Oil Chevrolet	110		Running
33	1	24	Jeff Gordon	DuPont Chevrolet	110	32	Running
34	18	25	Brian Vickers	GMAC/ditech.com Chevrolet	110		Running
35	19	49	Ken Schrader	Schwan's Home Service Dodge	109		Running
36	2	48	Jimmie Johnson	Lowe's Chevrolet	109		Running
37	21	29	Kevin Harvick	GM Goodwrench Chevrolet	109		Running
38	23	99	Carl Edwards	Office Depot Ford	107		Running
39	31	0	Mike Bliss	Net Zero Best Buy Chevrolet	102		Running
40	13	5 #	Kyle Busch	Kellogg's Chevrolet	97		Running
41	26	9	Kasey Kahne	Dodge Dealers/UAW Dodge	92		Running
42	10	8	Dale Earnhardt Jr.	Budweiser Chevrolet	88		Running
43	35	27	Tom Hubert	Napa Valley Ford	33		Oil Pressure

Raybestos Rookie of the Year Contender.

NASCAR NEXTEL Cup Series Point Standings

(After 16 Races)

Pos.	Driver	Points	Behind	Change
1	**Greg Biffle**	2250	—	+1
2	Jimmie Johnson	2228	-22	-1
3	Elliott Sadler	2073	-177	—
4	Tony Stewart	2052	-198	+2
5	Mark Martin	2022	-228	—
6	Rusty Wallace	2013	-237	+2
7	Ryan Newman	1994	-256	—
8	Kurt Busch	1978	-272	+1
9	Carl Edwards	1963	-287	-5
10	Jamie McMurray	1923	-327	+1

Gordon and Johnson got their momentum going early with strong qualifying runs that placed Gordon on the pole after a track-record lap at 94.325 miles per hour, just a tick faster than Johnson, who would complete the all-Hendrick front row ahead of Martin and road-racing ace Boris Said.

Gordon took advantage of his start from the pole and set the early pace as the field sorted itself out. Behind him, Stewart mounted an immediate charge, moving up to second place as the opening laps unfolded.

Gordon led the first 32 trips around the 1.99-mile course and appeared to be having things his way until transmission problems began to plague the DuPont Monte Carlo. Ultimately, Hendrick drivers Johnson and Kyle Busch also suffered transmission woes, dropping all three out of contention.

As the race played out, the usual suspects emerged at the front, with two-time Sonoma winners Rusty Wallace and Ricky Rudd taking turns at the point along with Stewart. Rudd took the lead from Wallace with just under 30 laps remaining and focused on running a smooth, consistent line, having already made the decision to go the distance on his existing tires and fuel.

Stewart moved into second behind Rudd and began to hound the driver of the famed Wood Brothers Ford, challenging the veteran known for his ability on road courses. Time and again Stewart charged, pressuring Rudd from behind and looking for an opening to place the nose of The Home Depot Chevrolet, only to have Rudd slam the door closed.

Finally, Stewart remembered what he and crew chief Greg Zipadelli had discussed prior to the race — that patience would be the key to a good finish at Infineon. "At that point, the best thing to do was to not overdrive the car, slow down a little bit," Stewart recalled. "It was better for me to let the tires cool off, and once I did that, I got my speed back and it gave me a chance to make another run at him."

That was exactly what Stewart needed. With 10 laps remaining he made his move, diving to the inside of Rudd on the demanding Turn 11 hairpin and wrestling the lead away for the final time. Once in front, Stewart opened a 2.266-second advantage to bring a welcome end to a victory drought that dated back to August 2004 at Watkins Glen, 31 races ago.

PEPSI 400

It should not have come as any great surprise that Tony Stewart won the Pepsi 400 at Daytona International Speedway. In the 2005 season opener, the Daytona 500, Stewart led 107 laps, more than twice as many as any other driver, and appeared to be on the way to victory before a late-race caution bunched the field and disrupted Stewart's bid for victory. He fell to seventh place after suddenly finding himself without any friends in the draft over final green-white-checkered-flag dash to the finish.

To the crowd's delight, Tony Stewart pumps his arms in victory after climbing up the fence and onto the flagstand at Daytona. His second win in as many starts was also his first at the famous "World Center of Racing."

TOP 10 QUALIFIERS

Pos.	Driver	Seconds	mph
1	Tony Stewart	48.496	185.582
2	Scott Riggs	48.539	185.418
3	Jimmie Johnson	48.577	185.273
4	Boris Said	48.595	185.204
5	Joe Nemechek	48.674	184.904
6	Elliott Sadler	48.789	184.468
7	Kevin Harvick	48.789	184.468
8	Jason Leffler	48.800	184.426
9	Rusty Wallace	48.813	184.377
10	Kerry Earnhardt	48.850	184.237

(Above) Boris Said takes a spin through the tri-oval to bring out the seventh of nine cautions at Lap 114. Said, who had qualified fourth for the second straight week, spun again later but continued in the race and finished one lap down to the leaders.

(Right) Dale Jarrett looks relaxed and confident as he readies to tackle the high banks. A fifth-place run in the Pepsi 400 matched his finish a week ago at Sonoma and moved the UPS driver into the top 10 in points for the first time since Talladega, eight weeks ago.

One year earlier, Stewart also led all drivers, fronting the field for 98 of 200 laps, but finished second to Dale Earnhardt Jr., who found a burst of speed late in the race after overcoming handling problems early in the event.

In last year's Pepsi 400, Stewart was in command with less than 10 laps to go but could not hold off the Hendrick duo of Jeff Gordon and Jimmie Johnson, who drafted past on their way to a 1-2 finish, dropping Stewart into a late-race scrum in which he wound up fifth.

And in this year's Aaron's 499 at Talladega, the other superspeedway using restrictor plates, Stewart had a very strong outing, besting all drivers except Gordon, whose DuPont Chevrolet clearly was in a class by itself.

That Gordon, with four wins in his last six restrictor-plate outings, had effectively put an end to the dominance the DEI Chevrolets of Earnhardt and Michael Waltrip had enjoyed for several years, perhaps overshadowed Stewart's consistently strong performances on the big superspeedways. But to careful observers, the strength of the Chevrolet bearing the orange and white of The Home Depot at Daytona was no revelation.

For Tony Stewart, recent strong outings on the restrictor-plate tracks had not translated to victory for one reason or another. In this race, however, a focused and deliberate Stewart left little to chance by leading all but 22 of the event's 400-mile distance.

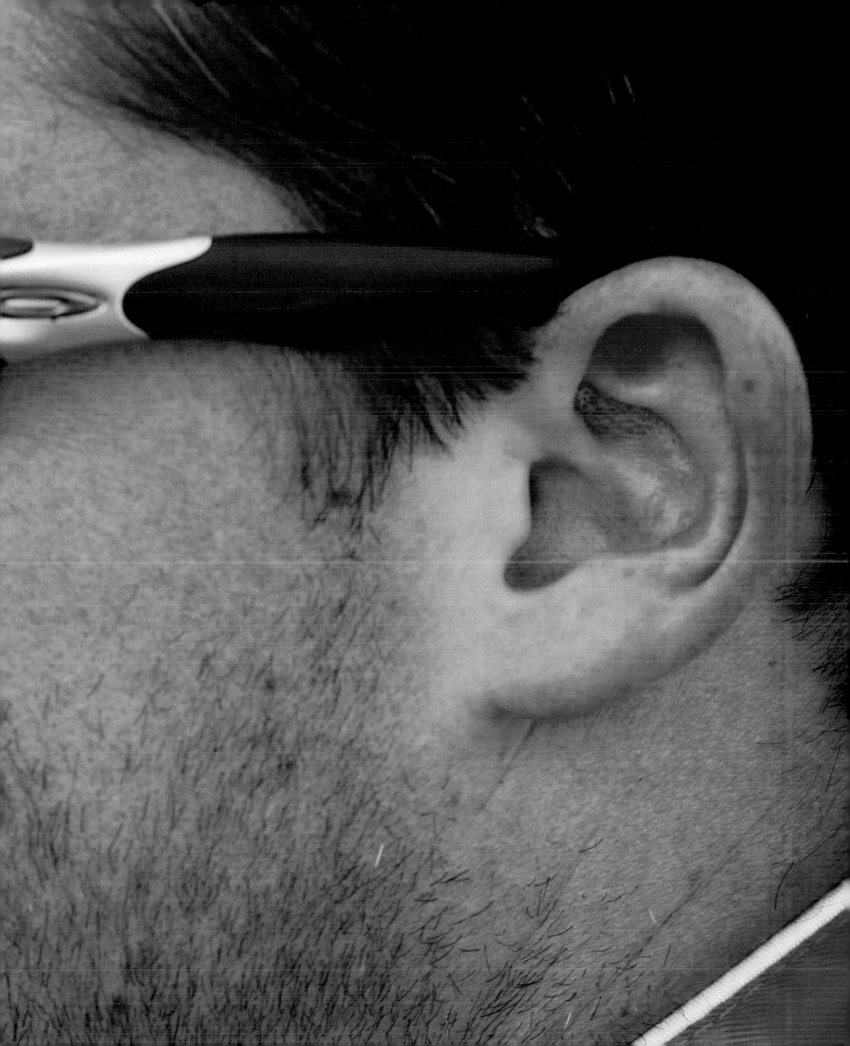

With that said, Stewart's win was nonetheless shocking. To wit: Races at Daytona are typically known for furious action at the front of the pack — the last three events, for example, saw averages of 24 lead changes among 11 different drivers. But Stewart was having none of that. He quite simply crushed his competition in a dazzling display of skill and power.

Stewart led all but nine of the event's 160 laps — a record for a 400-mile race at Daytona. He was never passed on the track, giving up the lead only while pitting, and if anyone doubted his dominance, all questions were put to rest following a restart after the eighth of nine caution flags during the race.

With 17 laps remaining, Stewart lined up fifth behind Kasey Kahne, Johnson, Dave Blaney and Matt Kenseth, and as the field roared into the first turn after its first lap under green, Stewart drove to the top of the banking, bringing Jamie McMurray with him in a three-wide

(Above) Carl Edwards (99) scrapes the wall after getting together with Kevin Harvick (29) while entering the tri-oval. The incident eventually involved a total of seven cars, including Kyle Busch (5), and brought out the final caution with less than 15 laps remaining in the race.

(Left) Kasey Kahne (9) and Matt Kenseth (17) duel for the lead following the final restart of the night. When this group made it to the first turn, Jimmie Johnson (48) dove to the low side while Tony Stewart (20) and Jamie McMurray (42) went high to form a four-wide struggle for the lead.

PEPSI 400

NASCAR NEXTEL Cup Series Race No. 17

Fin. Pos.	Start Pos.	Car No.	Driver	Team	Laps	Laps Led	Status
1	1	20	Tony Stewart	The Home Depot Chevrolet	160	151	Running
2	33	42	Jamie McMurray	Home123/Havoline Dodge	160		Running
3	39	8	Dale Earnhardt Jr.	Budweiser Chevrolet	160		Running
4	9	2	Rusty Wallace	Miller Lite Dodge	160		Running
5	13	88	Dale Jarrett	UPS Ford	160	1	Running
6	3	48	Jimmie Johnson	Lowe's Chevrolet	160		Running
7	15	24	Jeff Gordon	DuPont/Pepsi Chevrolet	160		Running
8	43	4	Mike Wallace	Lucas Oil Chevrolet	160		Running
9	38	17	Matt Kenseth	DeWalt Power Tools Ford	160		Running
10	40	49	Ken Schrader	Schwan's Home Service Dodge	160		Running
11	42	31	Jeff Burton	Cingular Chevrolet	160		Running
12	31	19	Jeremy Mayfield	Dodge Dealers/UAW Dodge	160		Running
13	35	21	Ricky Rudd	Motorcraft Genuine Parts Ford	160		Running
14	27	12	Ryan Newman	Alltel Dodge	160		Running
15	5	01	Joe Nemechek	U.S. Army Chevrolet	160		Running
16	19	9	Kasey Kahne	Dodge Dealers/UAW Dodge	160	3	Running
17	20	09	Johnny Sauter	Miccosukee Resort Dodge	160		Running
18	8	11	Jason Leffler	FedEx Express Chevrolet	160	1	Running
19	36	45	Kyle Petty	Stars and Stripes G-P Dodge	160		Running
20	14	0	Mike Bliss	Net Zero Best Buy Chevrolet	160		Running
21	6	38	Elliott Sadler	M&M's Ford	160	4	Running
22	37	40	Sterling Marlin	Prilosec OTC Dodge	160		Running
23	25	77 #	Travis Kvapil	Kodak/Jasper Eng. & Trans. Dodge	160		Running
24	7	29	Kevin Harvick	GM Goodwrench Chevrolet	160		Running
25	24	37	Kevin Lepage	R&J Racing Dodge	160		Running
26	11	7	Robby Gordon	Fruit of the Loom Chevrolet	160		Running
27	30	07	Dave Blaney	Jack Daniel's Chevrolet	159		Running
28	4	36	Boris Said	CENTRIX Financial Chevrolet	159		Running
29	16	25	Brian Vickers	GMAC/ditech.com Chevrolet	158		Running
30	21	92	Hermie Sadler	Taco Bell Chevrolet	156		Running
31	32	5 #	Kyle Busch	Kellogg's/Cheez-it® Chevrolet	146		Accident
32	26	22	Scott Wimmer	Caterpillar Dodge	146		Accident
33	34	99	Carl Edwards	Pennzoil Ford	146		Accident
34	41	43	Jeff Green	Chex Most Popular Driver Dodge	141		Running
35	22	18	Bobby Labonte	Interstate Batteries Chevrolet	134		Running
36	18	16	Greg Biffle	National Guard Ford	129		Running
37	28	97	Kurt Busch	Smirnoff Ice/Sharpie Ford	102		Running
38	12	32	Bobby Hamilton Jr.	Tide Chevrolet	101		Accident
39	23	6	Mark Martin	Viagra Ford	88		Running
40	17	15	Michael Waltrip	NAPA Auto Parts Chevrolet	87		Accident
41	2	10	Scott Riggs	Valvoline/"Herbie Fully Loaded" Chevrolet	64		Running
42	10	33	Kerry Earnhardt	Bass Pro Shops/Tracker Chevrolet	53		Brakes
43	29	41	Casey Mears	Target Dodge	35		Accident

\# Raybestos Rookie of the Year Contender.

NASCAR NEXTEL Cup Series Point Standings
(After 17 Races)

Pos.	Driver	Points	Behind	Change
1	**Jimmie Johnson**	**2378**	—	+1
2	Greg Biffle	2305	-73	-1
3	Tony Stewart	2242	-136	+1
4	Elliott Sadler	2178	-200	-1
5	Rusty Wallace	2173	-205	+1
6	Ryan Newman	2115	-263	+1
7	Jamie McMurray	2093	-285	+3
8	Mark Martin	2068	-310	-3
9	Kurt Busch	2030	-348	-1
10	Dale Jarrett	2030	-348	+2

challenge on the leaders. At the same time, Johnson dove to the inside to make it four-abreast in an electrifying battle for the late-race lead, one which lasted but a moment before Stewart powered past on the outside. Once again in front, Stewart was simply unstoppable on the way to his first Daytona victory in 14 career starts.

When asked if he knew before the race just how good his car would be, Stewart responded, "Normally in July, we're all fighting grip and being loose or tight or drifting up the race track. [But] we really never had a complaint with the race car. We just kept working on trying to make it faster.

"You know you've got a car that's close when you make the changes that we made and the car was responding to it," Stewart continued. "I didn't know going into the race that we were going to be *this* good."

And thus began "The Race to the Chase," the stretch of 10 events ending at Richmond in September that would determine the field of drivers eligible to compete in the 2005 Chase for the NASCAR NEXTEL Cup.

For Stewart, his second consecutive win pushed him to third in the points, a jump of seven spots over the last three events, while McMurray held on to finish second in the race and climbed three positions to seventh in the standings.

Others who left Daytona carrying momentum included Dale Jarrett, who used a fourth-place finish to climb back into the top 10 for the first time in eight weeks, while Earnhardt got a much needed boost from his third-place finish, moving up to 16th in points and within striking distance of 10th place, 158 points out.

Finishing seventh in the race, Jeff Gordon kept his championship hopes alive as well, rising to 13th in the standings but just 48 points away from 10th, while Kenseth's ninth-place effort resurrected his chances by showing newfound consistency, although he was still listed in 19th place.

Daytona was far less kind to the rest of the drivers from Roush Racing, however, as Greg Biffle, Mark Martin, Kurt Busch and Carl Edwards all were involved in accidents that resulted in each driver falling in the points, with Edwards dropping out of the top 10 after a five-week run that had him as high as fourth place in the championship standings.

USG SHEETROCK 400

Everyone's eyes were firmly fixed on the Race to the Chase as competitors rolled into Chicagoland Speedway, but for two drivers, the pressure of clawing their way into contention for the Chase for the NASCAR NEXTEL Cup over the next nine events was compounded by the burden of carrying the label, "winless in his last …"

Matt Kenseth and Dale Earnhardt Jr. had suffered through the first half of the 2005 season, both looking for the competitive form they had become accustomed to in recent years.

Kenseth had made a living on consistency, charging through the last three seasons gathering top fives and top 10s at an uncanny rate highlighted by occasional visits to Victory Lane. This year, however, Kenseth and longtime crew chief Robbie Riser had found the going quite a bit tougher, so far scoring only one top five — a fourth place at Michigan — to go with just three other top-10 performances over the season's first 17 events.

Nineteenth in points, Kenseth was far behind his Roush Racing teammates in the standings, with Greg Biffle, Mark Martin and Kurt Busch all within the top 10, while Carl Edwards was just outside in 12th after a five-week stint among the leaders.

The entire race-day crew on the Budweiser Chevrolet assists driver Dale Earnhardt Jr. across the tri-oval grass toward Victory Lane for a long-awaited and much-anticipated winner's celebration.

Strapped-in and ready to go, Matt Kenseth prepares for some track time during practice at Chicagoland. Kenseth led all drivers in the second round of practice and was fourth best in qualifying before leading nearly two-thirds of the race on Sunday.

Worse yet for Kenseth was the fact that Roush drivers had already captured eight wins in addition to Martin's victory in the NASCAR NEXTEL All-Star Challenge, while the No. 17 DeWalt team had to look all the back to early March of last year — 50 races ago — to recall their last trip to Victory Lane.

The good news for Kenseth, however, was that his team was gaining momentum of late, picking up finishes of 11th or better in their last three starts while moving up five positions in the points. A fourth-place qualifying effort at Chicagoland added fuel to their fire, and Kenseth was confident he could continue gaining momentum this week.

For Earnhardt, the news was not very good. After floundering over the first 10 races of the season, the Budweiser Chevrolet driver fell into a six-race funk that dropped him from ninth place in the standings all the way to 18th. Replacing crew chief Pete Rondeau with DEI Technical Director Steve Hmiel hadn't helped much, and the pressure of not having won a race since Phoenix near the end of last season, 19 races ago, weighed heavy on the shoulders of the driver whose fans hope for — even expect — a win every time out.

TOP 10 QUALIFIERS

Pos.	Driver	Seconds	mph
1	Jimmie Johnson	28.701	*188.147
2	Ryan Newman	28.715	188.055
3	Casey Mears	28.773	187.676
4	Matt Kenseth	28.816	187.396
5	Brian Vickers	28.827	187.324
6	Greg Biffle	28.867	187.065
7	Scott Riggs	28.899	186.858
8	Dale Jarrett	28.929	186.664
9	Kevin Harvick	28.971	186.393
10	Dave Blaney	28.989	186.278

* Track Record

(Above) Jimmie Johnson (48) and Ryan Newman (12) lead the starting field through Turns 3&4 on the way to the green flag to begin the 267-lap, 400-mile USG SHEETROCK 400.

(Left) Ricky Rudd (21) tries the outside groove on Jeremy Mayfield (19) in their struggle for position. Mayfield got the best of it, finishing one spot ahead of Rudd, who scored his fourth top 10 of the season.

(Top Right) A crewman scrapes rubber buildup off of a used tire to expose the wear indicators underneath.

A third place last week at Daytona lifted team spirits some, but with a 25th-place start in Chicago this week, everyone knew there was still work to be done.

As the USG SHEETROCK 400 took the green flag under bright, sunny skies, the 80,000 fans in attendance watched as pole-sitter Jimmie Johnson, Ryan Newman and Greg Biffle swapped the lead over the first 65 laps. That would be all any of them would see of the front spot, however, as Kenseth seized control on Lap 66 and began to run away with the show.

Kenseth and the No. 17 Ford, painted this week in the colors of the event's title sponsor, clearly had the field covered, leading four times in large chunks for 175 of the next 180 laps and giving up the point only while pitting during four of the seven caution periods that occurred during that span.

With the race firmly in hand, Kenseth stretched his advantage until the ninth yellow flag flew for debris with less than 25 laps remaining. That's when anyone else with designs on winning the race knew their only chance to beat the swift-running Ford would rest solely on track position.

Tony Stewart (20) drops to the apron while Matt Kenseth (17) and Jeremy Mayfield (19) race past. Stewart had J.J. Yeley qualify the car after taking a hard lick in a practice accident and started at the rear due to a driver change. He made it all the way to second place before having to settle for a finish of fifth.

"We were kind of a sitting duck," Kenseth said of that moment in the race. "We knew we wanted to put four tires on the car because we ran so good all day, but you knew a bunch of [other drivers] were going to get two."

And one of those was Earnhardt, who had spent the race to that point slowly picking his way through the field and into the top five. Running fourth at the time of the caution, Earnhardt got the call from Hmiel to pit for two tires and fuel.

"When you have the best car, you come get four tires every chance you get," Hmiel explained later. "On the other hand, [Kenseth] beat us all day on four tires, so with 20 [laps] to go we gambled."

(Left) Dale Earnhardt Jr. (8) challenges Scott Wimmer (22) for the late-race lead. Wimmer, who had stayed on the track under caution, led on the final two restarts but couldn't hold off the Budweiser driver once victory was within his reach.

(Below) The Budweiser crew erupts in celebration after their driver crossed the finish line to earn his first win of the 2005 season. Of his team Earnhardt said, "I've had fun with this team. I never anticipated them being as good a bunch of guys as they are. … I feel like part of them."

(Opposite Page) Victory at last! Dale Earnhardt Jr. proclaims his triumph to end a frustrating winless streak dating back to fall 2004, 20 races ago.

USG SHEETROCK 400

NASCAR NEXTEL Cup Series Race No. 18

Fin. Pos.	Start Pos.	Car No.	Driver	Team	Laps	Laps Led	Status
1	25	8	Dale Earnhardt Jr.	Budweiser Chevrolet	267	11	Running
2	4	17	Matt Kenseth	USG SHEETROCK/DeWalt Ford	267	176	Running
3	1	48	Jimmie Johnson	Lowe's Chevrolet	267	21	Running
4	5	25	Brian Vickers	GMAC/ditech.com Chevrolet	267		Running
5	13	20	Tony Stewart	The Home Depot Chevrolet	267		Running
6	22	19	Jeremy Mayfield	Dodge Dealers/UAW Dodge	267		Running
7	28	21	Ricky Rudd	Motorcraft Genuine Parts Ford	267		Running
8	19	97	Kurt Busch	Sharpie Ford	267		Running
9	3	41	Casey Mears	Target/Kraft Dodge	267		Running
10	20	6	Mark Martin	Viagra Ford	267		Running
11	6	16	Greg Biffle	National Guard/Post-It Ford	267	34	Running
12	33	2	Rusty Wallace	Miller Genuine Draft Dodge	267		Running
13	26	18	Bobby Labonte	Boniva Chevrolet	267		Running
14	24	5 #	Kyle Busch	Kellogg's Chevrolet	267		Running
15	15	01	Joe Nemechek	U.S. Army Chevrolet	267		Running
16	31	39	David Stremme	U.S. Navy Dodge	267		Running
17	30	22	Scott Wimmer	Caterpillar Dodge	267	10	Running
18	8	88	Dale Jarrett	UPS Ford	267		Running
19	9	29	Kevin Harvick	GM Goodwrench Chevrolet	267		Running
20	43	11	Jason Leffler	FedEx Express Chevrolet	267		Running
21	17	32	Bobby Hamilton Jr.	Tide Chevrolet	267	1	Running
22	36	42	Jamie McMurray	Home123/Havoline Dodge	267		Running
23	7	10	Scott Riggs	Valvoline Chevrolet	267		Running
24	40	43	Jeff Green	Cheerios/Betty Crocker Dodge	267		Running
25	42	4	Mike Wallace	Lucas Oil Chevrolet	267	1	Running
26	41	49	Ken Schrader	Schwan's Home Service Dodge	267	1	Running
27	29	45	Kyle Petty	Georgia-Pacific/Brawny Dodge	267	1	Running
28	39	37	Kevin Lepage	Patron Tequila Dodge	267	1	Running
29	2	12	Ryan Newman	Mobil 1/Alltel Dodge	262	9	Running
30	35	31	Jeff Burton	Bass Pro Shops/Cingular Chevrolet	260		Running
31	32	51	Stuart Kirby	Marathon Multipower-3 Chevrolet	259		Running
32	38	40	Sterling Marlin	Coors Light Dodge	253	1	Engine
33	14	24	Jeff Gordon	DuPont Chevrolet	249		Accident
34	11	0	Mike Bliss	Net Zero Best Buy Chevrolet	249		Accident
35	12	7	Robby Gordon	Menard's Dodge	222		Running
36	27	15	Michael Waltrip	NAPA Auto Parts Chevrolet	214		Accident
37	23	38	Elliott Sadler	Combos/M&M's Ford	210		Running
38	10	07	Dave Blaney	Jack Daniel's Chevrolet	200		Accident
39	21	99	Carl Edwards	Office Depot Ford	170		Running
40	37	00	Carl Long	Sunquest Vacations Dodge	148		Handling
41	18	9	Kasey Kahne	Dodge Dealers/UAW Dodge	138		Engine
42	34	44	Terry Labonte	Pizza Hut Chevrolet	124		Handling
43	16	77 #	Travis Kvapil	Jasper Engines/Kodak Dodge	13		Engine

Raybestos Rookie of the Year Contender.

NASCAR NEXTEL Cup Series Point Standings

(After 18 Races)

Pos.	Driver	Points	Behind	Change
1	Jimmie Johnson	2548	—	—
2	Greg Biffle	2440	-108	—
3	Tony Stewart	2397	-151	—
4	Rusty Wallace	2300	-248	+1
5	Elliott Sadler	2230	-318	-1
6	Mark Martin	2202	-346	+2
7	Ryan Newman	2196	-352	-1
8	Jamie McMurray	2190	-358	-1
9	Jeremy Mayfield	2179	-369	+2
10	Kurt Busch	2172	-376	-1

On the restart with 19 laps remaining, Scott Wimmer led off after staying out on the track, followed by Earnhardt, with Kenseth mired in ninth, the first of those who took four fresh Goodyears.

While Earnhardt began sizing up the Caterpillar Dodge, Kenseth started his charge toward the front, a run interrupted by a four-lap caution that ended with 13 circuits remaining.

Back under green, the Budweiser driver made his move quickly to assume the point with 11 to go. On fresh tires, Kenseth was bearing down, arriving in second place and closing with five laps to go. Time, however, was not on his side, as Earnhardt was able to capitalize on clean air and finish with a mere 0.291-second advantage to take his 16th career victory.

It had been a while since the No. 8 team had had a chance to celebrate in Victory Lane, but by the looks of things, they hadn't forgotten how. "That's the satisfaction of this win," Earnhardt said amongst the hoopla. "To see what [these guys] feel today means more to me than taking the trophy out and setting in on the mantle."

To be sure, they were "0-for" no more.

NEW ENGLAND 300

Pressure and momentum are two important facets in any sport — intangible aspects of human nature that are impossible to pin down but imperative in dictating the flow of competition. Further, the two ideals coexist in a balance that is nearly impossible to manage but yet essential to performance, be it good or bad.

Going into the New England 300, momentum and pressure clearly were affecting a number of teams in a variety of ways.

Momentum was unmistakably on the side of Tony Stewart and the No. 20 outfit from Joe Gibbs Racing. After floundering over the first half of the season, Stewart and company seemed to have simply changed gears and rocketed away from their competition.

Crewmen on Brian Vickers' Chevrolet hustle through a four-tire stop under caution at New Hampshire. Vickers won the Bud Pole for the race, his first of the year and the second of his career, and led 10 laps early in the event before settling down into the top 10 for most of the race.

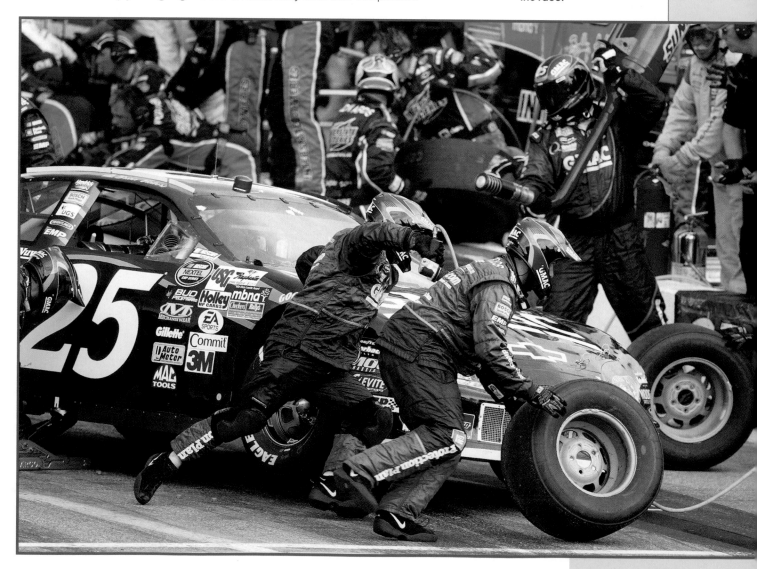

(Above) Dale Earnhardt Jr. streaks down the straightaway on his way to a ninth-place finish at New Hampshire. That, on the heels of his win at Chicago and a third place at Daytona, lifted his spirits — and his position in the point standings.

(Right) Jeremy Mayfield breaks out the Sharpie to sign a fan's copy of *The Official NASCAR Preview and Press Guide*. Mayfield cracked the top 10 in points for the first time this season last week in Chicago, and he moved up another spot after the New England 300.

That shift into high gear came at Michigan where Stewart, after three straight races finishing no better than 15th, battled amongst a bevy of Roush drivers to take a hard-fought second place. He followed that with back-to-back wins at Sonoma, Calif., and Daytona — as different as any two tracks can be — and left Chicago last week with his fourth straight top-five finish after starting at the rear of the field in a backup car, having wrecked his primary mount in practice.

TOP 10 QUALIFIERS

Pos.	Driver	Seconds	mph
1	Brian Vickers	29.225	130.327
2	Kasey Kahne	29.250	130.215
3	Elliott Sadler	29.344	129.798
4	Ryan Newman	29.349	129.776
5	Kurt Busch	29.351	129.767
6	Rusty Wallace	29.358	129.736
7	Kyle Busch #	29.363	129.714
8	Kevin Harvick	29.370	129.683
9	Greg Biffle	29.385	129.617
10	Bobby Labonte	29.390	129.595

Kasey Kahne (9) charges into the turn with Brian Vickers (25) and Ryan Newman (12) hot on his tail. Kahne qualified on the front row next to Vickers and led laps early, eventually dropping to sixth at finish, one spot ahead of Newman.

As if to indicate that his fifth place at Chicagoland was somewhat of an "off" day, Stewart merely obliterated the competition at New Hampshire International Speedway. Using the first 50 laps to move up from his 13th-place start, Stewart took the point on Lap 51 and proceeded to lead 232 of the next 250 laps, including the last 55, in a display of dominance akin to his overwhelming run at Daytona two weeks before.

Undoubtedly, positive momentum was on Stewart's side, and watching him climb the fence and into the flagstand to personally capture the checkered flag made it equally as obvious that he was feeling very little pressure.

With others, momentum appeared to be building — slowly — while pressure to perform eased ever so slightly. Kurt Busch had gained the most of late, able to negate an unfortunate 37th place at Daytona by sandwiching that around a third-place run on the road course at Sonoma and an eighth-place result at Chicago. Busch added energy to his title defense here at New Hampshire as the "best of the rest" behind Stewart, jumping five positions to fifth in the standings and squarely into the field of championship contenders.

(Right) Ryan Newman (12) chooses the outside groove to face a challenge from Tony Stewart (20) down low. Stewart, however, was simply passing by on his way to the front where he spent most of the afternoon.

(Below) Bobby Labonte receives full service from his Interstate Batteries crew during one of 10 cautions during the race. Labonte had a sparkling day, picking up a strong third-place finish, the first top five in his last seven tries.

While Busch let out a small sigh of relief, Dale Earnhardt Jr. and Matt Kenseth were still holding their breath. Finishing 1-2, respectively, a week ago at Chicago had given both drivers renewed hope, and they capitalized with top 10s in the New England 300.

Earnhardt's ninth-place finish on the flat, 1.058-mile oval unofficially formed a top-10 streak at three, which moved him from 18th to a challenging 13th in the standings, where he sat just 59 points away from the magical 10th-place position, currently occupied by Dale Jarrett.

Kenseth's 10th-place effort at New Hampshire formed a string for him as well, with five consecutive races running 11th or better at the finish. Still feeling plenty of heat, Kenseth and crew chief Robbie Reiser could sense the steam building as they crept up the point ladder from 24th to 16th over that same five-race span.

Joining Busch, Earnhardt and Kenseth as drivers pushing upward was Jeremy Mayfield. The Dodge driver's season so far had not been outstanding, but consistency was the name

Tony Stewart's Home Depot machine leads the way for Kurt Busch in the IRWIN car, with Kyle Busch looking to stick his Kellogg's Chevrolet on the inside. The brothers Busch enjoyed good outings, with Kurt second best to Stewart and Kyle finishing two spots back, in fourth.

NEW ENGLAND 300

NASCAR NEXTEL Cup Series Race No. 19

Fin. Pos.	Start Pos.	Car No.	Driver	Team	Laps	Laps Led	Status
1	13	20	Tony Stewart	The Home Depot Chevrolet	300	232	Running
2	5	97	Kurt Busch	IRWIN Industrial Tools Ford	300	6	Running
3	10	18	Bobby Labonte	Interstate Batteries Chevrolet	300		Running
4	7	5 #	Kyle Busch	Kellogg's Chevrolet	300		Running
5	9	16	Greg Biffle	National Guard/Post-It Ford	300		Running
6	2	9	Kasey Kahne	Dodge Dealers/UAW Dodge	300	18	Running
7	4	12	Ryan Newman	Alltel Dodge	300	22	Running
8	6	2	Rusty Wallace	Miller Lite Dodge	300		Running
9	24	8	Dale Earnhardt Jr.	Budweiser Chevrolet	300		Running
10	16	17	Matt Kenseth	DeWalt Power Tools Ford	300		Running
11	1	25	Brian Vickers	GMAC/ditech.com Chevrolet	300	10	Running
12	20	99	Carl Edwards	Office Depot/Scotts Ford	300		Running
13	12	48	Jimmie Johnson	Lowe's Chevrolet	300		Running
14	25	31	Jeff Burton	Cingular Wireless Chevrolet	300		Running
15	19	6	Mark Martin	Viagra Ford	300		Running
16	34	88	Dale Jarrett	UPS Ford	300		Running
17	28	15	Michael Waltrip	NAPA Auto Parts Chevrolet	300		Running
18	22	01	Joe Nemechek	U.S. Army Chevrolet	300		Running
19	11	19	Jeremy Mayfield	Dodge Dealers/UAW Dodge	299		Running
20	37	07	Dave Blaney	Jack Daniel's Chevrolet	299		Running
21	18	0	Mike Bliss	Net Zero Best Buy Chevrolet	299		Running
22	8	29	Kevin Harvick	GM Goodwrench Chevrolet	299		Running
23	14	21	Ricky Rudd	Motorcraft Genuine Parts Ford	299		Running
24	27	11	Jason Leffler	FedEx Ground Chevrolet	299	1	Running
25	21	24	Jeff Gordon	DuPont Chevrolet	299		Running
26	41	49	Ken Schrader	Schwan's Home Service Dodge	299		Running
27	30	77 #	Travis Kvapil	Kodak/Jasper Eng. & Trans. Dodge	299		Running
28	36	32	Bobby Hamilton Jr.	Tide Chevrolet	299		Running
29	42	45	Kyle Petty	Georgia-Pacific/Brawny Dodge	299	1	Running
30	31	7	Robby Gordon	Harrah's Chevrolet	299		Running
31	15	43	Jeff Green	Cheerios/Betty Crocker Dodge	298	1	Running
32	23	10	Scott Riggs	Valvoline Chevrolet	298		Running
33	26	41	Casey Mears	Target Dodge	298		Running
34	29	40	Sterling Marlin	Coors Light Dodge	298		Running
35	32	22	Scott Wimmer	Caterpillar Dodge	297	9	Running
36	33	66 #	Mike Garvey	Jani-King Ford	296		Running
37	43	37	Kevin Lepage	bospoker.net Dodge	296		Running
38	40	4	Mike Wallace	Lucas Oil Chevrolet	294		Running
39	3	38	Elliott Sadler	M&M's Ford	233		Accident
40	17	42	Jamie McMurray	Texaco/Havoline Dodge	145		Accident
41	39	89	Morgan Shepherd	Cornerstone Bancard Dodge	99		Handling
42	38	27	Ted Christopher	Freddie B's Ford	29		Brakes
43	35	00	Carl Long	Buyer's Choice Auto Warranty Chevrolet	8		Brakes

\# Raybestos Rookie of the Year Contender.

NASCAR NEXTEL Cup Series Point Standings

(After 19 Races)

Pos.	Driver	Points	Behind	Change
1	Jimmie Johnson	2672	—	—
2	Greg Biffle	2595	-77	—
3	Tony Stewart	2587	-85	—
4	Rusty Wallace	2442	-230	—
5	Kurt Busch	2347	-325	+5
6	Ryan Newman	2347	-325	+1
7	Mark Martin	2320	-352	-1
8	Jeremy Mayfield	2285	-387	+1
9	Elliott Sadler	2276	-396	-4
10	Dale Jarrett	2254	-418	+1

of the game for Mayfield. Twenty-sixth in points early in the year, Mayfield had quietly collected finishes in the upper teens with occasional forays into the top 10, all the while ascending in the points until breaking the top-10 barrier last week in Chicago. Even a 19th place here in New England couldn't reverse his trend, as he moved from ninth to eighth on the sub-par performance.

For several teams, the forces of upward impetus and downward stress seemed to be in relative balance. Jimmie Johnson, Greg Biffle, Rusty Wallace, Mark Martin and Ryan Newman all had been able to maintain a competitive stance with minor variations in point positions from week to week, all looking like good bets to remain among the top 10.

For Jarrett, Jamie McMurray, Carl Edwards and Kevin Harvick, however, stagnation was a growing concern. Each of them had cracked the top 10 at some point during the season, but all were hovering very close to the cut-off position. Jarrett was tops among them in 10th place, and with each passing event, point positions would become more and more difficult to gain, adding pressure in increasing doses as the schedule progressed.

Two other drivers had momentum, but it was unfortunately of the downward variety. Elliott Sadler had been within the top 10 in points since the fourth week of the season. Solidly in third place for five straight weeks, Sadler began slipping after finishing 21st in the Pepsi 400 and then 37th at Chicago. That slip turned into an all out slide at New Hampshire with his second DNF of the year resulting in a plummet from fifth to ninth in points.

Finally there was Jeff Gordon. The four-time champ began the year on a serious roll, winning three times in the first nine races and solidly among the top five in points. That ended abruptly, however, with accidents resulting in three straight DNFs that sent Gordon into a free-fall. Six finishes of 30th or worse in the previous eight races leading up to a 25th place in the New England 300 had the DuPont driver mired at 15th in points with little relief in sight. The question for Gordon and his team now had become whether pure pressure would reverse the trend — or burst the bubble for good.

Only time would tell. And with just seven races to go in the Race to the Chase, time was running out.

PENNSYLVANIA 500

When Jack Roush arrived at Pocono Raceway in June several weeks ago, he had yet to reach Victory Lane at the triangular-shaped super speedway in 17 years of fielding entries. His teams had run well there to be sure — Mark Martin alone had recorded six runner-up finishes among his 18 top fives and 25 top 10s over 36 career starts — but Roush had yet to find the magic it took to conquer the oddly-configured tri-oval.

That all ended when Carl Edwards, competing on the track for the first time, drove to victory in the Pocono 500 for his second career win. Martin took seventh in that race, with Kurt Busch the best of the remaining three Roush drivers way back in 22nd place.

This time around, things would be different.

Jamie McMurray set the pace in qualifying for the Pennsylvania 500 with a 53.330-second lap at 168.761 miles per hour to capture the second Bud Pole of his career, but right on his heels sat Roush drivers Busch and Martin in second and third, with Greg Biffle not far behind in seventh on the starting grid.

Kurt Busch (97) hugs the inside of Turn 3 ahead of Tony Stewart (20) and Jimmie Johnson (48) at the front of the Pocono field. Busch led 131 laps — 105 more than any other driver — on the way to his second win of the season.

June winner Edwards lined up at the rear of the field in 41st place after Bobby Gerhart qualified the car while Edwards was in Colorado, competing in the NASCAR Busch Series where he currently sat fourth in the point standings.

Busch wasted no time staking his claim as the man to beat, charging straight into the lead as the green flag flew to begin the 500-mile affair. In a word, Busch was gone. Stretching his advantage to a gaudy five seconds early in the race, Busch allowed P.J. Jones, Mike Wallace and Ryan Newman to lead one lap each while he pitted for tires and fuel, with his only real challenge over the first half of the race coming from Joe Nemechek, who took the point during the day's second caution at the 50-lap mark.

(Right) Crew chief Ryan Pemberton likes what he sees on the stopwatch as he clocks his driver, Joe Nemechek. The U.S. Army Chevrolet clearly was one of the strongest cars on the track but a cut tire, a broken shock and a penalty for pitting too soon under caution all combined to thwart Nemechek's top-five bid.

(Below) Dave Blaney (07), Jeff Green (43) and Jeremy Mayfield (19) form a three-wide drag race down Pocono's Long Pond Straight, all hoping to settle things before entering the single-groove Tunnel Turn. Mayfield eventually triumphed by finishing 18th ahead of Green in 19th and Blaney in 20th.

Nemechek, with a strong U.S. Army Chevrolet under him, was able to hold the lead for five laps under green before Busch motored past to reassume his position at the point in the first of only two passes he was forced to make on the track during the entire race.

Busch's day got interesting when the fourth yellow flag flew on Lap 121 for debris. Having already led 110 trips around the 2.5-mile oval, Busch pitted for four tires but experienced problems on the left rear during the stop and left pit road in eighth place.

Biffle and Rusty Wallace, both of whom took just two tires, led on the restart with 75 laps remaining, while Busch began his march toward the leaders, a march interrupted five times over the next 50 laps as the event succumbed to a flurry of yellow flags that had Biffle, Martin and Wallace each taking a turn at the front.

By the time the green flag flew on Lap 181 following the day's ninth caution, Busch decided he had had enough and dropped the hammer in his powerful IRWIN-sponsored Ford, using just two laps to retake the point from then-leader Wallace.

Three more cautions appeared over the final 10 laps, the third of which set up a green-white-checkered finish with Busch in front followed by Wallace and Martin.

The final restart on Lap 202 presented little challenge for Busch, as he immediately drove away to a comfortable lead. Fittingly, the race ended under caution after Kasey Kahne hit the wall, leaving Wallace and Martin to follow Busch across the line for the final time.

(Above) Elliott Sadler collects his personal belongings from the M&M's Ford, substantially shortened in an accident during practice. Behind it sits the No. 48 Chevrolet, Jimmie Johnsons' primary mount, damaged in practice prior to qualifying.

(Right, Above) Kyle Busch finds the Turn 1 wall after a faulty wheel bearing sent the Kellogg's Monte Carlo spinning at the 150-lap mark. Unable to continue, Busch was listed 39th in the final rundown.

(Right, Below) The slightly-battered pole-winning Dodge of Jamie McMurray receives care under caution. The Texaco crew kept McMurray on the lead lap where he was able to finish 11th and maintain his 11th position in the points.

TOP 10 QUALIFIERS

Pos.	Driver	Seconds	mph
1	Jamie McMurray	53.330	168.761
2	Kurt Busch	53.402	168.533
3	Mark Martin	53.450	168.382
4	Ryan Newman	53.492	168.249
5	Ricky Rudd	53.617	167.857
6	Tony Stewart	53.721	167.532
7	Greg Biffle	53.818	167.230
8	Brian Vickers	53.818	167.230
9	Jimmie Johnson	53.869	167.072
10	Kevin Harvick	53.869	167.072

Edwards managed to keep his Office Depot Ford out of trouble and charged all the way to fourth place, giving Roush three of the top four positions in a dominant performance by the multi-car team based in Concord, N.C.

With the win, his fourth top-eight run in the last five events, Busch solidified his fifth-place position in the points, while Biffle fell to 17th at the finish and dropped to third in the standings behind Jimmie Johnson and Tony Stewart after a nine-week run in one of the top two spots.

(Above) Rusty Wallace (2) and Mark Martin (6) vie for position in the late stages of the race. Both drivers took turns at the front while Kurt Busch worked through traffic, and they finished together with Wallace taking second ahead of Martin in third.

(Left) Kurt Busch (97) sails through Pocono's sweeping third turn ahead of Roush teammate Matt Kenseth (17). Busch led nearly the entire first half of the race before being shuffled back in the field on a faulty pit stop.

(Opposite Page) Kurt Busch claims the Pocono win. Although not without its challenges, the Pennsylvania 500 was a convincing victory for the defending NASCAR NEXTEL Cup Series champion.

PENNSYLVANIA 500

NASCAR NEXTEL Cup Series Race No. 20

Fin. Pos.	Start Pos.	Car No.	Driver	Team	Laps	Laps Led	Status
1	2	97	Kurt Busch	IRWIN Industrial Tools Ford	203	131	Running
2	13	2	Rusty Wallace	Miller Lite Dodge	203	18	Running
3	3	6	Mark Martin	Viagra Ford	203	26	Running
4	41	99	Carl Edwards	Office Depot/Scotts Ford	203		Running
5	4	12	Ryan Newman	Mobil 1/Alltel Dodge	203	1	Running
6	10	29	Kevin Harvick	GM Goodwrench Chevrolet	203		Running
7	6	20	Tony Stewart	The Home Depot Chevrolet	203		Running
8	23	18	Bobby Labonte	Interstate Batteries Chevrolet	203		Running
9	34	0	Mike Bliss	Net Zero Best Buy Chevrolet	203		Running
10	5	21	Ricky Rudd	Motorcraft Genuine Parts Ford	203		Running
11	1	42	Jamie McMurray	Havoline-Texaco Dodge	203		Running
12	9	48	Jimmie Johnson	Lowe's Chevrolet	203		Running
13	21	24	Jeff Gordon	DuPont Chevrolet	203		Running
14	8	25	Brian Vickers	GMAC/ditech.com Chevrolet	203		Running
15	20	88	Dale Jarrett	UPS Ford	203		Running
16	39	38	Elliott Sadler	M&M's Ford	203		Running
17	7	16	Greg Biffle	National Guard Ford	203	17	Running
18	16	19	Jeremy Mayfield	Dodge Dealers/UAW Dodge	203		Running
19	26	43	Jeff Green	Cheerios/Betty Crocker Dodge	203		Running
20	22	07	Dave Blaney	Jack Daniel's Chevrolet	203		Running
21	42	41	Casey Mears	Target Dodge	203		Running
22	14	01	Joe Nemechek	U.S. Army Chevrolet	203	8	Running
23	27	32	Bobby Hamilton Jr.	Tide Chevrolet	203		Running
24	19	11	Jason Leffler	FedEx Ground Chevrolet	203		Running
25	11	22	Scott Wimmer	Caterpillar Dodge	203		Running
26	24	15	Michael Waltrip	NAPA Auto Parts Chevrolet	203		Running
27	15	9	Kasey Kahne	Dodge Dealers/UAW Dodge	202		Running
28	25	40	Sterling Marlin	Coors Light Dodge	202		Running
29	31	4	Mike Wallace	Lucas Oil/Wide Open Chevrolet	202	1	Running
30	33	45	Kyle Petty	Kyle Petty Charity Ride/Brawny Dodge	202		Running
31	12	49	Ken Schrader	Schwan's Home Service Dodge	202		Running
32	38	8	Dale Earnhardt Jr.	Budweiser Chevrolet	201		Running
33	18	10	Scott Riggs	Valvoline Chevrolet	201		Running
34	32	66 #	Mike Garvey	Peak Fitness Ford	201		Running
35	37	37	Kevin Lepage	BoSPOKER.net Dodge	201		Running
36	30	17	Matt Kenseth	DeWalt Power Tools Ford	195		Running
37	17	31	Jeff Burton	Cingular Wireless Chevrolet	192		Running
38	40	77 #	Travis Kvapil	Kodak/Jasper Eng. & Trans. Dodge	179		Running
39	28	5 #	Kyle Busch	Kellogg's Chevrolet	150		Accident
40	29	7	Robby Gordon	Jim Beam Chevrolet	143		Engine
41	36	34	P.J. Jones	Mach I Inc. Chevrolet	23	1	Transmission
42	43	27	Kirk Shelmerdine	L.R. Lyons & Sons Ford	11		Overheating
43	35	13	Greg Sacks	Sacks Motorsports Dodge	5		Brakes

Raybestos Rookie of the Year Contender.

NASCAR NEXTEL Cup Series Point Standings

(After 20 Races)

Pos.	Driver	Points	Behind	Change
1	**Jimmie Johnson**	**2799**	—	—
2	Tony Stewart	2733	-66	+1
3	Greg Biffle	2712	-87	-1
4	Rusty Wallace	2617	-182	—
5	Kurt Busch	2537	-262	—
6	Ryan Newman	2607	-292	—
7	Mark Martin	2490	-309	—
8	Jeremy Mayfield	2394	-405	—
9	Elliott Sadler	2391	-408	—
10	Dale Jarrett	2372	-427	—

Other notables in the race included sixth-place Kevin Harvick, who had struggled since he last saw the top 10 six races ago here at Pocono; Bobby Labonte, whose eighth place came on the heels of his third-place run last week at New Hampshire; Mike Bliss, with his first top 10 of the season in ninth; and Ricky Rudd, who posted his third top-10 finish in the last five events.

Matt Kenseth, most in need of a good finish among the Roush drivers, had a difficult day and finished 36th, ending his recent surge and severely hampering his drive in the Race to the Chase, while Dale Earnhardt Jr. suffered a similar fate, finishing 32nd in the Pennsylvania 500.

ALLSTATE 400
AT THE BRICKYARD

Tony Stewart (far left) and crew chief Greg Zipadelli (far right) join crewmen in scaling the frontstretch fence after a stirring victory at Indianapolis Motor Speedway. This was the third fence-climbing for Stewart over a five-race stretch, but none meant more to the Indiana native than this one.

E very racer has that special event — the single race he wants to win more than any other, more than anything. For a kid growing up in Indiana, cutting his racing teeth in open-wheel divisions around the Midwest, winning at Indianapolis Motor Speedway is that special event.

Winning at The Brickyard — hallowed ground for any such kid, any such racer — is the pinnacle of a career, and for Tony Stewart, anything less than victory was pure and simple defeat. Six times before, Stewart had attacked the 400-mile event with everything his soul could muster; six times ending in bitter disappointment. Frustration that ran so deep it sometimes spilled over into outright anger.

Three years ago, that anger showed its ugly head as Stewart shunned media types after climbing from his car following the race, sparking a week-long Stewart-bashing fest that overshadowed Bill Elliott's hugely popular triumph. Stewart, however, found a way to channel that negative energy into an all-out assault on the remainder of the season that culminated in the 2002 NASCAR NEXTEL Cup Series championship, a title he since said he would gladly trade for a single victory — at The Brickyard.

(Right) Casey Mears (41) leads fellow Dodge driver Kasey Kahne through the low-banked turns at Indianapolis. Mears had to start at the back of the field after an unapproved impound adjustment to his Dodge, but still managed to improve 34 positions to finish sixth.

(Below) The cars of Elliott Sadler (38) and Jeremy Mayfield (19) occupy the front row for the start of the Allstate 400 at The Brickyard. Sadler posted a qualifying lap more than a full mile per hour faster than Mayfield's but was more than two mph off Casey Mears' track record set last year.

TOP 10 QUALIFIERS

Pos.	Driver	Seconds	mph
1	Elliott Sadler	48.882	184.116
2	Jeremy Mayfield	49.166	183.053
3	Michael Waltrip	49.187	182.975
4	Kasey Kahne	49.224	182.837
5	Brian Vickers	49.238	182.785
6	Ryan Newman	49.270	102.666
7	Jeff Gordon	49.324	182.466
8	Sterling Marlin	49.324	182.466
9	Ricky Rudd	49.373	182.285
10	Mark Martin	49.376	182.274

(Above) The teams of Elliott Sadler (38) and Brian Vickers (25) go head-to-head on pit road. Both drivers had turns at the front in the first half of the race, with Vickers able to stay among the leaders and score his fourth top five of the season.

(Left) Team members attend to details on Kevin Harvick's GM Goodwrench Chevrolet in the Indy garage. Needing a good run to stay competitive in the points, Harvick, the 2003 winner of this event, made it into the top 10 briefly but fell to a disappointing 19th place at the finish.

That would no longer be necessary. This was Tony Stewart's day.

It wasn't too hard to see this one coming. The engine that drives the Home Depot team was definitely firing on all cylinders, powering Stewart to finishes of second, first, first, fifth, first and seventh in the six races leading up to the Allstate 400 at The Brickyard. The "20" team had used that streak to climb from 10th place in the point standings all the way to second and was banging on leader Jimmie Johnson's rear bumper, just 66 points behind and closing fast.

Stewart was relaxed — even jovial. Communication was good within the team and confidence was high. Stewart had even taken the opportunity to practice climbing frontstretch fences following wins at Daytona and New Hampshire in anticipation of scaling the grand-daddy of all fences, the one lining the "canyon" that contains the famous strip of bricks.

If ever there was karma, this was it.

Stewart began his 400-mile quest a mediocre 22nd after qualifying three-quarters of a second behind pole-winner Elliott Sadler. Using the patience he employed to reach victory on

Fans enjoy the view of the canyon-like frontstretch as the field roars toward Turn 1. The crowd at Indianapolis, estimated at 280,000, is traditionally the largest on the annual NASCAR NEXTEL Cup Series schedule.

(Above) Tony Stewart (20) holds the outside line through the corner against an inside challenge from Kasey Kahne (9). Stewart was chasing his friend and former Sprint Car teammate in the late stages of the race, until a caution provided him the winning opportunity.

(Left) Tony Stewart offers a huge smile and a thumbs-up while clutching the trophy he covets above all others. The popular win crafted by Stewart, crew chief Greg Zipadelli (right) and the Home Depot team put them on top of the point standings for the first time this season.

the road course at Sonoma, Stewart carefully, if not gingerly, picked his way through traffic while avoiding trouble over the first half of the race. Six cautions before the 80-lap mark neither helped nor hindered his steady advance into the top five by the midway point of the race.

Stewart reached the leaders by Lap 100 and eased past Brian Vickers to take his first lead of the day, an advantage he stretched to three seconds over the next 18 laps until the race

ALLSTATE 400

NASCAR NEXTEL Cup Series Race No. 21

Fin. Pos.	Start Pos.	Car No.	Driver	Team	Laps	Laps Led	Status
1	22	20	Tony Stewart	The Home Depot Chevrolet	160	44	Running
2	4	9	Kasey Kahne	Dodge Dealers/UAW Dodge	160	39	Running
3	5	25	Brian Vickers	Garnier Fructis Chevrolet	160	14	Running
4	2	19	Jeremy Mayfield	Dodge Dealers/UAW Dodge	160		Running
5	20	17	Matt Kenseth	DeWalt Power Tools Ford	160	9	Running
6	40	41	Casey Mears	Target Dodge	160	10	Running
7	10	6	Mark Martin	Viagra Ford	160		Running
8	7	24	Jeff Gordon	DuPont Chevrolet	160		Running
9	8	40	Sterling Marlin	Coors Light Dodge	160		Running
10	16	5 #	Kyle Busch	Kellogg's/Delphi Chevrolet	160		Running
11	12	0	Mike Bliss	Net Zero Best Buy Chevrolet	160		Running
12	38	99	Carl Edwards	AAA Ford	160		Running
13	28	45	Kyle Petty	Georgia-Pacific/Marsh Stores Dodge	160	1	Running
14	24	88	Dale Jarrett	UPS Ford	160		Running
15	15	43	Jeff Green	Box Tops/Cheerios/Betty Crocker Dodge	160		Running
16	3	15	Michael Waltrip	NAPA Auto Parts Chevrolet	160		Running
17	23	42	Jamie McMurray	Havoline-Texaco Dodge	160		Running
18	37	97	Kurt Busch	Crown Royal Ford	160		Running
19	14	29	Kevin Harvick	GM Goodwrench Chevrolet	160		Running
20	29	31	Jeff Burton	Cingular Chevrolet	160		Running
21	31	16	Greg Biffle	National Guard Ford	160		Running
22	11	49	Ken Schrader	Red Baron Pizza Dodge	160		Running
23	33	91	Bill Elliott	Stanley Tools Dodge	160		Running
24	13	7	Robby Gordon	Fruit-of-the Loom Chevrolet	160	1	Running
25	41	2	Rusty Wallace	Miller Lite Dodge	160		Running
26	26	22	Scott Wimmer	Caterpillar Dodge	160	1	Running
27	35	04	Bobby Hamilton	Bailey's/Hunter Barge Dodge	160		Running
28	19	01	Joe Nemechek	U.S. Army Chevrolet	160		Running
29	34	23	Mike Skinner	The History Channel Dodge	160		Running
30	30	07	Dave Blaney	Jack Daniel's Chevrolet	160		Running
31	32	36	Boris Said	CENTRIX Financial Chevrolet	160		Running
32	1	38	Elliott Sadler	M&M's Ford	159	39	Running
33	18	11	Jason Leffler	FedEx Express Chevrolet	159		Running
34	6	12	Ryan Newman	Alltel Dodge	158		Running
35	21	10	Scott Riggs	Rally's Chevrolet	152		Running
36	43	44	Terry Labonte	dltech.com Chevrolet	151	2	Handling
37	39	77 #	Travis Kvapil	Kodak/Jasper Eng. & Trans. Dodge	146		Running
38	42	48	Jimmie Johnson	Lowe's Chevrolet	143		Accident
39	25	32	Bobby Hamilton Jr.	Tide Chevrolet	119		Running
40	36	18	Bobby Labonte	Interstate Batteries Chevrolet	116		Accident
41	9	21	Ricky Rudd	Motorcraft Genuine Parts Ford	73		Accident
42	17	1	Martin Truex Jr.	Bass Pro Shops/Tracker Chevrolet	62		Accident
43	27	8	Dale Earnhardt Jr.	Budweiser Chevrolet	62		Accident

Raybestos Rookie of the Year Contender.

NASCAR NEXTEL Cup Series Point Standings
(After 21 Races)

Pos.	Driver	Points	Behind	Change
1	**Tony Stewart**	2923	—	+1
2	Jimmie Johnson	2848	-75	-1
3	Greg Biffle	2812	-111	—
4	Rusty Wallace	2705	-218	—
5	Kurt Busch	2646	-277	—
6	Mark Martin	2636	-287	+1
7	Ryan Newman	2568	-355	-1
8	Jeremy Mayfield	2554	-369	—
9	Dale Jarrett	2493	-430	+1
10	Carl Edwards	2487	-436	+2

was interrupted by the race's eighth caution when a cut tire sent Bobby Labonte's Chevrolet into the third-turn wall.

Back under green, Stewart's stiffest competition arrived in the form of Kasey Kahne, who flexed the muscle of his powerful Dodge on the low side of Turn 4, moving past Stewart on Lap 134 to take the role of the hare with Stewart relegated to that of the hound.

For 16 agonizing laps, Stewart chased the red-and-white Dodge around the 2.5-mile track, looking for but unable to find a chink in Kahne's armor. But the finger of fate can indeed be fickle, and that finger pointed directly to Johnson, whose Chevrolet cut a tire, sending him into the fourth-turn wall to produce the 10th and final caution of the day.

With the field bunched tightly behind, Kahne took the green flag on the final restart with 11 laps to go. Screaming into the first turn, Kahne left the slightest opening — small, but just enough for Stewart to challenge. This, Stewart knew, would be his best shot.

"I knew Kasey wasn't going to do anything stupid," Stewart recalled of the moment. "I knew I *was* going to do something stupid."

Ill-advised or not, Stewart dropped to the inside and masterfully swept past and into the lead for the final time.

"Just the tires cooling off (from the caution) ... lightened my car up a little bit, and my car didn't need to be tightened because it was perfect before," Kahne bemoaned after the race. "I just pushed off all four corners after that and just couldn't get the runs down the straightaways."

Safely in clean air and with no traffic to hamper his advance, the native of nearby Rushville opened a gap of nearly a second over the final 10-lap sprint as the 280,000 fans on hand witnessed destiny fulfilled.

"You dream about something for so long, you become consumed by it," Stewart admitted. "Finally, today I got to feel what it feels like, see what the view is of coming down that front straightaway and seeing those checkered flags as the first driver to go under versus the third of fourth driver.

"This is probably — well, it's definitely — the greatest day of my life up to this point, professionally and personally. I couldn't ask for more."

SIRIUS SATELLITE RADIO AT THE GLEN

As the saying goes: When you're hot, you're hot. And absolutely no one associated with the NASCAR NEXTEL Cup Series was about to deny that Tony Stewart was, indeed, hot. Red hot.

Basking the aftermath of the biggest, most significant win of his highly successful career, Stewart had a mere 120 hours or so to celebrate what he described as "the best day of my life" before returning to work, this time on the road course at Watkins Glen, N.Y.

Could it have been any better for Stewart? Winner of the last two road-course events, including this race one year ago, the driver from Joe Gibbs Racing sauntered into Upstate New York having won four of his last six starts while vaulting from 10th to first in the point standings. He did not need to be reminded that this was the place where, three years ago, he began an astounding run that culminated in the 2002 NASCAR NEXTEL Cup Series championship. Still floating on an emotional cloud, Stewart climbed aboard his Home Depot Chevrolet on Friday afternoon

Led by point leader Tony Stewart (20), the drivers at the top of the standings bring the field around the road course at Watkins Glen International in front of an estimated crowd of 85,000. The starting grid was set by car owner points after Bud Pole qualifying was washed out.

(Above) Scott Pruett prepares to compete in the No. 40 Coors Light Dodge in place of regular driver Sterling Marlin. No stranger to road racing, Pruett gave the team its best finish of the season with a strong fourth-place showing.

(Above Right) Robby Gordon had to bring his Jim Beam Chevrolet up through the field twice after starting 39th and then being caught by an untimely caution. Gordon was fast, however, and bested everyone but Stewart in his first top-10 run of the season.

(Right) Terry Labonte, also known for his ability on the road courses, took the wheel of the FedEx Chevrolet for Joe Gibbs Racing in place of Jason Leffler, who was released from the team following Indianapolis.

and quickly set the tone for the weekend by posting practice laps one full second faster than anyone else could muster.

To no one's surprise, Stewart carried that speed into Bud Pole qualifying where he easily set the pace, with only Robby Gordon able to get "close" to him, nearly a half-second behind. Unfortunately for Gordon, however, his lap would not benefit the owner/driver, as rain blanketed the area before the session was complete, forcing the field for the SIRIUS Satellite Radio at The Glen to be set according to car owner points.

(Left) Dale Earnhardt Jr. (right) chats with Paul Menard prior to race time. Menard, a NASCAR Busch Series regular with experience in open-wheel racing, was on hand to drive the No. 1 Monte Carlo fielded by DEI in his second career NASCAR NEXTEL Cup Series start.

(Right) Boris Said (36) leads a single-file line that includes Jeff Burton (31) and Mark Martin (6) through the backstretch chicane. In his seventh start of the year, Said grabbed a season-best third place for MB/Sutton Motorsports.

Tony Stewart's orange-and-white Chevrolet was a rocket ship at Watkins Glen, leading all but nine laps in Stewart's third straight road-course win.

That blow to Gordon — who would now be forced to start all the way back in 39th place — was of little consequence to Stewart, who would start on the pole either way. And that, as it turned out, was all the advantage he would need.

At the drop of the green flag on Sunday, Stewart charged into Turn 1, successfully fending off whatever challenge the other point leaders could muster and began to put a thrashing on the rest of the field. Roughly two-and-a-half hours later, 42 drivers had chased the "20" car around the 2.45-mile, 11-turn road course for 83 of the event's 92 laps — a record — with Stewart leaving the top spot only for pit stops to refresh his tires and fuel supply.

The only hiccups in an otherwise flawless day came late in the race when a failed alternator forced the driver to switch off non-essential electrical devices and when the seventh and final caution flag flew with just two of the scheduled 90 laps remaining. The resulting green-white-checkered finish gave Gordon, who put on a marvelous exhibition in driving from the back to the front on two separate occasions, one last shot to challenge Stewart for the win.

Masterful on restarts all day long, Stewart played this one perfectly, getting the jump as the field hit the frontstretch and handily beating Gordon into the first turn.

"If I could make it through Turn 1 (ahead of Gordon), I didn't have any concerns," Stewart said of the final restart. No concerns indeed, as Stewart used the final two trips around the track to open a healthy advantage of 1.927 seconds to take his fifth win of the season, the 24th of his career. In so doing, he led the most laps for the eighth time this year and the sixth time in the last eight races while increasing his lead in the standings over Jimmie Johnson to 105 points.

(Above) Mark Martin (6) flies through the Esses with Jamie McMurray (42) hot on his tail. McMurray, fighting for a top-10 spot in the standings, succeeded by jumping two positions to ninth after finishing 13th at The Glen. Martin, winner of three straight here in the mid 1990s, also moved up one position with a sixth-place finish in the race.

(Opposite Page) Tony Stewart doesn't mind taking a champagne shower following his convincing victory. The win, his second straight and fifth in the last seven races, gave him a 105-point cushion at the top of the standings.

SIRIUS SATELLITE RADIO AT THE GLEN
NASCAR NEXTEL Cup Series Race No. 22

Fin. Pos.	Start Pos.	Car No.	Driver	Team	Laps	Laps Led	Status
1	1	20	Tony Stewart	The Home Depot Chevrolet	92	83	Running
2	39	7	Robby Gordon	Jim Beam Chevrolet	92	2	Running
3	41	36	Boris Said	CENTRIX Financial Chevrolet	92		Running
4	25	40	Scott Pruett	Coors Light Dodge	92		Running
5	2	48	Jimmie Johnson	Lowe's Chevrolet	92	2	Running
6	4	2	Rusty Wallace	SIRIUS/Miller Lite Dodge	92		Running
7	6	6	Mark Martin	Viagra Ford	92		Running
8	22	25	Brian Vickers	ditech.com/GMAC Financial Chevrolet	92		Running
9	17	01	Joe Nemechek	U.S. Army Chevrolet	92		Running
10	16	8	Dale Earnhardt Jr.	Budweiser Chevrolet	92		Running
11	8	19	Jeremy Mayfield	Dodge Dealers/UAW Dodge	92		Running
12	12	38	Elliott Sadler	M&M's Ford	92		Running
13	11	42	Jamie McMurray	Home123/Havoline Dodge	92		Running
14	14	24	Jeff Gordon	DuPont Chevrolet	92	2	Running
15	13	29	Kevin Harvick	GM Goodwrench Chevrolet	92		Running
16	26	21	Ricky Rudd	Motorcraft Genuine Parts Ford	92		Running
17	21	9	Kasey Kahne	Dodge Dealers/UAW Dodge	92		Running
18	15	17	Matt Kenseth	DeWalt Power Tools Ford	92		Running
19	10	99	Carl Edwards	Office Depot Ford	92		Running
20	29	45	Kyle Petty	Georgia-Pacific/Brawny Dodge	92		Running
21	34	22	Scott Wimmer	Caterpillar Dodge	92		Running
22	9	88	Dale Jarrett	UPS Ford	92		Running
23	24	41	Casey Mears	Target Dodge	92		Running
24	32	43	Jeff Green	Cheerios/Betty Crocker Dodge	92		Running
25	37	32	Ron Fellows	Tide Chevrolet	92		Running
26	27	0	Mike Bliss	Net Zero/Best Buy Chevrolet	92		Running
27	42	1	Paul Menard	Kraft/Ritz Chevrolet	92		Running
28	38	37	Anthony Lazzaro	Tequila Patron Dodge	92		Running
29	40	92	Johnny Miller	Oak Glove Co. Chevrolet	92		Running
30	7	12	Ryan Newman	Alltel Dodge	92	1	Running
31	31	10	Scott Riggs	Valvoline Chevrolet	92		Running
32	28	49	Ken Schrader	Schwan's Home Service Dodge	92		Running
33	20	5 #	Kyle Busch	Kellogg's Chevrolet	92		Running
34	30	07	Dave Blaney	Jack Daniel's Chevrolet	92		Running
35	43	50	Jorge Goeters	CU National/Red Cactus Salsa Dodge	91	1	Running
36	23	18	Bobby Labonte	Interstate Batteries Chevrolet	86		Engine
37	35	11	Terry Labonte	FedEx Kinko's Chevrolet	86		Running
38	3	16	Greg Biffle	Subway/National Guard Ford	84		Running
39	5	07	Kurt Busch	Sharpie Ford	80		Accident
40	33	77 #	Travis Kvapil	Kodak/Jasper Eng. & Trans. Dodge	76		Running
41	19	15	Michael Waltrip	NAPA Auto Parts Chevrolet	71	1	Accident
42	36	4	P.J. Jones	Lucas Oil Chevrolet	41		Accident
43	18	31	Jeff Burton	Cingular Wireless Chevrolet	31		Accident

Raybestos Rookie of the Year Contender.

NASCAR NEXTEL Cup Series Point Standings
(After 22 Races)

Pos.	Driver	Points	Behind	Change
1	Tony Stewart	3113	—	—
2	Jimmie Johnson	3008	-105	—
3	Greg Biffle	2861	-252	—
4	Rusty Wallace	2855	-258	—
5	Mark Martin	2782	-331	+1
6	Kurt Busch	2692	-421	-1
7	Jeremy Mayfield	2684	-429	+1
8	Ryan Newman	2646	-467	-1
9	Jamie McMurray	2599	-514	+2
10	Carl Edwards	2593	-520	—

Gordon held off a challenge from road-racing ace Boris Said over the final two laps to finish second — an impressive, albeit unsatisfying, run for the 2003 winner of this event — while Said finished third ahead of Scott Pruett, subbing this week for Sterling Marlin, who returned to his native Tennessee due to the passing of his father, former NASCAR driver Coo Coo Marlin.

Jeff Gordon was hoping the friendly confines of Watkins Glen, site of half of his record eight road-course wins, would provide a boost in his effort to advance in the Race to the Chase, but bad luck followed him from Indianapolis, this time showing up in the form of a cut tire after advancing to the front early in the race. Gordon recovered well enough to finish 14th, which provided a slight boost in the points where he now was listed 13th, just 67 out of 10th place.

Finishing ahead of the DuPont Chevrolet was Jamie McMurray (13th), who rejoined the top 10 in points after a three-week absence, and Elliott Sadler (12th), who halted his recent slide in the standings and moved into an 11th-place tie with Dale Jarrett, both drivers a slim three points behind 10th-place Carl Edwards and squarely within striking distance with four races remaining in the 2005 Race to the Chase.

GFS MARKETPLACE 400

Victory! Surrounded by jubilant team members, Jeremy Mayfield salutes the fans after outlasting the competition to snatch the win at Michigan. The finish nearly assured the driver a place in the Chase for the NASCAR NEXTEL Cup for the second straight year.

Gambling, by definition, is betting on the unknown. Strategy on the other hand, concerns the application of knowledge. In the GFS Marketplace 400 at Michigan International Speedway, there were gamblers and there were strategists.

The gamblers lost.

For nearly 300 of the scheduled 400-mile distance, things had gone pretty much according to expectations. Joe Nemechek lived up to his "Front Row Joe" nickname by posting the best lap in qualifying, and he squirted out to an early lead at the drop of the initial green flag. And while Nemechek, third-place starter Kasey Kahne and fourth-fastest qualifier Kyle Busch jostled at the front of the field for the first 100 miles, the odds-on favorites gathered in their wake.

Yes, this was Michigan, and the Roush contingent was quickly weaving its way toward the front. From mid-pack starting spots, Carl Edwards (12th), Matt Kenseth (13th), Mark Martin (14th) and Kurt Busch (17th) steadily progressed through the field, chased by teammate Greg Biffle (31st) and Tony Stewart (36th), the 1-2 finishers at this track in June.

Busch reached the point first when a cut tire sent Nemechek's U.S. Army Chevrolet into the first-turn wall while leading to bring out the third caution flag at Lap 75. By then, all five Roush drivers, along with Stewart, had reached the top 10.

Before 50 more laps had passed, Stewart and the five Roush Fords were listed in six of the top seven positions. Only Nemechek's teammate, Scott Riggs, was able to spoil their party with a particularly strong Valvoline Chevrolet.

The race had begun to take on a look eerily similar to the event run here in June — when Stewart joined four Roush cars to make up the final top five — until Stuart Kirby and Travis Kvapil tangled in Turn 3 to slow the pace for the seventh time. With slightly more than 50 laps remaining, it was decision time.

Driver Joe Nemechek consults with crew members in the Michigan garage between practice runs. They had the U.S. Army Chevrolet dialed-in for the race, with the pole-winner showing great speed until cutting a tire while leading the event.

TOP 10 QUALIFIERS

Pos.	Driver	Seconds	mph
1	Joe Nemechek	37.582	191.581
2	Jeff Gordon	37.627	191.352
3	Kasey Kahne	37.645	191.260
4	Kyle Busch	37.687	191.047
5	Ryan Newman	37.692	191.022
6	Mike Bliss	37.709	190.936
7	Brian Vickers	37.744	190.759
8	Elliott Sadler	37.837	190.290
9	Ricky Rudd	37.844	190.255
10	Jimmie Johnson	37.895	189.999

In Jeremy Mayfield's pit, a plan was quickly formulated. "History says this place, from Lap 150 on, goes green," crew chief Richard "Slugger" Labbe stated later. "We ran 52 laps here at the test (run recently by the team at Michigan) and then ran out of gas coming to 53. We knew we had the car to do it and the engine that could do it and the carburetor that could do it, and Jeremy is really good on saving fuel."

(Above) Kurt Busch (97) leads a trio of Roush cars that includes Mark Martin (6) and Matt Kenseth (17), with Tony Stewart lurking from behind in The Home Depot Chevrolet. Busch led more laps than anyone but didn't have the fuel needed to secure the win.

(Left) Scott Riggs (10) runs alongside Sterling Marlin (40) on Michigan's frontstretch. Like teammate Joe Nemechek, Riggs had a very quick Chevrolet, and like Jeremy Mayfield, he benefited from fuel management to take a career-best second-place finish.

Jeremy Mayfield's stop for a new set of tires and a full load of fuel came at the perfect time in the race — at least for him. With others unsure about their mileage at Michigan, Mayfield knew, based on test data, that he had enough on board to complete the distance.

So a strategy was set. Mayfield and others peeled onto pit road for what they hoped would be their final pit stops of the day, while the frontrunners, including leader Busch, Kenseth and Martin, remained on the track, betting that another yellow flag would appear before their fuel cells ran dry.

Exactly 51 laps remained as Mayfield took the green flag, buried at mid-field in the 26th position. One by one as the laps clicked by, those who had gambled on one more caution reluctantly dropped to the apron and headed down pit road under green, needing an additional splash of fuel to complete the required distance.

Jeremy Mayfield sails through the frontstretch tri-oval in his Dodge Dealers/UAW Dodge. Crew chief "Slugger" Labbe freely admitted their car was not the fastest in the race, but proved again that speed alone does not always determine the victor.

GFS MARKETPLACE 400

NASCAR NEXTEL Cup Series Race No. 23

Fin. Pos.	Start Pos.	Car No.	Driver	Team	Laps	Laps Led	Status
1	11	19	Jeremy Mayfield	Dodge Dealers/UAW Dodge	200	6	Running
2	19	10	Scott Riggs	Valvoline Chevrolet	200	13	Running
3	13	17	Matt Kenseth	DeWalt Power Tools Ford	200	9	Running
4	12	99	Carl Edwards	AAA Ford	200	17	Running
5	36	20	Tony Stewart	The Home Depot Chevrolet	200		Running
6	31	16	Greg Biffle	National Guard/Prism-the Game Ford	200	3	Running
7	17	97	Kurt Busch	Crown Royal Ford	200	65	Running
8	1	01	Joe Nemechek	U.S. Army Chevrolet	200	30	Running
9	7	25	Brian Vickers	GMAC/ditech.com Chevrolet	200		Running
10	10	48	Jimmie Johnson	Lowe's Chevrolet	200		Running
11	29	91	Bill Elliott	Auto Value/Bumper-to-Bumper Dodge	200		Running
12	5	12	Ryan Newman	Alltel Dodge	200		Running
13	38	2	Rusty Wallace	Miller Lite Dodge	200		Running
14	30	41	Casey Mears	Target Dodge	200		Running
15	2	24	Jeff Gordon	DuPont Chevrolet	200		Running
16	18	18	Bobby Labonte	Interstate Batteries Chevrolet	200		Running
17	14	6	Mark Martin	Viagra Ford	200	10	Running
18	16	8	Dale Earnhardt Jr.	Budweiser Chevrolet	200	1	Running
19	9	21	Ricky Rudd	Motorcraft Genuine Parts Ford	200		Running
20	28	42	Jamie McMurray	Havoline-Texaco Dodge	200		Running
21	37	40	Sterling Marlin	Coors Light Dodge	200	1	Running
22	42	29	Kevin Harvick	GM Goodwrench Chevrolet	200		Running
23	22	22	Scott Wimmer	Caterpillar Dodge	200		Running
24	26	43	Jeff Green	Cheerios/Betty Crocker Dodge	200		Running
25	27	49	Ken Schrader	Schwan's Home Service Dodge	200		Running
26	40	31	Jeff Burton	Cingular Wireless Chevrolet	200		Running
27	24	15	Michael Waltrip	NAPA Auto Parts Chevrolet	200		Running
28	23	4	John Andretti	Lucas Oil Chevrolet	199		Running
29	3	9	Kasey Kahne	Dodge Dealers/UAW Dodge	199	15	Running
30	39	7	Robby Gordon	Menard's Chevrolet	199		Running
31	15	37	Tony Raines	BoSPOKER.net Dodge	198	2	Running
32	25	07	Dave Blaney	Jack Daniel's Chevrolet	198		Running
33	35	45	Kyle Petty	Georgia-Pacific/Brawny Dodge	198		Running
34	33	88	Dale Jarrett	UPS Ford	198		Running
35	43	32	Bobby Hamilton Jr.	Tide Chevrolet	197		Running
36	32	66	Jimmy Spencer	Arbor Mortgage Ford	196		Running
37	6	0	Mike Bliss	Net Zero/Best Buy Chevrolet	185		Running
38	41	77 #	Travis Kvapil	Kodak/Jasper Eng. & Trans. Dodge	179		Accident
39	8	38	Elliott Sadler	Pedigree/M&Ms Ford	174		Running
40	20	11	Terry Labonte	FedEx Express Chevrolet	159		Engine
41	21	51	Stuart Kirby	Marathon American Spirit Motor Oil Chev.	140		Accident
42	34	00	Johnny Benson	State Fair Corn Dogs Dodge	127		Oil Line
43	4	5 #	Kyle Busch	Kellogg's Chevrolet	81	28	Overheating

Raybestos Rookie of the Year Contender.

NASCAR NEXTEL Cup Series Point Standings

(After 23 Races)

Pos.	Driver	Points	Behind	Change
1	**Tony Stewart**	**3268**	—	—
2	Jimmie Johnson	3142	-126	—
3	Greg Biffle	3016	-252	—
4	Rusty Wallace	2979	-289	—
5	Mark Martin	2899	-369	—
6	Jeremy Mayfield	2869	-399	+1
7	Kurt Busch	2848	-420	-1
8	Ryan Newman	2773	-495	—
9	Carl Edwards	2758	-510	+1
10	Jamie McMurray	2702	-566	-1

By Lap 190, race leader Edwards could go no farther and pitted, handing the point to Dale Earnhardt Jr., who headed to pit road the next time around. That put Sterling Marlin in front for a lap before he reported in, giving the lead to Tony Raines, who stayed in front for two laps before his fuel cell ran dry. That allowed Mayfield to inherit the lead for the first time in the race with just six laps remaining.

From that point on, Mayfield fed his Dodge just enough throttle to maintain position over Riggs, who was also playing the mileage game, and finish with a margin of victory of 1.974-seconds for his first win of the season, the fifth of his career and the first since his win last September at Richmond that boosted him into the inaugural Chase for the NASCAR NEXTEL Cup.

"I was trying to stay ahead of the '10' car just to win the race," an excited Mayfield said. "There were times I thought I was going to run out [of fuel] on the backstretch. I knew it was close, but I [made it across] the start/finish line."

Riggs held on for a career-best second place, while Roush drivers took four of the next five positions, with Stewart sandwiched behind Kenseth and Edwards, but ahead of Biffle and Busch.

With the win, Mayfield moved up a spot to sixth in the point standings to solidify his position within the top 10, displacing Kurt Busch, who dropped to seventh, while Edwards climbed to ninth ahead of Jamie McMurray, who wound up 20th.

Others vying for a foothold in the Race to the Chase had mixed results. Kenseth improved his stock considerably by moving 61 points closer to the 10th position; he now sat 15th in the standings, 104 markers away. Dale Jarrett remained 11th but was no longer in a tie with teammate Elliott Sadler, who was involved in an accident and fell two positions after finishing 39th.

Jeff Gordon started on the front row with Nemechek but spent his race wrestling an ill-handling DuPont Chevrolet to a 15th-place finish. He left Michigan 12th in points but still within reach of 10th place, 58 behind McMurray with three races remaining in the Race to the Chase.

SHARPIE 500

In racing, the results of good teamwork often take time to become apparent — especially to the casual observer. For Matt Kenseth and the No. 17 team, those results had been showing for several weeks. But by the end of the Sharpie 500 at Bristol Motor Speedway, anyone who hadn't already noticed the resurgence of the team led by crew chief Robbie Reiser, surely did now.

Kenseth and the team had been fighting an uphill battle right from the beginning of the year, when a blown engine in the Daytona 500 put them in a hole at 42nd place in the standings. The team's recovery had been slow, with DNFs due to accidents at Phoenix and Charlotte serving as brief setbacks to a slow but steady progression though the points.

Kenseth cracked the top 20 for the first time at Infineon Raceway, the 16th event on the schedule, with only three top-10 runs to show for his efforts up to that point. In the following week's Pepsi 400 at Daytona, Kenseth finished ninth, and he followed that with a second-place effort at Chicagoland, driving arguably the best car in the field.

A pumped fist emerges from the window opening seconds after driver Matt Kenseth finished thumping the field on the way to his first victory of the season. The win boosted Kenseth up to 11th in the point standings and put him squarely in contention in the Race to the Chase.

(Above) NASCAR NEXTEL Cup Series cars sit neatly parked on their respective team haulers during Friday night's NASCAR Busch Series action. That race was won by Ryan Newman, who captured his third straight victory in the series.

(Right) Kevin Harvick fires away from his pit box during Saturday night's 500-lapper. Harvick's hopes of moving up in the points took a huge hit — literally — when he became an unfortunate victim of an on-track tussle.

The five races that followed yielded three more top 10s, and by the time the team arrived in Eastern Tennessee for the Sharpie 500, Kenseth had climbed to 15th in the standings. More importantly, however, he had closed to within 102 points of 10th place, the cut-off position for this year's Chase for the NASCAR NEXTEL Cup, set to begin after the Richmond event, three races away.

Hard work and positive attitudes had permeated the team, and after coming this far — seven top 10s in the last 11 races — and arriving on the top-10 doorstep, they weren't about to let up now.

Team morale was boosted further at the start of the Bristol weekend when, in Bud Pole qualifying, Kenseth posted a lap at 127.3 mph to win just the second pole position of his NASCAR NEXTEL Cup Series career, his first in more than three years.

(Left) Jeff Burton (31) charges into the corner on his way toward the front pack. Burton made it all the way to second place after starting 24th and secured his best finish in more than two years.

(Below) Dale Earnhardt Jr. (8) chases Carl Edwards (99) out of Turn 4 and onto Bristol's short frontstretch. The defending event champion, Earnhardt picked up a much-needed top-10 finish to keep the point leaders in sight.

TOP 10 QUALIFIERS

Pos.	Driver	Seconds	mph
1	Matt Kenseth	15.073	127.300
2	Jeff Gordon	15.085	127.199
3	Dave Blaney	15.090	127.157
4	Greg Biffle	15.107	127.014
5	Ricky Rudd	15.111	126.980
6	Ryan Newman	15.114	126.955
7	Ken Schrader	15.114	126.955
8	Bobby Hamilton Jr.	15.122	126.888
9	Elliott Sadler	15.140	126.737
10	Kasey Kahne	15.158	126.587

When the Sharpie 500 took the green flag in front of 160,000 on a balmy Saturday night, Kenseth took immediate advantage of his front-row starting spot and jumped to the early lead. Thus began an overwhelming performance rarely seen on the tricky and treacherous high-banked half mile.

(Above) Tempers flared and sparks flew when Dale Jarrett (88) took exception to an earlier bump by Ryan Newman (12) that sent the UPS Ford spinning. This incident put Newman in the garage (after the Alltel Dodge got nailed by Harvick) and earned Jarrett a two-lap penalty on pit road.

(Right) Kyle Petty (right) holds an impromptu counseling session with Carl Edwards immediately following the race. Earlier, Edwards turned Jeff Green around in Petty's No. 43 car, and then spun Kyle's Georgia-Pacific Dodge with just five laps to go.

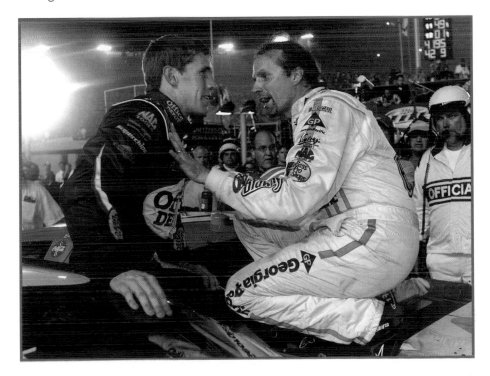

Simply put, the Wisconsin native drove off and left his 42 competitors to fight amongst themselves for whatever scraps he left on the table. By the time the checkered flag waved some three-plus hours later, Kenseth had led 415 of the event's 500 laps. He was never passed on the track, giving up the lead only while pitting, which forced others into a variance of pit strategies in their attempts to negate Kenseth's obvious advantage on the track. Even at that, Kenseth merely rocketed straight back to the front

Kenseth's crew outfits their Ford Taurus with new Goodyears and a load of fuel under one of the night's 16 cautions. Consistent teamwork had become a hallmark of the effort from the Roush stable while the team climbed into contention in the standings.

SHARPIE 500

NASCAR NEXTEL Cup Series Race No. 24

Fin. Pos.	Start Pos.	Car No.	Driver	Team	Laps	Laps Led	Status
1	1	17	Matt Kenseth	DeWalt Power Tools Ford	500	415	Running
2	24	31	Jeff Burton	Cingular Wireless Chevrolet	500		Running
3	4	16	Greg Biffle	National Guard Ford	500	1	Running
4	5	21	Ricky Rudd	Motorcraft Genuine Parts Ford	500		Running
5	20	2	Rusty Wallace	Miller Lite Dodge	500	9	Running
6	2	24	Jeff Gordon	DuPont Chevrolet	500	27	Running
7	27	0	Mike Bliss	CertainTeed Chevrolet	500	4	Running
8	17	20	Tony Stewart	The Home Depot Chevrolet	500		Running
9	41	8	Dale Earnhardt Jr.	Budweiser Chevrolet	500		Running
10	13	97	Kurt Busch	Sharpie Minis Ford	500		Running
11	7	49	Ken Schrader	Schwan's Home Service Dodge	500		Running
12	35	01	Joe Nemechek	U.S. Army Chevrolet	500		Running
13	9	38	Elliott Sadler	M&M's Ford	500	2	Running
14	32	22	Scott Wimmer	Caterpillar Dodge	500		Running
15	22	15	Michael Waltrip	NAPA Auto Parts Chevrolet	500		Running
16	25	6	Mark Martin	Viagra Ford	500		Running
17	15	4	Mike Wallace	Food City/Lucas Oil Chevrolet	500		Running
18	16	19	Jeremy Mayfield	Dodge Dealers/UAW Dodge	500	18	Running
19	31	77 #	Travis Kvapil	Kodak/Jasper Eng. & Trans. Dodge	500		Running
20	23	25	Brian Vickers	GMAC/ditech.com Chevrolet	500		Running
21	42	18	Bobby Labonte	PowerADE Flava23 Chevrolet	500	21	Running
22	28	43	Jeff Green	Cheerios/Hamburger Helper Dodge	500		Running
23	3	07	Dave Blaney	Jack Daniel's Chevrolet	500		Running
24	37	99	Carl Edwards	Office Depot Ford	499		Running
25	26	45	Kyle Petty	Georgia-Pacific/Northern Quilted Dodge	499		Running
26	18	42	Jamie McMurray	Havoline/Texaco Dodge	498		Running
27	39	11	Terry Labonte	FedEx Express Chevrolet	497		Running
28	34	50	Jimmy Spencer	Allied Buildings Dodge	493		Running
29	40	40	Sterling Marlin	Coors Light Dodge	491		Running
30	38	92	Hermie Sadler	Kingsport Iron & Metal Chevrolet	491		Running
31	30	88	Dale Jarrett	UPS Ford	478		Running
32	43	80	Carl Long	Royal Admin Svc./carloan.com Chevrolet	472		Running
33	11	5 #	Kyle Busch	Kellogg's Chevrolet	448		Running
34	14	41	Casey Mears	Target Dodge	427		Running
35	8	32	Bobby Hamilton Jr.	Tide Chevrolet	411		Running
36	29	48	Jimmie Johnson	Lowe's Chevrolet	410		Engine
37	19	29	Kevin Harvick	GM Goodwrench/Reese's Big Cup Chev.	352	3	Accident
38	33	7	Robby Gordon	Jim Beam Chevrolet	332		Oil Leak
39	6	12	Ryan Newman	Alltel Dodge	317		Accident
40	12	10	Scott Riggs	Checkers/Rally's Chevrolet	309		Engine
41	36	95 #	Stanton Barrett	Langley Properties Chevrolet	251		Engine
42	10	9	Kasey Kahne	Dodge Dealers/UAW Dodge	212		Accident
43	21	00	Johnny Benson	Bryan Chevrolet	78		Electrical

Raybestos Rookie of the Year Contender.

NASCAR NEXTEL Cup Series Point Standings

(After 24 Races)

Pos.	Driver	Points	Behind	Change
1	**Tony Stewart**	**3410**	—	—
2	Jimmie Johnson	3197	-213	—
3	Greg Biffle	3186	-224	—
4	Rusty Wallace	3139	-271	—
5	Mark Martin	3014	-396	—
6	Jeremy Mayfield	2983	-427	—
7	Kurt Busch	2982	-428	—
8	Carl Edwards	2849	-561	+1
9	Ryan Newman	2819	-591	-1
10	Jeff Gordon	2799	-611	+2

within a few laps under green. His 0.511-second margin of victory was immensely misleading, given that the final restart following the 16th caution of the evening occurred with just two laps remaining in the event.

In the end, Kenseth's win, the 10th of his career, broke an agonizing 56-race winless string and boosted him from 15th all the way to 11th in the standings, where he now sat just 11 points away from the all-important 10th spot and a chance to compete for his second NASCAR NEXTEL Cup Series crown.

Despite his dominance, Kenseth's rise in the standings was not without help from other drivers in the Race to the Chase mix upon arriving at Bristol. One of the more significant occurrences of the evening took place when Ryan Newman clipped the UPS Ford of Dale Jarrett near the 300-lap mark to bring out the 11th yellow flag of the night. Incensed by the incident, Jarrett retaliated 17 laps later by driving into the side of the Alltel Dodge as Newman attempted to pass by in Turn 2. Getting the worst of that altercation was Kevin Harvick who, unable to avoid the accident scene, plowed into the side of Newman. The resulting poor finishes dropped Harvick two spots to 16th in the standings and Jarrett from 11th to 14th, leaving both drivers with little chance to make the top-10 cut.

Unable to continue, Newman's 39th-place finish lowered him one position to ninth in the points, 20 markers ahead of Jeff Gordon, who kept his championship hopes alive with a sixth-place finish and broke into the top 10 for the first time since mid-June.

Jamie McMurray finished a lap off the pace and fell two positions to 12th in the points, one spot ahead of Elliott Sadler, who remained 13th, 34 points behind Gordon.

Defending event champion Dale Earnhardt Jr. had a relatively uneventful race and brought the Budweiser Chevrolet home in ninth place to rise one position to 15th in the standings. Now 117 points out of the 10th position with just two races remaining in the Race to the Chase, Earnhardt's chances to compete for his first title were looking very bleak indeed.

SONY HD 500

Rick Hendrick (center) examines his team's newest trophy, won by Kyle Busch (left) in his initial NASCAR NEXTEL Cup Series win, partly the result of quick thinking in the pits by crew chief Alan Gustafson (right).

Not long ago, a rookie driver in the NASCAR NEXTEL Cup Series had some breathing room. After all, competing in the world's top stock car series would take a little getting used to. Heavier cars, faster speeds and racing against the most accomplished professional drivers around were all things a rookie needed to learn about. It would come in time, but a freshman season was expected to be a learning experience. In short, rookies weren't *supposed* to win.

Even Jeff Gordon soldiered through his initial campaign of 1993 without a win. And when he made that first trip to Victory Lane after the 1994 Coca-Cola 600, the talk centered on a bright young star winning in *only* his 42nd start.

All that changed in 1999 when Tony Stewart descended on the scene. It took Stewart 23 tries to notch his first victory, and he added two more before the end of the season and won Raybestos Rookie of the Year honors with a "remarkable" three wins.

(Right) Jeff Burton's Cingular Chevrolet gets fitted by one of many body templates during inspection at California.

(Below) Bud Pole winner Carl Edwards (99) takes the early lead at California followed by (in order) teammates Mark Martin, Kurt Busch and Greg Biffle. After sweeping the top four qualifying positions, Roush drivers – all five of them — swapped the top spot over the first 81 laps of the SONY HD 500.

Like Gordon, Matt Kenseth got his first win in the Coca-Cola 600, but Kenseth's came during his rookie season of 2000 in his 18th career start. That was the same year Dale Earnhardt Jr. moved up to the NASCAR NEXTEL Cup Series, and Earnhardt drove to two wins, the first coming early in the season at Texas Motor Speedway in his 12th big-league attempt.

TOP 10 QUALIFIERS

Pos.	Driver	Seconds	mph
1	Carl Edwards	38.906	185.061
2	Mark Martin	38.954	184.833
3	Kurt Busch	39.045	184.403
4	Greg Biffle	39.052	184.370
5	Jimmie Johnson	39.120	184.049
6	Jeff Gordon	39.166	183.833
7	Kasey Kahne	39.172	183.805
8	J.J. Yeley	39.182	183.758
9	Brian Vickers	39.194	183.702
10	Scott Riggs	39.241	183.482

Kevin Harvick shocked the racing world early the next season when he drove to victory at Atlanta in just his third race. Harvick won again in 2001 on the way to taking his rookie crown.

The bar was ratcheted up further in 2002. Ryan Newman won rookie honors with a single victory, while Jimmie Johnson took three checkered flags, the first in his native California — the 13th race of his career. That was the same year Jamie McMurray took over for the injured Sterling Marlin and shocked everyone by winning at Charlotte in only his second race.

(Above) Brian Vickers sails through California's Turn 2 in his ditech.com Monte Carlo. Vickers, whose team shares shop facilities with Kyle Busch's No. 5 effort at Hendrick Motorsports, had a very fine run to third place, his fourth top 10 in the last five events.

(Left) Tony Stewart (20) and Carl Edwards (99) battle for the fourth position in the final laps of the race. Edwards prevailed in this fight, dropping Stewart to fifth for his 11th consecutive top-10 finish.

McMurray didn't win during his official rookie season of 2003, but Greg Biffle did, and although no rookies won last year, Kasey Kahne kept pounding on the winner's circle door with five runner-up finishes, some of them by merely a few feet. Kahne's freshman campaign was brilliant to be sure, but the 24-year-old driver still was frustrated at not getting that first win.

Enter Kyle Busch, the 20-year-old sensation from Las Vegas, Nevada. The 2004 NASCAR Busch Series Rookie of the Year (five wins, second in points) slid into the No. 5 Kellogg's Chevrolet from Hendrick Motorsports with plenty of expectations riding on his lean shoulders. And Busch responded. At Las Vegas in the third race of 2005, he nearly grabbed that magical first win, finishing second to Johnson but ahead of big brother Kurt, the defending NASCAR NEXTEL Cup Series champion.

Another runner-up finish at Dover in June mixed with three more top fives confirmed the promise team owner Rick Hendrick had seen in his young driver, and when the Kellogg's Chevrolet rolled out this Labor Day weekend at California Speedway — site of Busch's first Bud Pole back in February — a quiet confidence could be sensed within the team.

Ironically, it was two years prior that the No. 5 team had last been to Victory Lane. Then, Terry Labonte drove to his 22nd career win at Darlington in the Southern 500. Even more ironic was that Labonte took the lead in that race by beating his competition off pit road

Kurt Busch (97) watches from behind as younger brother Kyle (5) begins to open up a lead. Kyle took the top spot away from Kurt on Lap 82, his first of five appearances at the front during the race.

First-time victor Kyle Busch acknowledges the fans amidst the aftermath of celebratory burnouts. Just four days ahead of the record, this race was the 20-year-old's last opportunity to become the youngest winner in NASCAR NEXTEL Cup Series history.

SONY HD 500

NASCAR NEXTEL Cup Series Race No. 25

Fin. Pos.	Start Pos.	Car No.	Driver	Team	Laps	Laps Led	Status
1	25	5 #	Kyle Busch	Kellogg's Chevrolet	254	95	Running
2	4	16	Greg Biffle	National Guard/Charter Ford	254	16	Running
3	9	25	Brian Vickers	GMAC/ditech.com Chevrolet	254		Running
4	1	99	Carl Edwards	Office Depot Ford	254	21	Running
5	14	20	Tony Stewart	The Home Depot Chevrolet	254	56	Running
6	7	9	Kasey Kahne	Dodge Dealers/UAW Dodge	254		Running
7	23	17	Matt Kenseth	DeWalt Power Tools Ford	254	14	Running
8	40	42	Jamie McMurray	Home 123/Havoline Dodge	254		Running
9	39	21	Ricky Rudd	Motorcraft Genuine Parts Ford	254		Running
10	22	01	Joe Nemechek	U.S. Army Chevrolet	254		Running
11	2	6	Mark Martin	Viagra Ford	254	4	Running
12	3	97	Kurt Busch	Smirnoff Ice/Sharpie Ford	254	39	Running
13	19	15	Michael Waltrip	NAPA Auto Parts Chevrolet	254	3	Running
14	18	29	Kevin Harvick	GM Goodwrench Chevrolet	254		Running
15	34	2	Rusty Wallace	Miller Lite Dodge	254		Running
16	5	48	Jimmie Johnson	Lowe's Chevrolet	254		Running
17	15	38	Elliott Sadler	M&M's Ford	254		Running
18	28	12	Ryan Newman	SONY HD TV/Alltel Dodge	254		Running
19	12	40	Sterling Marlin	Coors Light Dodge	254		Running
20	42	18	Bobby Labonte	AsthmaControl.com Chevrolet	254		Running
21	6	24	Jeff Gordon	DuPont Chevrolet	254		Running
22	21	07	Dave Blaney	Jack Daniel's Chevrolet	254		Running
23	11	32	Bobby Hamilton Jr.	Tide Chevrolet	254		Running
24	37	88	Dale Jarrett	UPS Ford	254		Running
25	17	43	Jeff Green	Wheaties Dodge	254	1	Running
26	13	19	Jeremy Mayfield	Dodge Dealers/UAW Dodge	254	1	Running
27	38	0	Mike Bliss	Net Zero Best Buy Chevrolet	254		Running
28	32	37	Tony Raines	Patron Tequila/BoSPOKER.net Dodge	254		Running
29	31	49	Ken Schrader	Red Barron Pizza Dodge	253		Running
30	26	36	Boris Said	CENTRIX Financial Chevrolet	253		Running
31	27	22	Scott Wimmer	Caterpillar Dodge	250		Accident
32	33	41	Casey Mears	Target Dodge	249		Running
33	29	77 #	Travis Kvapil	Kodak/Jasper Eng. & Trans. Dodge	249		Running
34	24	7	Robby Gordon	Fruit of the Loom Chevrolet	248	2	Accident
35	16	31	Jeff Burton	Cingular Wireless Chevrolet	248		Accident
36	10	10	Scott Riggs	Valvoline Chevrolet	246		Accident
37	36	66	Mike Garvey	Jani King Ford	232		Running
38	41	8	Dale Earnhardt Jr.	Budweiser Chevrolet	211	2	Engine
39	8	11	J.J. Yeley	FedEx Freight Chevrolet	209		Running
40	30	91	Bill Elliott	McDonald's Dodge	180		Engine
41	20	45	Kyle Petty	Brawny/Georgia-Pacific Dodge	171		Engine
42	43	92	Hermie Sadler	Oak Gloves Dodge	87		Brakes
43	35	51	Stuart Kirby	Marathon American Spirit Chevrolet	31		Brakes

Raybestos Rookie of the Year Contender.

NASCAR NEXTEL Cup Series Point Standings

(After 25 Races)

Pos.	Driver	Points	Behind	Change
1	**Tony Stewart**	3570	—	—
2	Greg Biffle	3361	-209	+1
3	Jimmie Johnson	3312	-258	-1
4	Rusty Wallace	3257	-313	—
5	Mark Martin	3149	-421	—
6	Kurt Busch	3114	-456	+1
7	Jeremy Mayfield	3073	-497	-1
8	Carl Edwards	3014	-556	—
9	Matt Kenseth	2939	-631	+2
10	Jamie McMurray	2929	-641	+2

during a late-race pit stop and managed to hold his position over the final laps to score the win — a scenario similar to what was about to play out at California.

In the SONY HD 500, Kyle Busch started 25th and spent the first 50 laps working his way toward the front where he found upon his arrival, big brother Kurt and his Roush Racing friends — Biffle, Kenseth, Carl Edwards and Mark Martin — along with Stewart.

The Roush drivers were taking turns at the front, each gathering five bonus points for leading the race, until the young Hendrick driver crashed their party by seizing the top spot on Lap 82.

Stewart and the younger Busch controlled the middle portion of the race, with Stewart leading on eight occasions for 56 laps, while Busch led a total of five times for an event-high 95 laps.

As the race entered its final stages, a caution for debris set into motion a critical series of events. In the frantic round of pit stops, Busch brought the Kellogg's machine in too close to the wall. Realizing there wasn't enough room to change left-side tires, crew chief Alan Gustafson called off the four-tire stop and ordered right sides only in a heady mid-stop call, sending his driver out ahead of the pack.

Third on the restart behind Robby Gordon and Jeff Green, both of whom stayed out during the yellow, Busch quickly reassumed the lead and held off a strong charge by Biffle over the closing laps that included a green-white-checked finish to take the much-anticipated win. In so doing, Busch became the youngest driver in history to win a NASCAR NEXTEL Cup Series race at 20 years, 4 months and 2 days, beating the prior mark set in 1952 by Donald Thomas by a mere four days.

In describing the triumph, Gustafson remarked, "It's the biggest win of my life. … We really wanted to win the race for Kyle to get the youngest winner award. That all came together at the last minute. We got our first pole [at California] and now our first win. It's unbelievable."

As for Kyle Busch, it was apparent while watching him celebrate in Victory Lane that the heavy weight of rookie expectations had lightened considerably.

CHEVY ROCK & ROLL 400

Kyle Busch had barely begun his victory celebration at California Speedway when calculators and scratch pads were pulled out by team members from several organizations to figure out how the California results affected their chances to make it into the Chase for the NASCAR NEXTEL Cup.

Twenty-five races had been completed, leaving only the Chevy Rock & Roll 400 to determine how the field for the 2005 NASCAR NEXTEL Cup Series championship would shape up. For some, the Richmond event would be merely a chance to move up or down a position or two — an opportunity to gain or lose five or 10 points when the totals were adjusted for the championship contenders following the race. For others, the 400-lapper on the three-quarter-mile oval would define their seasons as either successful or disappointing.

Tony Stewart had no such worries as he strolled into Richmond. Eleven straight top-10 runs, nine of those in the top five, put him alone atop the heap. With a 209-point margin over

Let the celebration begin! Kurt Busch starts the party in Victory Lane after his third win of the 2005 NASCAR NEXTEL Cup Series season. With it, Busch moved into the fifth position for the Chase for the NASCAR NEXTEL Cup, dropping Mark Martin to sixth.

(Above) Jeff Gordon wears a stoic expression prior to the start of the Chevy Rock & Roll 400. Sitting 12th in the standings and 30 points away from the top 10 going in, the four-time champion knew he had his work cut out for him this night.

(Above Right) Mark Martin sits ready to begin the battle at Richmond. Already assured of a place in the Chase for the NASCAR NEXTEL Cup, Martin would be gunning for his first points-paying win of the season.

second-place Greg Biffle, Stewart didn't even need to enter the Richmond race to remain the driver everyone would chase as the final 10-race stretch got underway next week at New Hampshire.

Biffle, Jimmie Johnson, Rusty Wallace and Mark Martin also were locked in as members of the championship field, while Kurt Busch needed only to start the event to be assured a chance to defend his series crown. Jeremy Mayfield, who drove into the inaugural Chase for the NASCAR NEXTEL Cup with a victory in this event one year ago, only needed to gain a finishing position better than 40th.

Things got a bit more interesting beginning with Carl Edwards, the eighth-place driver entering the weekend. A strong fourth place at California had padded his cushion over 10th place by 35 points. Now 85 ahead of the cut-off spot, Edwards could control his own destiny with a finish of 19th or better at Richmond. With all of the knowledge of the Roush organization and plenty of power under the hood of his Ford, Edwards just needed to stay out of trouble to get his shot at the title.

The three drivers behind Edwards were sitting on pins and needles. Ninth-place Matt Kenseth held a narrow margin of 10 points over Jamie McMurray, who was separated from 11th-place Ryan Newman by a single point. The 11-point span that covered all three drivers equated to only a few finishing positions in the race, and each one knew they would need to go as hard as they could while realizing that one mistake or bit of bad luck could easily derail their efforts to make the elite field of 10.

Jeff Gordon, 12th in points after falling from the top 10 at California, and Elliott Sadler in 13th place, were the dark horses in the field. A two-time Richmond winner, Gordon certainly could finish well, but making up 30 points on 10th place with everything on the line would

Kevin Harvick (29) yields the inside line to the hard-charging Kurt Busch (97) in a lead change near mid-distance. Harvick, who started from the pole, his second of the year, ruled the first half of the race before his GM Goodwrench Chevrolet got too tight.

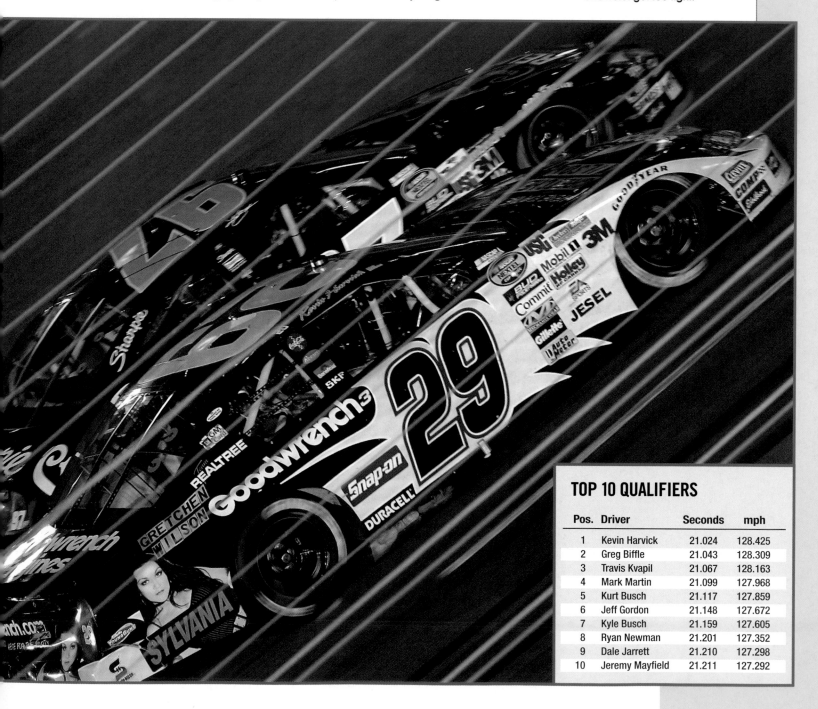

TOP 10 QUALIFIERS

Pos.	Driver	Seconds	mph
1	Kevin Harvick	21.024	128.425
2	Greg Biffle	21.043	128.309
3	Travis Kvapil	21.067	128.163
4	Mark Martin	21.099	127.968
5	Kurt Busch	21.117	127.859
6	Jeff Gordon	21.148	127.672
7	Kyle Busch	21.159	127.605
8	Ryan Newman	21.201	127.352
9	Dale Jarrett	21.210	127.298
10	Jeremy Mayfield	21.211	127.292

A capacity crowd estimated at 107,000 stands to watch Kurt Busch bring the field into Turn 1 on a restart. As the final race leading to the Chase for the NASCAR NEXTEL Cup, the event has become one of the most anticipated on the series schedule.

Ryan Newman was all business at Richmond in his Alltel Dodge. Entering the event 11th in points, Newman qualified eighth, ran a clean race among the top 10 and finished 12th — good enough to gain the final position in the championship-contending field.

be a difficult task at best, especially considering the DuPont team had not been showing the early-season form that brought them three wins. For Sadler, 52 points out of the top 10, a flawless run would need to be combined with bad luck on the part of several drivers immediately ahead of him if he were to join the championship field for the second year in a row.

With the stage set, Bud Pole winner Kevin Harvick led the field under the green flag to begin the race on Saturday night and immediately exerted the power of his GM Goodwrench Chevrolet to lead 167 of the first 199 laps.

(Above) The No. 97 Crown Royal Ford receives service under caution while driver Kurt Busch waits to return to action. The crew did an outstanding job with the race on the line, keeping their driver in front on three critical restarts in the late going.

(Left) Rookie Travis Kvapil (77) holds the inside line against Jimmie Johnson (48), with Greg Biffle (16) moving up from behind. Kvapil had a fine outing at Richmond, first by qualifying a career-best third for the race, and then by driving to a lead-lap finish just outside the top 10.

CHEVY ROCK & ROLL 400 — NASCAR NEXTEL Cup Series Race No. 26

Fin. Pos.	Start Pos.	Car No.	Driver	Team	Laps	Laps Led	Status
1	5	97	Kurt Busch	Crown Royal Ford	400	185	Running
2	13	17	Matt Kenseth	DeWalt Power Tools Ford	400	3	Running
3	2	16	Greg Biffle	National Guard Ford	400	3	Running
4	7	5 #	Kyle Busch	Kellogg's/Delphi Chevrolet	400	10	Running
5	15	2	Rusty Wallace	Miller Lite Dodge	400		Running
6	10	19	Jeremy Mayfield	Dodge Dealers/UAW Dodge	400	17	Running
7	25	20	Tony Stewart	The Home Depot Chevrolet	400		Running
8	14	9	Kasey Kahne	Dodge Dealers/UAW Dodge	400	6	Running
9	39	11	Terry Labonte	FedEx/Kinko's Chevrolet	400	7	Running
10	1	29	Kevin Harvick	GM Goodwrench/Gretchen Wilson Chev.	400	167	Running
11	3	77 #	Travis Kvapil	Kodak/Jasper Eng. & Trans. Dodge	400	1	Running
12	8	12	Ryan Newman	Alltel Dodge	400		Running
13	4	6	Mark Martin	Viagra Ford	400		Running
14	26	4	Mike Wallace	Lucas/MusikMafia Chevrolet	400		Running
15	31	0	Mike Bliss	Net Zero/Best Buy Chevrolet	400		Running
16	20	43	Jeff Green	Cheerios/Betty Crocker Dodge	400		Running
17	19	38	Elliott Sadler	M&M's Ford	400		Running
18	12	31	Jeff Burton	Cingular Wireless/Big & Rich Chevrolet	400		Running
19	42	49	Ken Schrader	Schwan's Home Service Dodge	400		Running
20	29	8	Dale Earnhardt Jr.	Budweiser True Music Chevrolet	400		Running
21	18	99	Carl Edwards	Scotts/Winterizer Ford	400		Running
22	23	18	Bobby Labonte	Interstate Batteries Chevrolet	399		Running
23	17	41	Casey Mears	Target/Lysol Dodge	399		Running
24	30	22	Scott Wimmer	Caterpillar Dodge	399		Running
25	24	48	Jimmie Johnson	Lowe's Chevrolet	399		Running
26	11	01	Joe Nemechek	U.S. Army Chevrolet	399		Running
27	40	45	Kyle Petty	Georgia-Pacific/Brawny Dodge	399		Running
28	36	09	Johnny Sauter	Miccosukee Resort Dodge	399		Running
29	37	10	Scott Riggs	Valvoline/Nickelback Chevrolet	398		Running
30	6	24	Jeff Gordon	DuPont Chevrolet	398		Running
31	28	15	Michael Waltrip	NAPA Auto Parts Chevrolet	396		Running
32	10	66	Mike Garvey	CAO Ford	395		Running
33	27	07	Dave Blaney	Jack Daniel's Chevrolet	395		Running
34	21	37	Tony Raines	BoSPOKER.net Dodge	394		Running
35	38	7	Robby Gordon	Jim Beam Black Chevrolet	394	1	Running
36	35	50	Jimmy Spencer	Allied Steel Buildings Dodge	393		Running
37	22	25	Brian Vickers	Green Day/GMAC Chevrolet	374		Running
38	16	21	Ricky Rudd	U.S. Air Force/Motorcraft Ford	366		Accident
39	9	88	Dale Jarrett	UPS Ford	364		Accident
40	32	42	Jamie McMurray	Havoline/Texaco Dodge	362		Accident
41	41	40	Sterling Marlin	Coors Light Dodge	358		Running
42	34	39	David Stremme	U.S. NAVY Dodge	321		Accident
43	33	32	Bobby Hamilton Jr.	Tide Chevrolet	193		Accident

Raybestos Rookie of the Year Contender.

NASCAR NEXTEL Cup Series Point Standings
(After 26 Races)

Pos.	Driver	Points	Behind	Change
1	**Tony Stewart**	**3716**	—	—
2	**Greg Biffle**	3531	-185	—
3	**Rusty Wallace**	3412	-304	+1
4	**Jimmie Johnson**	3400	-316	-1
5	**Kurt Busch**	3304	-412	+1
6	**Mark Martin**	3273	-443	-1
7	**Jeremy Mayfield**	3228	-488	—
8	**Carl Edwards**	3114	-602	—
	Matt Kenseth	3114	-602	—
10	**Ryan Newman**	3055	-661	+1

But as the evening evolved from twilight to darkness, the handling of Harvick's Monte Carlo began to tighten. Behind him, Kurt Busch had been moving ever closer, and as the halfway point approached, Busch surged ahead of Harvick to take command of the event.

Command may not adequately describe the hold Busch had from that point on. In all, he led five times for 185 laps, including the last 78 on the way to his third win of the season. Finishing behind him were Roush teammates Kenseth and Biffle, and with the runner-up finish, Kenseth completed an amazing run that began in June and took the former champion from 24th place in the standings to a berth in the Chase for the NASCAR NEXTEL Cup.

When the points were totaled, Kenseth was tied for eighth place with teammate Edwards, who made the championship field on a 21st-place finish as the last car on the lead lap.

The 10th and final driver to earn a chance to contend for the title was Newman, who did exactly what he needed to do in the race. Starting eighth, Newman placed his Alltel Dodge among the top 10 and kept it there throughout most of the event, avoiding trouble presented by 10 accidents and two spins over the course of the race before finishing 12th.

Formerly in the 10th position, McMurray suffered bitter disappointment at Richmond for the second year in a row. Starting in a hole from the 38th position, McMurray's Dodge never showed enough speed to catch Newman on the track. Finally, a bump from Tony Raines sent the Ganassi driver spinning into the inside wall along the backstretch where his race — along with his chances to make the top-10 field — abruptly ended.

Sadler managed a 17th-place, lead-lap finish, but his deficit going into the event was simply too much to overcome, while Jeff Gordon struggled with his DuPont Monte Carlo and eventually smacked the wall and finished two laps off the pace, officially ending his "Drive for Five."

So the field was set, and everyone immediately turned their attention toward New Hampshire International Speedway where, in one week's time, the 2006 edition of the Chase for the NASCAR NEXTEL Cup would begin.

INTRODUCTION TO
THE CHASE FOR THE NASCAR NEXTEL CUP 2005

Twenty-six events had been completed in the 2005 NASCAR NEXTEL Cup Series season, run on 20 different race tracks ranging from the high-banked superspeedways at Daytona and Talladega to the tight grueling bull-rings at Bristol and Martinsville to the twisting road courses of Watkins Glen and Infineon Raceway — all in a schedule designed to asses the muster of drivers and teams in a test of skill, preparation and endurance.

And over that span, 10 drivers emerged to prove themselves the best in the field, the top of the class, able to achieve the outstanding performance and consistency needed to attain the right to compete in the 2006 Chase for the NASCAR NEXTEL Cup.

Ten races remained to determine who among the 10 would be crowned champion, with a year-end bonus worth at least $5 million waiting to be awarded to the winner at the NASCAR NEXTEL Cup Series Awards Ceremony in New York City the first weekend of December.

For those who made it, point totals were adjusted on a five-point sliding scale that pitted all 10 against each other within a 45-point margin, top to bottom, making the coveted title within reach of every one.

Now it was time to put the rubber to the asphalt, drop the green flag and see which driver, which team, could out-run, out-think, out-last nine of the best other drivers and teams the sport has to offer. Now it was time to go racing.

Qualifying Field for the 2005 Chase for the NASCAR NEXTEL Cup

Pos.	Driver	Starts	Wins	Top 5	Top 10	DNF	Points
1	Tony Stewart	26	5	12	18	1	5050
2	Greg Biffle	26	5	10	15	1	5045
3	Rusty Wallace	26	0	7	14	0	5040
4	Jimmie Johnson	26	2	9	15	4	5035
5	Kurt Busch	26	3	8	14	3	5030
6	Mark Martin	26	0	6	12	1	5025
7	Jeremy Mayfield	26	1	4	7	1	5020
8	Carl Edwards	26	2	8	10	1	5015
9	Matt Kenseth	26	1	6	11	3	5015
10	Ryan Newman	26	0	5	10	3	5005

1 TONY STEWART

Race #	Location	Start	Finish	Status	Points Pos.
1	Daytona	4	7	Running	6
2	California	29	17	Running	7
3	Las Vegas	23	10	Running	6
4	Atlanta	9	17	Running	7
5	Bristol	11	3	Running	3
6	Martinsville	7	26	Running	5
7	Texas	10	31	Engine	11
8	Phoenix	6	33	Running	14
9	Talladega	11	2	Running	6
10	Darlington	15	10	Running	7
11	Richmond	3	2	Running	6
12	Lowe's	9	24	Running	6
13	Dover	6	15	Running	5
14	Pocono	26	29	Running	10
15	Michigan	3	2	Running	6
16	Infineon	7	1	Running	4
17	Daytona	1	1	Running	3
18	Chicagoland	13	5	Running	3
19	New Hampshire	13	1	Running	3
20	Pocono	6	7	Running	2
21	Indianapolis	22	1	Running	1
22	Watkins Glen	1	1	Running	1
23	Michigan	36	5	Running	1
24	Bristol	17	8	Running	1
25	California	14	5	Running	1
26	Richmond	25	7	Running	1

2 GREG BIFFLE

Race #	Location	Start	Finish	Status	Points Pos.
1	Daytona	23	25	Running	25
2	California	5	1	Running	5
3	Las Vegas	3	6	Running	3
4	Atlanta	6	3	Running	2
5	Bristol	10	9	Running	2
6	Martinsville	8	29	Running	2
7	Texas	5	1	Running	2
8	Phoenix	3	41	Overheat	3
9	Talladega	29	13	Running	4
10	Darlington	3	1	Running	3
11	Richmond	9	6	Running	2
12	Lowe's	29	6	Running	2
13	Dover	2	1	Running	2
14	Pocono	23	30	Running	2
15	Michigan	25	1	Running	2
16	Infineon	41	14	Running	1
17	Daytona	18	36	Running	2
18	Chicagoland	6	11	Running	2
19	New Hampshire	9	5	Running	2
20	Pocono	7	17	Running	3
21	Indianapolis	31	21	Running	3
22	Watkins Glen	3	38	Running	3
23	Michigan	31	6	Running	3
24	Bristol	4	3	Running	3
25	California	4	2	Running	2
26	Richmond	2	3	Running	2

3

4

RUSTY WALLACE

JIMMIE JOHNSON

Race #	Location	Start	Finish	Status	Points Pos.
1	Daytona	36	10	Running	10
2	California	23	10	Running	8
3	Las Vegas	21	12	Running	7
4	Atlanta	32	27	Running	9
5	Bristol	3	13	Running	9
6	Martinsville	4	5	Running	7
7	Texas	6	10	Running	3
8	Phoenix	9	36	Running	10
9	Talladega	20	22	Running	13
10	Darlington	12	12	Running	14
11	Richmond	8	19	Running	12
12	Lowe's	20	10	Running	11
13	Dover	11	5	Running	7
14	Pocono	12	11	Running	8
15	Michigan	12	10	Running	8
16	Infineon	14	4	Running	6
17	Daytona	9	4	Running	5
18	Chicagoland	33	12	Running	4
19	New Hampshire	6	8	Running	4
20	Pocono	13	2	Running	4
21	Indianapolis	41	25	Running	4
22	Watkins Glen	4	6	Running	4
23	Michigan	38	13	Running	4
24	Bristol	20	5	Running	4
25	California	34	15	Running	4
26	Richmond	15	5	Running	3

Race #	Location	Start	Finish	Status	Points Pos.
1	Daytona	2	5	Running	5
2	California	8	2	Running	2
3	Las Vegas	9	1	Running	2
4	Atlanta	3	2	Running	1
5	Bristol	14	6	Running	1
6	Martinsville	37	8	Running	1
7	Texas	18	3	Running	1
8	Phoenix	12	15	Running	1
9	Talladega	6	20	Accident	1
10	Darlington	9	7	Running	1
11	Richmond	28	40	Accident	1
12	Lowe's	5	1	Running	1
13	Dover	1	4	Running	1
14	Pocono	21	6	Running	1
15	Michigan	16	19	Running	1
16	Infineon	2	36	Running	2
17	Daytona	3	6	Running	1
18	Chicagoland	1	3	Running	1
19	New Hampshire	12	13	Running	1
20	Pocono	9	12	Running	1
21	Indianapolis	42	38	Accident	2
22	Watkins Glen	2	5	Running	2
23	Michigan	10	10	Running	2
24	Bristol	29	36	Engine	2
25	California	5	16	Running	3
26	Richmond	24	25	Running	4

5

KURT BUSCH

6

MARK MARTIN

Race #	Location	Start	Finish	Status	Points Pos.
1	Daytona	13	2	Running	2
2	California	20	3	Running	1
3	Las Vegas	5	3	Running	1
4	Atlanta	24	32	Running	4
5	Bristol	26	35	Accident	7
6	Martinsville	9	19	Running	9
7	Texas	19	7	Running	4
8	Phoenix	2	1	Running	2
9	Talladega	10	7	Running	2
10	Darlington	11	37	Running	4
11	Richmond	4	17	Running	5
12	Lowe's	35	43	Accident	10
13	Dover	10	9	Running	8
14	Pocono	2	22	Running	11
15	Michigan	13	12	Running	9
16	Infineon	6	3	Running	8
17	Daytona	28	37	Running	9
18	Chicagoland	19	8	Running	10
19	New Hampshire	5	2	Running	5
20	Pocono	2	1	Running	5
21	Indianapolis	37	18	Running	5
22	Watkins Glen	5	39	Accident	6
23	Michigan	17	7	Running	7
24	Bristol	13	10	Running	7
25	California	3	12	Running	6
26	Richmond	5	1	Running	5

Race #	Location	Start	Finish	Status	Points Pos.
1	Daytona	32	6	Running	7
2	California	18	7	Running	3
3	Las Vegas	19	30	Running	9
4	Atlanta	12	4	Running	5
5	Bristol	34	31	Running	10
6	Martinsville	22	3	Running	4
7	Texas	16	20	Running	7
8	Phoenix	22	16	Running	6
9	Talladega	16	33	Running	11
10	Darlington	20	4	Running	6
11	Richmond	14	15	Running	10
12	Lowe's	13	28	Accident	12
13	Dover	12	3	Running	6
14	Pocono	13	7	Running	5
15	Michigan	15	3	Running	5
16	Infineon	3	15	Running	5
17	Daytona	23	39	Running	8
18	Chicagoland	20	10	Running	6
19	New Hampshire	19	15	Running	7
20	Pocono	3	3	Running	7
21	Indianapolis	10	7	Running	6
22	Watkins Glen	6	7	Running	5
23	Michigan	14	17	Running	5
24	Bristol	25	16	Running	5
25	California	2	11	Running	5
26	Richmond	4	13	Running	6

JEREMY MAYFIELD 7

CARL EDWARDS 8

Race #	Location	Start	Finish	Status	Points Pos.
1	Daytona	24	23	Running	22
2	California	3	28	Running	26
3	Las Vegas	26	20	Running	26
4	Atlanta	14	13	Running	21
5	Bristol	8	17	Running	18
6	Martinsville	3	15	Running	17
7	Texas	2	11	Running	16
8	Phoenix	8	13	Running	16
9	Talladega	22	4	Running	12
10	Darlington	8	33	Accident	15
11	Richmond	15	13	Running	16
12	Lowe's	36	4	Running	13
13	Dover	13	14	Running	12
14	Pocono	6	14	Running	13
15	Michigan	5	22	Running	13
16	Infineon	32	7	Running	11
17	Daytona	31	12	Running	11
18	Chicagoland	22	6	Running	9
19	New Hampshire	11	19	Running	8
20	Pocono	16	18	Running	8
21	Indianapolis	2	4	Running	8
22	Watkins Glen	8	11	Running	7
23	Michigan	11	1	Running	6
24	Bristol	16	18	Running	6
25	California	13	26	Running	7
26	Richmond	10	6	Running	7

Race #	Location	Start	Finish	Status	Points Pos.
1	Daytona	27	12	Running	13
2	California	19	5	Running	4
3	Las Vegas	20	14	Running	5
4	Atlanta	4	1	Running	3
5	Bristol	42	26	Running	4
6	Martinsville	36	38	Running	11
7	Texas	20	19	Running	13
8	Phoenix	11	7	Running	8
9	Talladega	21	32	Running	14
10	Darlington	10	9	Running	13
11	Richmond	11	21	Running	13
12	Lowe's	12	3	Running	8
13	Dover	8	16	Running	9
14	Pocono	29	1	Running	4
15	Michigan	23	5	Running	4
16	Infineon	23	38	Running	9
17	Daytona	34	33	Accident	12
18	Chicagoland	21	39	Running	12
19	New Hampshire	20	12	Running	12
20	Pocono	41	4	Running	12
21	Indianapolis	38	12	Running	10
22	Watkins Glen	10	19	Running	10
23	Michigan	12	4	Running	9
24	Bristol	37	24	Running	8
25	California	1	4	Running	8
26	Richmond	18	21	Running	8

9 MATT KENSETH

Race #	Location	Start	Finish	Status	Points Pos.
1	Daytona	14	42	Engine	42
2	California	6	26	Running	36
3	Las Vegas	8	8	Running	28
4	Atlanta	23	31	Running	31
5	Bristol	25	16	Running	28
6	Martinsville	18	11	Running	21
7	Texas	39	18	Running	21
8	Phoenix	17	42	Accident	28
9	Talladega	23	11	Running	23
10	Darlington	31	26	Running	24
11	Richmond	26	12	Running	21
12	Lowe's	3	37	Accident	23
13	Dover	23	7	Running	22
14	Pocono	10	32	Running	24
15	Michigan	21	4	Running	21
16	Infineon	24	11	Running	20
17	Daytona	38	9	Running	19
18	Chicagoland	4	2	Running	16
19	New Hampshire	16	10	Running	16
20	Pocono	30	36	Running	17
21	Indianapolis	20	5	Running	15
22	Watkins Glen	15	18	Running	16
23	Michigan	13	3	Running	15
24	Bristol	1	1	Running	11
25	California	23	7	Running	9
26	Richmond	13	2	Running	9

10 RYAN NEWMAN

Race #	Location	Start	Finish	Status	Points Pos.
1	Daytona	9	20	Running	19
2	California	9	9	Running	12
3	Las Vegas	1	9	Running	8
4	Atlanta	1	14	Running	6
5	Bristol	7	30	Running	11
6	Martinsville	2	4	Running	8
7	Texas	1	16	Running	9
8	Phoenix	7	14	Running	7
9	Talladega	5	39	Accident	15
10	Darlington	2	5	Running	10
11	Richmond	2	3	Running	7
12	Lowe's	1	5	Running	4
13	Dover	4	8	Running	4
14	Pocono	17	34	Accident	6
15	Michigan	1	15	Running	7
16	Infineon	11	9	Running	7
17	Daytona	27	14	Running	6
18	Chicagoland	2	29	Running	7
19	New Hampshire	4	7	Running	6
20	Pocono	4	5	Running	6
21	Indianapolis	6	34	Running	7
22	Watkins Glen	7	30	Running	8
23	Michigan	5	12	Running	8
24	Bristol	6	39	Accident	9
25	California	28	18	Running	11
26	Richmond	8	12	Running	10

SYLVANIA 300

When the NASCAR NEXTEL Cup Series teams began preparations for the Sylvania 300 at New Hampshire International Speedway, the tension in the air hung over the track like a thick New England fog. It wasn't lost on any one of the competitors who prepared for the first event of the 2006 Chase for the NASCAR NEXTEL Cup what had happened here one year ago.

In that race, Kurt Busch stormed into the lead just before the halfway point and led 153 of the final 166 laps on the way to a resounding win. Seventh in the championship standings going in, Busch left New England in a tie for first place with Dale Earnhardt Jr. Busch fell back to second place the following week at Dover but regained the top spot the next week at Talladega and never gave it up on the way to winning the NASCAR NEXTEL Cup Series championship.

Ryan Newman's Mobil 1/Alltel Dodge didn't reach the front of the field until Lap 181 of the Sylvania 300. From there, he led a total of 66 laps, including the all-important final two.

(Above) Kurt Busch spins through New Hampshire's Turn 2 after tagging the outside wall, the result of being hit from behind by Scott Riggs. Busch returned to the event after a lengthy stay behind the wall but lost 122 points on the day.

(Right) Accompanied by NASCAR officials, Kurt Busch makes his way toward Scott Riggs' pit stall to express his displeasure to crew chief Rodney Childers regarding the Lap-3 incident.

Conversely, Tony Stewart arrived at New Hampshire fourth in points, but was involved in an accident and wound up 39th and fell four spots to eighth by the end of the day. A sixth-place effort the following week at Dover actually dropped him to ninth in the standings, and despite his best efforts over the next eight races, Stewart never regained a position higher than sixth place, where he finished at the end of the season.

Ryan Newman started 10th in last year's title chase and promptly blew an engine and left New Hampshire 136 points behind the leaders. A win the following week at Dover only moved the Dodge driver up to eighth place, and he was never able to reach higher than seventh the rest of the way.

TOP 10 QUALIFIERS

Pos.	Driver	Seconds	mph
1	Tony Stewart	29.043	131.143
2	Jeff Gordon	29.058	131.075
3	Dale Earnhardt Jr.	29.124	130.777
4	Matt Kenseth	29.149	130.666
5	Scott Riggs	29.194	130.465
6	Elliott Sadler	29.230	130.304
7	Rusty Wallace	29.247	130.228
8	Jeremy Mayfield	29.285	130.059
9	Kevin Harvick	29.332	129.851
10	Jimmie Johnson	29.339	129.820

(Left) Crewmen pull the tire from Matt Kenseth's Ford after a lug nut lodged itself in the brake assembly, causing the wheel to lock up. Quick work by the team kept Kenseth on the lead lap, where he eventually rebounded for a third-place finish.

(Above) Pole-winner Tony Stewart (20) jumps to the early lead ahead of third-place qualifier Dale Earnhardt Jr. (8), with front-row starter Jeff Gordon (24) and Matt Kenseth (17) on the outside. Earnhardt, in his first race with Tony Eury Jr. as crew chief, picked up a fifth-place finish, his first top five since winning at Chicagoland nine races ago.

In the end, each driver in last year's Chase for the NASCAR NEXTEL Cup had at least one bad race — Busch included — but clearly, there was no discounting the notion that getting off to a good start was essential in making a bid for the coveted crown.

Strangely enough, this year's kick-off of the final 10-race stretch was nearly the antithesis of last year's event. Not three laps after taking the initial green flag, Scott Riggs, driving a very loose Chevrolet, tagged Busch in Turn 2 and sent the defending champion into the wall. Relegated to racing for points, the No. 97 crew returned Busch to the track 67 laps behind the leaders, where he soldiered to a 35th-place finish.

At the front of the field, Stewart, the fastest of 11 drivers to break the track record in qualifying, had maintained a lead from Lap 1. Easily the fastest on the track in racing conditions as well, Stewart led 143 of the first 180 trips around the 1.058-mile oval.

With numerous cautions (there were 10 over the 300-lap affair), teams began shuffling the running order by employing various pit strategies in their efforts to gain track position, while Stewart continued to run among the top 10.

(Left) Teammates Jeff Burton (31) and Kevin Harvick (29) battle for position over the event's final laps. Burton edged out Harvick to take ninth place, dropping Harvick to his second consecutive 10th-place finish.

(Below) Ryan Newman blasts out of his pit and back into action. The quick stop during the day's final caution put Newman in front of Tony Stewart for the restart with 15 laps to go in the race.

(Opposing Page) Ryan Newman celebrates his 12th career victory, the first since Dover last fall, 35 races ago. The timely win also pushed Newman up seven positions in the Chase for the NASCAR NEXTEL Cup standings.

A round of green-flag pit stops dropped Stewart back in the running order with 40 laps remaining, but The Home Depot driver worked his way back toward the leaders, and when the field lined up for the final restart at Lap 285, Stewart was listed second behind Newman.

Stewart tracked Newman down and re-took the lead with eight laps to go, but was unable to open up a significant margin on the hard-charging Alltel driver. As the two entered the

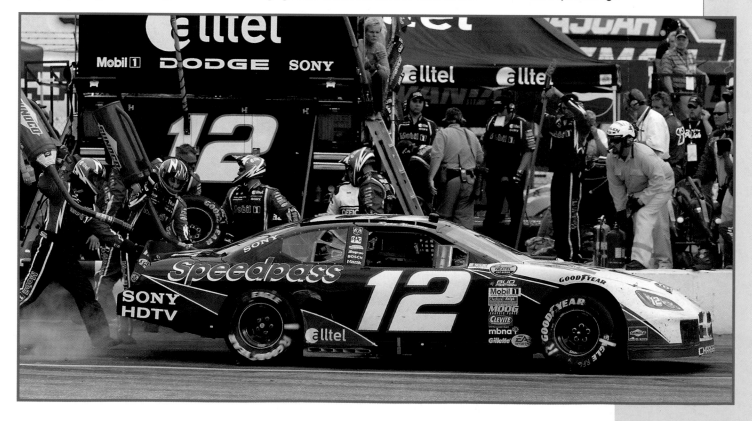

SYLVANIA 300

NASCAR NEXTEL Cup Series Race No. 27

Fin. Pos.	Start Pos.	Car No.	Driver	Team	Laps	Laps Led	Status
1	13	12	Ryan Newman	Mobil 1/Alltel Dodge	300	66	Running
2	1	20	Tony Stewart	The Home Depot Chevrolet	300	173	Running
3	4	17	Matt Kenseth	DeWalt Power Tools Ford	300		Running
4	26	16	Greg Biffle	National Guard Ford	300	1	Running
5	3	8	Dale Earnhardt Jr.	Budweiser Chevrolet	300	8	Running
6	7	2	Rusty Wallace	Miller Lite Dodge	300		Running
7	15	6	Mark Martin	Viagra Ford	300	31	Running
8	10	48	Jimmie Johnson	Lowe's Chevrolet	300		Running
9	14	31	Jeff Burton	Cingular Wireless Chevrolet	300		Running
10	9	29	Kevin Harvick	GM Goodwrench Chevrolet	300	1	Running
11	37	40	Sterling Marlin	Coors Light Dodge	300	4	Running
12	20	42	Jamie McMurray	Havoline/Texaco Dodge	300		Running
13	31	25	Brian Vickers	GMAC/ditech.com Chevrolet	300	8	Running
14	2	24	Jeff Gordon	DuPont Chevrolet	300	2	Running
15	36	15	Michael Waltrip	NAPA Auto Parts Chevrolet	300		Running
16	8	19	Jeremy Mayfield	Dodge Dealers/UAW Dodge	300		Running
17	18	43	Jeff Green	Cheerios/Betty Crocker Dodge	300	1	Running
18	33	88	Dale Jarrett	UPS Ford	300		Running
19	24	99	Carl Edwards	Office Depot/Scotts Ford	300		Running
20	28	21	Ricky Rudd	Motorcraft Genuine Parts Ford	300		Running
21	42	45	Kyle Petty	Georgia-Pacific/Brawny Dodge	300		Running
22	25	4	Mike Wallace	Lucas Oil Chevrolet	300		Running
23	23	41	Casey Mears	Target Dodge	299		Running
24	17	18	Bobby Labonte	Interstate Batteries Chevrolet	299		Running
25	11	01	Joe Nemechek	U.S. Army Chevrolet	299		Running
26	41	22	Scott Wimmer	Caterpillar Dodge	299		Running
27	30	5 #	Kyle Busch	Kellogg's Chevrolet	299		Running
28	5	10	Scott Riggs	Valvoline Chevrolet	299		Running
29	32	32	Bobby Hamilton Jr.	Tide Chevrolet	299		Running
30	6	38	Elliott Sadler	M&M's Ford	298	4	Running
31	39	92	Joey McCarthy	Trim Spa Dodge	295		Running
32	34	51	Stuart Kirby	Marathon American Spirit Oil Chevrolet	289		Running
33	16	07	Dave Blaney	Jack Daniel's Chevrolet	271		Running
34	29	11	J.J. Yeley	FedEx Express Chevrolet	251		Running
35	12	97	Kurt Busch	Sharpie Ford	233		Running
36	22	0	Mike Bliss	Net Zero/Best Buy Chevrolet	194		Accident
37	19	7	Robby Gordon	Jim Beam Chevrolet	190	1	Accident
38	21	9	Kasey Kahne	Dodge Dealers/UAW Dodge	164		Accident
39	43	50	Jimmy Spencer	Allied Steel Buildings Dodge	144		Accident
40	40	49	Ken Schrader	Schwan's Home Service Dodge	111		Accident
41	27	77 #	Travis Kvapil	Kodak/Jasper Eng. & Trans. Dodge	105		Accident
42	38	34	Ted Christopher	Mach 1 Motorsports Chevrolet	29		Transmission
43	35	75	Wayne Anderson	Rinaldi's Air Conditioning Service Dodge	16		Engine

\# Raybestos Rookie of the Year Contender.

Chase for the NASCAR NEXTEL Cup Standings
(With 9 Races Remaining)

Pos.	Driver	Points	Behind	Change
1	Tony Stewart	5230	—	—
2	Greg Biffle	5210	-20	—
3	Ryan Newman	5190	-40	+7
4	Rusty Wallace	5190	-40	-1
5	Matt Kenseth	5180	-50	+4
6	Jimmie Johnson	5177	-53	-2
7	Mark Martin	5176	-54	-1
8	Jeremy Mayfield	5135	-95	-1
9	Carl Edwards	5121	-109	-1
10	Kurt Busch	5088	-142	-5

second turn on Lap 299, Newman dropped to the inside, forcing Stewart to lift to avoid scraping the wall while coming off the corner. Side by side down the backstretch, Newman gained the advantage and dropped down low through Turns 3 & 4 to edge ahead as the two took the white flag. Unable to regain position, Stewart fell in line behind Newman, who took the win with a 0.292-second margin of victory.

"I never expected to have a second shot at Tony," Newman explained after his first win since Dover last fall. "We raced clean, we raced hard and we had fun. ... It felt like the old open-wheel days when we used to do that all the time."

"That's the way a race at Loudon should finish," stated Stewart, "with [two] guys in the Chase running hard. ... We did everything we could, but he (Newman) was faster."

Championship contenders Matt Kenseth and Greg Biffle finished third and fourth ahead of Earnhardt, who was driving his first race with Tony Eury Jr. as crew chief. Rusty Wallace overcame a pit road penalty and an accident to take sixth place ahead of Mark Martin and Jimmie Johnson, while four-time New Hampshire winner Jeff Burton had a solid run to ninth place ahead of Kevin Harvick.

Chase for the NASCAR NEXTEL Cup drivers Jeremy Mayfield and Carl Edwards had uneventful days, both finishing on the lead lap in the 16th and 19th positions, respectively.

MBNA RacePoints 400

With the Chase for the NASCAR NEXTEL Cup officially underway, the NASCAR NEXTEL Cup Series moved on to Dover, Del., for the running of the MBNA RacePoints 400.

For some, the "Monster Mile" was a welcome sight. Three championship contenders recently conquered the one-mile oval with season sweeps — Tony Stewart (2000), Jimmie Johnson (2002) and Ryan Newman (2003) — while Mark Martin collected finishes of first, second and third in his last three Dover starts, with the victory in the spring of 2004 upping his career total to four Dover wins.

Rusty Wallace could look back on three career victories and 10 top fives at Dover, the most recent of which was a fifth place earlier in the season in the race that was won by Greg Biffle.

Jeremy Mayfield's best Dover performance was a runner-up finish to Newman in 2003, which he followed last season by sweeping both poles at the track and collecting two top-10 finishes.

The Royal Crown crew leaps off the wall as driver Kurt Busch brings his Ford in for service under green, giving up the lead in the process. The stop proved crucial as the yellow flag flew moments later, dropping Busch off the lead lap for good.

Championship contenders Ryan Newman (left) and Jimmie Johnson relax on pit road prior to strapping in for 400 laps around the Monster Mile. At the end of the day, both drivers had three Dover wins apiece and were separated by just 12 points in the standings.

TOP 10 QUALIFIERS

Pos.	Driver	Seconds	mph
1	Ryan Newman	22.770	158.102
2	Kasey Kahne	22.919	157.074
3	Kyle Busch	22.952	156.849
4	Dale Earnhardt Jr.	22.986	156.617
5	Jimmie Johnson	22.993	156.569
6	Rusty Wallace	23.003	156.501
7	Mark Martin	23.004	156.494
8	Bobby Hamilton Jr.	23.017	156.406
9	Joe Nemechek	23.018	156.399
10	Kurt Busch	23.050	156.182

Others in the championship field faced the concrete oval with some trepidation. Matt Kenseth's Dover record reflected consistency — seven top 10s in 13 career starts — but he couldn't shake the memory of last year's disastrous run that ended with the DeWalt Ford stuck on top of the water-filled barriers at the entrance to pit road. For all intents and purposes, the resulting DNF dropped Kenseth from championship contention.

Like Kenseth, Carl Edwards and Kurt Busch had been able to post decent finishes at Dover, but they had not enjoyed great success, either. The bottom two in the Chase for the NASCAR NEXTEL Cup standings after New Hampshire, both drivers knew they needed to perform well this weekend to get back in the thick of the championship hunt.

Not surprisingly, Newman smoked everyone in Bud Pole qualifying by posting a lap more than a full mile per hour faster than his closest competitor, Kasey Kahne, to win his sixth pole position of the season — four more than anyone else. In all, seven of the Chase for the NASCAR NEXTEL Cup drivers started within the first six rows, with Biffle three rows back in the 18th position. Stewart and Edwards, however, lined up together, all the way back in row No 16. With 30 cars in front of them at the drop of the green flag, both drivers were starting at a distinct disadvantage.

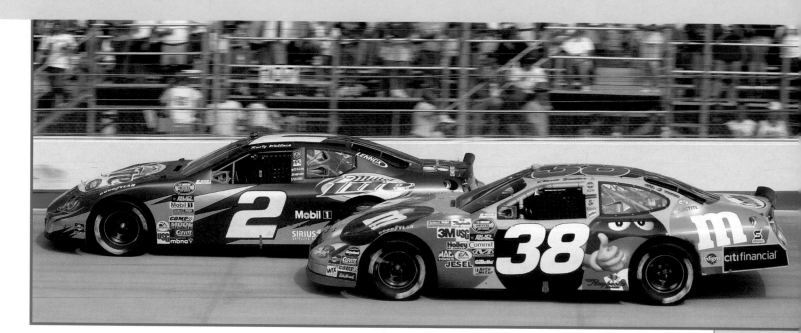

Newman and Johnson got things going early. The Penske Racing South driver led the first 30 laps before giving way to Johnson's Hendrick Chevrolet, and by the time the second yellow flag flew at Lap 70, Wallace, Mayfield and all of the Roush drivers except Edwards had joined Newman and Johnson in and around the top 10. Stewart, meanwhile, was struggling mightily with an ill-handling race car and fighting just to maintain his position on the lead lap.

(Above) Elliott Sadler (38) and Rusty Wallace (2) run together down the Dover frontstretch. Sadler got a great two-tire call from new crew chief Kevin Buskirk that gave him the mid-race lead. With a sixth-place finish, Sadler moved into the pivotal 11th position in the points, while Wallace advanced to second place, seven points behind Johnson.

(Left) In his sixth start of the season, Stanton Barrett, a NASCAR Busch Series regular, smacks the inside wall to bring out the first of 11 cautions on Lap 10.

(Right) Kyle Busch (5) attacks Dover's 24-degree banks with Mark Martin on his tail. Busch ran among the top 10 for the entire race, the top five for the last 100 laps and nearly stole the win from Johnson.

(Below) Four-time Dover winner Ricky Rudd (21) looks low on Kyle Petty, who won here in 1995. Petty gained more positions than any other driver during the day and matched his best run of the year with an eighth-place finish.

Kurt Busch took over the top spot during the next caution, and by the midpoint of the race, the leader board was dominated by Chase for the NASCAR NEXTEL Cup drivers. They were joined by strong-running Kahne, Kyle Busch, Joe Nemechek and Jamie McMurray, all with competitive cars.

Past the halfway mark, tire problems struck the Roush machines of Kenseth and Biffle, with each reporting cut tires at different times and each going a lap down due to unscheduled stops for new rubber.

Jimmie Johnson collects the checkered flag a scant 0.080 second ahead of Kyle Busch, who applied plenty of pressure over the green-white-checkered finish. Johnson's 17th career victory put him back on top of the point standings after a seven-week absence.

MBNA RacePoints 400

NASCAR NEXTEL Cup Series Race No. 28

Fin. Pos.	Start Pos.	Car No.	Driver	Team	Laps	Laps Led	Status
1	5	48	Jimmie Johnson	Lowe's Chevrolet	404	134	Running
2	3	5 #	Kyle Busch	Kellogg's Chevrolet	404		Running
3	6	2	Rusty Wallace	Miller Lite Dodge	404		Running
4	7	6	Mark Martin	Viagra Ford	404	7	Running
5	1	12	Ryan Newman	Alltel Dodge	404	30	Running
6	22	38	Elliott Sadler	M&M's Ford	404	26	Running
7	12	19	Jeremy Mayfield	Dodge Dealers/UAW Dodge	404		Running
8	34	45	Kyle Petty	Georgia-Pacific/Brawny Dodge	404		Running
9	32	99	Carl Edwards	Office Depot Ford	404		Running
10	23	41	Casey Mears	Target Dodge	404		Running
11	36	31	Jeff Burton	Cingular Wireless Chevrolet	404		Running
12	20	21	Ricky Rudd	Motorcraft Genuine Parts Ford	403		Running
13	18	16	Greg Biffle	National Guard Ford	403	14	Running
14	26	25	Brian Vickers	GMAC/ditech.com Chevrolet	403		Running
15	15	88	Dale Jarrett	UPS Ford	403		Running
16	2	9	Kasey Kahne	Dodge Dealers/UAW Dodge	403		Running
17	9	01	Joe Nemechek	U.S. Army Chevrolet	403		Running
18	31	20	Tony Stewart	The Home Depot Chevrolet	402		Running
19	17	29	Kevin Harvick	GM Goodwrench Chevrolet	402		Running
20	24	07	Dave Blaney	Jack Daniel's Chevrolet	402		Running
21	13	77 #	Travis Kvapil	Kodak/Jasper Eng. & Trans. Dodge	402		Running
22	38	4	Mike Wallace	Lucas Oil Chevrolet	402		Running
23	10	97	Kurt Busch	Crown Royal Ford	401	192	Running
24	29	10	Scott Riggs	Valvoline Chevrolet	401		Running
25	37	11	J.J. Yeley	FedEx Freight Chevrolet	401		Running
26	27	15	Michael Waltrip	NAPA Auto Parts Chevrolet	401	1	Running
27	21	43	Jeff Green	Cheerios/Betty Crocker Dodge	401		Running
28	42	49	Ken Schrader	Red Baron Pizza Dodge	401		Running
29	19	42	Jamie McMurray	Havoline-Texaco Dodge	400		Running
30	30	0	Mike Bliss	Best Buy Chevrolet	399		Running
31	4	8	Dale Earnhardt Jr.	Budweiser Chevrolet	397		Running
32	28	18	Bobby Labonte	MBNA RacePoints Chevrolet	397		Running
33	8	32	Bobby Hamilton Jr.	Tide Chevrolet	386		Running
34	43	78	Kenny Wallace	Furniture Row Chevrolet	381		Running
35	11	17	Matt Kenseth	DeWalt Power Tools Ford	367		Accident
36	16	22	Scott Wimmer	Caterpillar Dodge	293		Accident
37	25	24	Jeff Gordon	DuPont Chevrolet	291		Accident
38	39	37	Tony Raines	BoSPOKER.net Dodge	288		Accident
39	33	7	Robby Gordon	Harrah's Chevrolet	279		Engine
40	35	66	Kevin Lepage	EAS Ford	197		Accident
41	14	40	Sterling Marlin	Coors Light Dodge	190		Engine
42	41	00	Carl Long	Sundance Vacations/carloan.com Chev.	144		Engine
43	40	95	Stanton Barrett	S. Barrett Motorsports Chevrolet	8		Accident

Raybestos Rookie of the Year Contender.

Chase for the NASCAR NEXTEL Cup Standings
(With 8 Races Remaining)

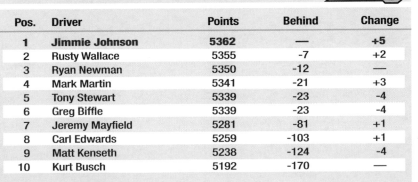

Pos.	Driver	Points	Behind	Change
1	Jimmie Johnson	5362	—	+5
2	Rusty Wallace	5355	-7	+2
3	Ryan Newman	5350	-12	—
4	Mark Martin	5341	-21	+3
5	Tony Stewart	5339	-23	-4
6	Greg Biffle	5339	-23	-4
7	Jeremy Mayfield	5281	-81	+1
8	Carl Edwards	5259	-103	+1
9	Matt Kenseth	5238	-124	-4
10	Kurt Busch	5192	-170	—

While his Roush teammates struggled to get back on the lead lap, Kurt Busch took control of the race. In all, Busch led an event-high 192 laps and looked to be a clear-cut favorite for the win. With less than 40 laps remaining, Busch reported to pit road to begin the final round of green-flag stops, and no sooner had he returned to action than Kenseth's right-front tire let go, sending the yellow-and-black Ford into the wall to bring out the ninth caution of the day and dropping Busch one lap down.

During the ensuing stops, crew chief Pat Tryson rolled the dice and called for right sides only on the Viagra Ford — a move that sent Martin back to the track in front followed by Johnson, Kyle Busch, Wallace and Newman, all shod with four fresh Goodyears.

Martin led the restart with 25 laps to go but was passed the next time around by Johnson, who immediately began to open a convincing lead — one he had stretched to nearly a second over Kyle Busch with five laps to go. That margin would not stand, however, as Nemechek nailed the inside wall to produce the 11th and final caution and force a green-white-checkered finish.

The debris cleared, Johnson took the final green flag with Hendrick teammate Kyle Busch hounding him from behind, hoping to loosen up the Lowe's Chevrolet in the final laps. Several times Busch tried to sneak the nose of his Monte Carol on the inside, only to have Johnson block the move as he kept his car glued to the bottom. Realizing that second place was preferable to wrecking both himself and his teammate, Busch tucked in to finish 0.080-second behind.

Wallace got past Martin in the closing laps, and the two veterans finished together for the second straight week, this time in third and fourth, while Newman held his ground and took fifth place in the closing laps.

The Monster Mile was particularly unkind to Stewart, who never got his car handling well and finished as the first car two laps down in 18th place, which broke his streak of 13 consecutive top-10 finishes. And Kurt Busch, in his effort to regain the lead lap, suffered yet another cut tire followed by a penalty for speeding on pit road and wound up 23rd at the finish — a devastating blow to his title defense.

UAW-FORD 500

The results from the RacePoints 400 at Dover shook things up considerably in the Chase for the NASCAR NEXTEL Cup. Eight of the 10 drivers changed positions, with five of those moving either up or down three or more spots.

The big winner, of course, was Jimmie Johnson, who gained the most by jumping from sixth on the list to the very top. Some of that could be attributed to Tony Stewart's struggles that negated his 20-point advantage and dropped him four positions to fifth place, where he found himself in a tie with Greg Biffle, who also dropped four spots after a 13th-place Dover run.

The good news for Stewart and Biffle, however, was that they were only 23 points behind Johnson, with Mark Martin, Ryan Newman and Rusty Wallace sandwiched in between. Clearly, all six drivers were still smack dab in the middle of the championship fight.

Dale Jarrett was admittedly exhausted after the UAW-Ford 500, but not enough to keep him from grinning ear-to-ear following the exciting finish that brought the former champion his 32nd career victory.

Jamie McMurray (42), Tony Stewart (20), Jimmie Johnson (48) and Matt Kenseth (17) stack it up four-high on Talladega's high banks. Among the strongest in the field, McMurray, Stewart and Kenseth combined to lead 126 laps in a race that had 20 different leaders.

TOP 10 QUALIFIERS

Pos.	Driver	Seconds	mph
1	Elliott Sadler	50.597	189.260
2	Dale Jarrett	50.727	188.775
3	Ryan Newman	50.775	188.596
4	Tony Stewart	50.782	188.570
5	Joe Nemechek	50.846	188.333
6	Bobby Labonte	50.853	188.307
7	Scott Riggs	50.863	188.270
8	Greg Biffle	50.872	188.237
9	Jimmie Johnson	50.878	188.215
10	Carl Edwards	50.909	188.100

At the other end of the spectrum were Matt Kenseth and Kurt Busch. Perhaps Kenseth could view his 35th-place finish at Dover as his an anomaly — the bad race in 10 that each of the contenders suffered last year. But with a 124-point deficit and eight drivers in front of him, Kenseth knew he could not withstand another one.

Kurt Busch, on the other hand, had a bad day at New Hampshire. Another off-day at Dover left him 170 points away from where he needed to be and with barely a flicker of hope of defending his crown.

But just when it seemed as though there was some sort of order taking hold within the Chase for the NASCAR NEXTEL Cup, all eyes turned south to a giant track in a small, central Alabama town named Talladega.

As motorsports scribes began to generate their pre-race storylines, words such as "wildcard" and "shakeup" started to appear in anticipation of the impact a visit to 2.66-mile tri-oval might have on the championship drive. And rightfully so. This was, after all, Talladega Superspeedway, where anything can, and often does, happen.

Such was the case in the UAW-Ford 500.

The pace car peels onto pit road, allowing front-row starters and teammates Elliott Sadler (38) and Dale Jarrett (88) to bring the field to the initial green flag. Sadler led nine of the first 16 laps before getting tangled up in the day's first multi-car accident.

(Above) The second big wreck of the race unfolds along the frontstretch after Casey Mears (41) got turned sideways in traffic. The race ended here for Mears, Jeff Gordon (24) and Scott Riggs (10), while championship contenders Rusty Wallace (2) and Greg Biffle (16) continued after repairs.

(Right) The Lowe's Chevrolet receives extensive repairs after Jimmie Johnson was involved in two major accidents before the halfway mark. The crew returned Johnson to the track where he finished 33 laps down, taking a big hit in the standings.

There were two significant accidents. The first came just 20 laps in when Johnson got into the back of pole-winner Elliott Sadler as they sailed through the high side of Turn 1. Johnson in turn was hit from behind by Dale Earnhardt Jr., and so it began. Michael Waltrip ended up getting some good roof time in his NAPA Chevrolet, and when it was all over, seven cars were involved. Among them was Martin, finished for the day in 41st place.

Down but not out, Johnson continued but was not able to avoid the second major incident, when Newman got a little too close to Casey Mears through the tri-oval on Lap 66, causing the Target Dodge to spin around in mid-pack. This time it was Scott Riggs who provided the acrobatics with multiple barrel-rolls, while seven other cars collected each other along the frontstretch. Newman escaped damage and continued but left contenders Wallace and Biffle sitting among the wreckage.

The action was no less furious at the front of the field, but it was of the intended variety. There were a whopping 50 lead changes spread among 20 different drivers as cars sliced, diced and bump-drafted in three- and four-wide packs over green-flag runs wedged between 10 caution periods.

(Above) Matt Kenseth (17), Jamie McMurray (42) and Ricky Rudd (21) guide the frontrunners around the mammoth super-speedway in three-wide formation. Among the group, Kenseth finished third ahead of (in order) Ryan Newman (12), Carl Edwards (99), Brian Vickers (25) and Sterling Marlin (40), while Joe Nemechek (01) grabbed another top 10 in ninth.

(Left) It had been 20 months since Dale Jarrett last uncorked the champagne, and he was quite happy to wet-down his teammates, who worked so hard for so long to make their return trip to Victory Lane.

UAW-FORD 500

NASCAR NEXTEL Cup Series Race No. 29

Fin. Pos.	Start Pos.	Car No.	Driver	Team	Laps	Laps Led	Status
1	2	88	Dale Jarrett	UPS Ford	190	2	Running
2	4	20	Tony Stewart	The Home Depot Chevrolet	190	65	Running
3	11	17	Matt Kenseth	DeWalt Power Tools Ford	190	23	Running
4	3	12	Ryan Newman	Alltel Dodge	190	12	Running
5	10	99	Carl Edwards	World Financial Group Ford	190	2	Running
6	27	25	Brian Vickers	GMAC/ditech.com Chevrolet	190	6	Running
7	16	40	Sterling Marlin	Coors Light Dodge	190		Running
8	21	97	Kurt Busch	Sharpie Ford	190	7	Running
9	5	01	Joe Nemechek	U.S. Army Chevrolet	190	1	Running
10	42	29	Kevin Harvick	GM Goodwrench Chevrolet	190	6	Running
11	6	18	Bobby Labonte	Interstate Batteries Chevrolet	190		Running
12	14	42	Jamie McMurray	Havoline/Texaco Dodge	190	38	Running
13	28	9	Kasey Kahne	Dodge Dealers/UAW Dodge	190		Running
14	32	19	Jeremy Mayfield	Dodge Dealers/UAW Dodge	190	1	Running
15	30	07	Dave Blaney	Jack Daniel's Chevrolet	190		Running
16	15	77 #	Travis Kvapil	Kodak/Jasper Eng. & Trans. Dodge	190	1	Running
17	36	22	Scott Wimmer	Caterpillar Dodge	190		Running
18	29	21	Ricky Rudd	Motorcraft Genuine Parts Ford	190	5	Running
19	33	4	Mike Wallace	Lucas Oil Chevrolet	190	1	Running
20	31	32	Bobby Hamilton Jr.	Tide Chevrolet	190		Running
21	40	43	Jeff Green	Cheerios/Betty Crocker Dodge	189	1	Running
22	43	37	Tony Raines	BoSPOKER.net Dodge	189		Running
23	22	7	Robby Gordon	Menard's Chevrolet	189		Running
24	38	45	Kyle Petty	Georgia-Pacific/Brawny Dodge	189		Running
25	41	2	Rusty Wallace	Miller Lite Dodge	185		Running
26	39	49	Ken Schrader	Red Baron Pizza Dodge	183	1	Accident
27	8	16	Greg Biffle	National Guard/Post-It Ford	172		Running
28	17	1	Martin Truex Jr.	Bass Pro Shops/Tracker Chevrolet	170		Engine
29	19	11	J.J. Yeley	FedEx Ground Chevrolet	165	1	Running
30	37	66	Kevin Lepage	Ace&TJ/Peak Fitness Ford	160		Running
31	9	48	Jimmie Johnson	Lowe's Chevrolet	158	3	Running
32	23	0	Mike Bliss	Best Buy Chevrolet	149		Accident
33	13	5 #	Kyle Busch	Kellogg's Chevrolet	146		Engine
34	1	38	Elliott Sadler	M&M's Ford	128	9	Running
35	18	31	Jeff Burton	Cingular Wireless Chevrolet	71		Accident
36	7	10	Scott Riggs	Checkers/Rally's Chevrolet	65		Accident
37	12	24	Jeff Gordon	DuPont Chevrolet	65		Accident
38	26	41	Casey Mears	Target Dodge	65	5	Accident
39	34	33	Kerry Earnhardt	Bass Pro Shops/Tracker Chevrolet	57		Accident
40	20	8	Dale Earnhardt Jr.	Budweiser Chevrolet	19		Accident
41	24	6	Mark Martin	Viagra Ford	19		Accident
42	25	15	Michael Waltrip	NAPA Auto Parts Chevrolet	19		Accident
43	35	00	Mike Skinner	Aaron's Ford	19		Accident

Raybestos Rookie of the Year Contender.

Chase for the NASCAR NEXTEL Cup Standings
(With 7 Races Remaining)

Pos.	Driver	Points	Behind	Change
1	Tony Stewart	5519	—	+4
2	Ryan Newman	5515	-4	+1
3	Rusty Wallace	5443	-76	-1
4	Jimmie Johnson	5437	-82	-3
5	Greg Biffle	5421	-98	+1
6	Carl Edwards	5419	-100	+2
7	Matt Kenseth	5408	-111	+2
8	Jeremy Mayfield	5407	-112	-1
9	Mark Martin	5381	-138	-5
10	Kurt Busch	5339	-180	—

Most prolific at the front were Kenseth, who led seven times for 23 laps, Jamie McMurray (nine times for 38 laps) and Stewart, who once again spent the most time leading a restrictor-plate race, this time for 65 laps on 11 different occasions.

The eighth caution ended with 57 of the prescribed 188 laps remaining to begin an extended green-flag run that would require one more stop for fuel. Stewart, McMurray, and then Kenseth took their turns pacing the field until Ken Schrader's spin in Turn 4 produced the ninth yellow flag. With a mere handful of laps left, a green-white-checkered dash to the finish would be required.

Dale Jarrett, whose sole lead to that point had come on Lap 3 after starting on the front row alongside Sadler, lined up fourth for the final restart and watched intently as Stewart and McMurray fanned out side by side. Glued to the bumper of Stewart's Monte Carlo, Jarrett pushed past McMurray, Newman and Kenseth before Stewart dropped to the inside in his bid to seal the win.

Now alongside the orange-and-white Chevrolet, Jarrett felt a sudden jolt from behind. Looking up, he could see that the boost had come from Kenseth's DeWalt Ford, and with the white flag in sight, the UPS machine pushed ahead to take a slight lead.

Just then Kyle Petty spun on the backstretch, which brought out the final caution and instantly finalized the event. With that, Jarrett ended an agonizing 98-race winless string dating back to February 2003 and simultaneously confirmed the appointment of Todd Parrott as the team's new crew chief slightly more than one week ago.

"I've been very fortunate in my career to win a lot of important races — big races," an elated Jarrett said, "a lot of them with this guy (Parrott). ... But at this point in time in my career, I'm not sure there's anything that was more important than getting that push down the backstretch from Matt Kenseth and taking the checkered flag here."

Stewart was credited with second place, which combined with Johnson's troubles, put him back atop the Chase for the NASCAR NEXTEL Cup standings. Kenseth was listed third over Newman by mere inches after a frame-by-frame review of official NASCAR timing and scoring video following the race, leaving Newman only four points shy of Stewart with seven races to go.

BANQUET 400
PRESENTED BY CONAGRA FOODS

When the Chase for the NASCAR NEXTEL Cup contenders left Talladega Superspeedway, a few were licking their chops, while others were licking their wounds.

Some escaped Talladega unscathed — even better off than when they had arrived. Tony Stewart was smiling the most. A strong, second-place showing buffeted by a few extra bonus points for leading the most laps allowed Stewart to turn his decline to fifth place following Dover into a momentary blip on an otherwise outstanding record over the past few months. Now back on top of the standings, Stewart faced Kansas comforted by the knowledge that three of his four career starts there had resulted in top-10 finishes, the other a 14th place one year ago.

Mark Martin (6) sets sail ahead of teammate Greg Biffle's National Guard Ford at Kansas Speedway. Martin took the lead for the first time on Lap 122 and stayed in front for 139 of the remaining 146 laps to claim his first points win of the year.

(Right) Crew Chief Larry Carter trims a bit of sheet metal off the bottom of the Miller Lite Dodge before driver Rusty Wallace goes racing at Kansas. Although Wallace started 33rd, he picked up 26 positions during the race to gain another top-10 finish.

(Below Right) Denny Hamlin (11), in his NASCAR NEXTEL Cup Series debut for Joe Gibbs Racing, slides past Stuart Kirby (51), who was making the sixth start of his young career. Hamlin raised a few eyebrows right off the bat by posting the seventh-fastest lap in Bud Pole qualifying.

(Below) Relaxed and confident, Tony Stewart strolls toward the starting grid where he would roll off from the ninth position. "Smoke" was fresh off a strong run at Talladega that put him back on top of the standings after a one-week hiatus.

TOP 10 QUALIFIERS

Pos.	Driver	Seconds	mph
1	Matt Kenseth	29.858	*180.856
2	Elliott Sadler	29.881	180.717
3	Jeff Gordon	29.922	180.469
4	Scott Wimmer	29.923	180.463
5	Carl Edwards	29.931	180.415
6	Kevin Lepage	29.938	180.373
7	Denny Hamlin	29.950	180.301
8	Greg Biffle	30.014	179.916
9	Tony Stewart	30.025	179.850
10	Kurt Busch	30.060	179.641

* Track Record

Like Stewart, Ryan Newman wore an obvious grin when he arrived at Kansas. His fourth-place run at Talladega cut his point deficit by eight, and combined with the fortunes of others, he was now just four points back of Stewart with no one else close enough to be breathing down his neck. A record of one win and three top fives in four career starts at Kansas gave Newman reason to be optimistic that the Banquet 400 would further galvanize his advantage in the standings.

For Jimmie Johnson, Rusty Wallace and Greg Biffle, looking ahead after Talladega was a matter of damage control. All three drivers went to Talladega solidly in the championship hunt but were caught up in accidents and now were separated from Stewart and Newman by a significant point gap. None of the three were out of it by any means, but each faced an uphill struggle from here on out that would leave little room for error.

All Mark Martin could do as he left the state of Alabama was shake his head and think about what might have been. He arrived at Talladega only 21 points away from the top of the standings but lost 117 points after being caught up in an accident that was no fault of his own. Now 138 behind and mired in ninth place, he considerd his shot at winning the championship all but over.

Not unexpectedly, Roush drivers Matt Kenseth (17), Kurt Busch (97) and Greg Biffle (16) cruise the 1.5-mile oval at the head of the field. Kenseth and Biffle dominated much of the race until their Roush teammate, Mark Martin, took control.

(Right) The Target crew attacks their Dodge on a quick stop for driver Casey Mears. Like Rusty Wallace, Mears picked up 26 spots during the day and grabbed his second top 10 in the last three events.

(Below) Jeff Green (43), Jimmie Johnson (48) and Rusty Wallace (2) use up the racing lines while Scott Wimmer (22) searches for an opening to advance. Wimmer showed great speed early on after a fourth-place qualifying run, but dropped to 27th by the finish, one spot behlnd Green.

But Martin, the consummate professional, mustered the inner strength to push his personal disappointment aside and strode into Kansas Speedway with the mindset that this race, like every other he's entered in his career, was an opportunity to score a victory.

Martin quietly posted the 19th-fastest lap in a qualifying session that produced some surprising results. Matt Kenseth, who entered the season with one Bud Pole in 184 career starts, put down a track-record lap at 180.856 mph to win his second pole in the last seven races. He was

(Above) Mark Martin waits for service under one of seven cautions during the race. A swift two-tire stop by his crew before the halfway point was the key to Martin's win. Later, he called them his "heroes."

(Left) Ricky Rudd (21) holds his line ahead of Jeff Gordon (24) on Kansas' 15-degree banks. Rudd kept his position and picked up his eighth top 10 of the season in ninth, one spot ahead of Gordon.

BANQUET 400
presented by ConAgra Foods

NASCAR NEXTEL Cup Series Race No. 30

Fin. Pos.	Start Pos.	Car No.	Driver	Team	Laps	Laps Led	Status
1	19	6	Mark Martin	Viagra Ford	267	139	Running
2	8	16	Greg Biffle	National Guard Ford	267	47	Running
3	5	99	Carl Edwards	Office Depot Ford	267	1	Running
4	9	20	Tony Stewart	The Home Depot Chevrolet	267	1	Running
5	1	17	Matt Kenseth	DeWalt Power Tools Ford	267	71	Running
6	22	48	Jimmie Johnson	Lowe's Chevrolet	267	1	Running
7	33	2	Rusty Wallace	Miller Lite Dodge	267	1	Running
8	34	41	Casey Mears	Target Dodge	267		Running
9	29	21	Ricky Rudd	Motorcraft Genuine Parts Ford	267		Running
10	3	24	Jeff Gordon	DuPont Chevrolet	267		Running
11	17	25	Brian Vickers	GMAC/ditech.com Chevrolet	267		Running
12	2	38	Elliott Sadler	M&M's Ford	267		Running
13	13	40	Sterling Marlin	Coors Light Dodge	267		Running
14	10	97	Kurt Busch	Sharpie Ford	267		Running
15	28	0	Mike Bliss	Net Zero Best Buy Chevrolet	267		Running
16	14	19	Jeremy Mayfield	Dodge Dealers/UAW Dodge	267	2	Running
17	24	49	Ken Schrader	Schwan's Home Service Dodge	267		Running
18	30	42	Jamie McMurray	Havoline/Texaco Dodge	267		Running
19	42	9	Kasey Kahne	Dodge Dealers/UAW Dodge	267		Running
20	16	01	Joe Nemechek	U.S. Army Chevrolet	267		Running
21	21	5 #	Kyle Busch	CARQUEST Chevrolet	267		Running
22	37	77 #	Travis Kvapil	Kodak Mammography/Jasper Dodge	267	1	Running
23	11	12	Ryan Newman	Alltel Dodge	267		Running
24	20	29	Kevin Harvick	GM Goodwrench Chevrolet	267	1	Running
25	26	07	Dave Blaney	Jack Daniel's Chevrolet	267		Running
26	12	43	Jeff Green	Cheerios/Betty Crocker Dodge	266		Running
27	4	22	Scott Wimmer	Caterpillar Dodge	266		Running
28	40	31	Jeff Burton	Cingular Wireless Chevrolet	266	1	Running
29	23	45	Kyle Petty	Georgia-Pacific/Northern Quilted Dodge	266		Running
30	41	10	Scott Riggs	Valvoline Chevrolet	265		Running
31	32	36	Boris Said	CENTRIX Financial Chevrolet	265		Running
32	7	11	Denny Hamlin	FedEx Kinko's Chevrolet	265		Running
33	35	44	Terry Labonte	Kellogg's Chevrolet	265		Running
34	38	8	Dale Earnhardt Jr.	Budweiser Chevrolet	265		Running
35	15	4	Mike Wallace	Lucas Oil Chevrolet	263	1	Running
36	6	66	Kevin Lepage	Peak Fitness/EAS Ford	263		Running
37	43	51	Stuart Kirby	Marathon American Spirit Chevrolet	263		Running
38	31	88	Dale Jarrett	UPS Ford	258		Running
39	39	18	Bobby Labonte	Interstate Batteries Chevrolet	222		Accident
40	36	15	Michael Waltrip	NAPA Auto Parts Chevrolet	215		Engine
41	27	92	P.J. Jones	Fox Collision Centers Dodge	184		Handling
42	18	02	Brandon Ash	Ash Racing Engines Ford	161		Rear End
43	25	32	Bobby Hamilton Jr.	Tide Chevrolet	63		Overheating

Raybestos Rookie of the Year Contender.

Chase for the NASCAR NEXTEL Cup Standings
(With 6 Races Remaining)

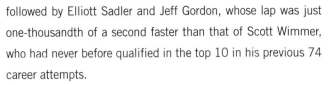

Pos.	Driver	Points	Behind	Change
1	Tony Stewart	5684	—	—
2	Ryan Newman	5609	-75	—
3	Greg Biffle	5596	-88	+2
4	Rusty Wallace	5594	-90	-1
5	Jimmie Johnson	5592	-92	-1
6	Carl Edwards	5589	-95	—
7	Mark Martin	5571	-113	+2
8	Matt Kenseth	5568	-116	-1
9	Jeremy Mayfield	5527	-157	-1
10	Kurt Busch	5460	-224	—

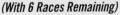

followed by Elliott Sadler and Jeff Gordon, whose lap was just one-thousandth of a second faster than that of Scott Wimmer, who had never before qualified in the top 10 in his previous 74 career attempts.

Carl Edwards was fifth fastest in the session followed by Kevin Lepage and Denny Hamlin. For Lepage, making his 17th start of the year, it was only the second time this season he had qualified better than 24th (he qualified eighth for the Daytona 500), while Hamlin's seventh-fastest time came in his NASCAR NEXTEL Cup Series debut.

Newman turned in the 11th-best effort in qualifying, but a faulty transmission in the Alltel Dodge had to be replaced before the start of the race, which put Newman at the back of the field on Sunday.

Kenseth verified his qualifying speed by jumping to the early lead, which he held for all but one of the first 72 laps. Biffle stepped up next and led all but two of the next 49 trips around the 1.5-mile oval while Roush teammates Martin, Edwards and Kenseth were joined by Wallace, Johnson, Jeff Gordon and Ricky Rudd to fill in the top 10.

The definitive moment in the race came when the fifth yellow flag flew on Lap 121, sending the leaders to pit road where crew chief Pat Tryson called for a two-tire stop on Martin's Ford — a move that pushed the No. 6 to the front of the field.

On the restart with 140 laps to go, Martin bolted at the drop of the green flag and never looked back. His car was superb and the veteran driver made no mistakes, giving up the lead only twice when he had to pit for fresh tires and fuel.

As the laps wound down, Biffle made one last charge, able to slowly but steadily close the gap on the leader. But 15 miles short of the finish, Biffle's advantage waned and Martin was able to edge away to a half-second lead, which he maintained to the checkered flag.

Beaming in Victory Lane after the 35th win of his career, Martin, predictably, deflected praise to his team. "[This win] was one that is well deserved by my team," Martin said, "and as long as I live I will remember it for the feeling that it feels like to give my team. They deserve to win so much.

"No matter what happens from here on out, we've had a great year, we've had a great race. We've won here. We won the All-Star race. We made the Chase, and these guys are my heroes."

UAW-GM QUALITY 500

Clouds break in front of the late-afternoon sun as team members view the action on the track during practice for the UAW-GM Quality 500 at Lowe's Motor Speedway.

Jimmie Johnson was happy to arrive at Lowe's Motor Speedway for the fifth event in the Chase for the NASCAR NEXTEL Cup. Troubles at Talladega Superspeedway two weeks ago had resulted in a 31st-place finish and dropped him from first place to fourth in the point standings, 82 points behind the leader. Last week at Kansas, Johnson had a solid sixth-place showing, but all five drivers who finished ahead of him were also Chase for the NASCAR NEXTEL Cup competitors. The end result was that Johnson dropped another position to fifth place and was now 92 points behind Tony Stewart, who was in first place.

Johnson was not discouraged, though. He remembered one year ago when he arrived at this event after finishing 37th at Talladega and 32nd at Kansas. Then, he was listed in ninth place in the Chase for the NASCAR NEXTEL Cup point standings, 247 points behind Kurt Busch, who was the leader at the time.

Johnson won the 2004 UAW-GM Quality 500 and then won three more times — at Martinsville, Atlanta and Darlington — in the last five races. He finished sixth at Phoenix during that five-race span, was second in the last race of the season at Homestead-Miami Speedway and nearly won the NASCAR NEXTEL Cup Series title. In the final point tally, Johnson was only eight points behind Kurt Busch, who won the 2004 NASCAR NEXTEL Cup Series championship.

With that in mind, Johnson took his Chevrolet onto the track in Bud Pole qualifying and posted the third-fastest lap behind Ryan Newman, who was second fastest, and Elliott

(Right) Elliott Sadler (left) and new crew chief Kevin Buskirk, congratulate each other after Sadler posted a track record of 193.216 miles per hour in Bud Pole qualifying. This was the team's third front-row start since Buskirk took the position four weeks ago at Dover.

(Below) Sadler was fast in the race as well; he led eight times for 112 laps before this spin on Lap 254 took him from winning contention.

TOP 10 QUALIFIERS

Pos.	Driver	Seconds	mph
1	Elliott Sadler	27.948	*193.216
2	Ryan Newman	27.961	193.126
3	Jimmie Johnson	28.001	192.850
4	Tony Stewart	28.022	192.706
5	Bobby Labonte	28.027	192.671
6	Mark Martin	28.123	192.014
7	Kurt Busch	28.131	191.959
8	Carl Edwards	28.145	191.864
9	Casey Mears	28.151	191.823
10	Jeff Gordon	28.167	191.714

* Track Record

(Above) Matt Kenseth (17) uses the low groove to challenge Casey Mears (41) for position. Mears continued to show recent strength with a sixth-place finish, his third top 10 in the last four events.

(Left) Chase for the NASCAR NEXTEL Cup contenders Kurt Busch (97) and Ryan Newman (12) race together through Lowe's Motor Speedway's 24-degree banking. Both drivers made significant gains in the standings; Busch picked up 82 points on his second-place run, while Newman closed to 17 points out of first on his seventh-place effort.

Sadler, who set a track record with a speed of 193.216 mph and won his fourth Bud Pole of the 2005 NASCAR NEXTEL Cup Series season.

The encouragement Johnson felt from his good qualifying effort did not last, however. A faulty engine required replacement prior to the race, which, according to the rules, meant Johnson would have to start the race near the back of the field.

Newman took the lead from Sadler on the first lap of the UAW-GM Quality 500 and led the first 21 laps before Sadler took over the first position. Sadler led eight times for a total of

(Right) The Home Depot team goes to work on their Chevrolet after Tony Stewart spun and hit the wall while leading the race. The incident proved costly as Stewart lost eight laps and ultimately his 75-point margin in the standings.

(Below) The entire field reports to pit road during the night's fourth caution at Lap 95. An event-record 15 yellow flags kept pit crews hopping throughout the evening.

(Above) Joe Nemechek (01) feels the heat of Jimmie Johnson's smoking Monte Carlo hot on his tail. Nemechek drove to the lead after a late-race restart, but it didn't take long for Johnson to track him down.

(Left) Jimmie Johnson (48) pulls alongside Joe Nemechek's U.S. Army Chevrolet as they battle for the top spot along the frontstretch. The two drivers traded the point three times over a seven-lap stretch before Johnson pulled away for good.

UAW-GM QUALITY 500

NASCAR NEXTEL Cup Series Race No. 31

Fin. Pos.	Start Pos.	Car No.	Driver	Team	Laps	Laps Led	Status
1	3	48	Jimmie Johnson	Lowe's Chevrolet	336	13	Running
2	7	97	Kurt Busch	IRWIN Industrial Tools Ford	336	2	Running
3	21	16	Greg Biffle	National Guard Ford	336	4	Running
4	12	01	Joe Nemechek	U.S. Army Chevrolet	336	11	Running
5	6	6	Mark Martin	Viagra Ford	336		Running
6	9	41	Casey Mears	Target Dodge	336	9	Running
7	2	12	Ryan Newman	Alltel Dodge	336	42	Running
8	39	11	Denny Hamlin	FedEx Express Chevrolet	336	1	Running
9	31	21	Ricky Rudd	Motorcraft Genuine Parts Ford	336	4	Running
10	8	99	Carl Edwards	Scotts Miracle-Gro Ford	336		Running
11	37	19	Jeremy Mayfield	Dodge Dealers/UAW Dodge	336	1	Running
12	25	25	Brian Vickers	GMAC/ditech.com Chevrolet	336		Running
13	22	07	Dave Blaney	Jack Daniel's Chevrolet	336		Running
14	19	31	Jeff Burton	Cingular Wireless Chevrolet	336		Running
15	16	45	Kyle Petty	Georgia-Pacific/Brawny Dodge	336		Running
16	43	09	Johnny Sauter	Miccosukee Resort Dodge	336		Running
17	42	77 #	Travis Kvapil	Kodak/Jasper Eng. & Trans. Dodge	336	1	Running
18	5	18	Bobby Labonte	Interstate Batteries Chevrolet	336		Running
19	41	43	Jeff Green	Petty Fan Fest/Bugles Dodge	336	1	Running
20	14	22	Scott Wimmer	Caterpillar Dodge	336	1	Running
21	17	66	Kevin Lepage	Peak Fitness Ford	336		Running
22	26	00	David Reutimann	State Farm Corn Dogs Chevrolet	336		Running
23	33	9	Kasey Kahne	Dodge Dealers/UAW Dodge	336	35	Running
24	27	2	Rusty Wallace	Miller Lite Dodge	336		Running
25	4	20	Tony Stewart	The Home Depot Chevrolet	328	61	Running
26	18	17	Matt Kenseth	Carhartt Ford	326		Running
27	1	38	Elliott Sadler	M&M's Ford	326	112	Running
28	35	29	Kevin Harvick	Snap-On/GM Goodwrench Chevrolet	291		Running
29	32	15	Michael Waltrip	NAPA Auto Parts Chevrolet	278	31	Accident
30	20	88	Dale Jarrett	UPS Ford	278		Accident
31	29	42	Jamie McMurray	Havoline/Texaco Dodge	278		Accident
32	23	7	Robby Gordon	Jim Beam Chevrolet	278		Accident
33	15	10	Scott Riggs	Valvoline Chevrolet	267		Accident
34	40	49	Ken Schrader	Schwan's Home Service Dodge	255		Engine
35	11	0	Mike Bliss	Net Zero Best Buy Chevrolet	252		Accident
36	34	39	David Stremme	Commit Lozenges Dodge	243		Accident
37	38	51	Stuart Kirby	Marathon American Spirit Oil Chevrolet	213		Handling
38	10	24	Jeff Gordon	DuPont Chevrolet	151		Accident
39	13	5 #	Kyle Busch	Kellogg's/Delphi Chevrolet	150	7	Accident
40	30	40	Sterling Marlin	Coors Light Dodge	124		Accident
41	24	32	Bobby Hamilton Jr.	Tide Chevrolet	94		Accident
42	28	8	Dale Earnhardt Jr.	Budweiser Chevrolet	61		Accident
43	36	4	Mike Wallace	Lucas Oil Chevrolet	40		Timing belt

\# Raybestos Rookie of the Year Contender.

Chase for the NASCAR NEXTEL Cup Standings
(With 5 Races Remaining)

Pos.	Driver	Points	Behind	Change
1	Tony Stewart	5777	—	—
2	Jimmie Johnson	5777	—	+3
3	Greg Biffle	5766	-11	—
4	Ryan Newman	5760	-17	-2
5	Mark Martin	5726	-51	+2
6	Carl Edwards	5723	-54	—
7	Rusty Wallace	5685	-92	-3
8	Jeremy Mayfield	5662	-115	+1
9	Matt Kenseth	5653	-124	-1
10	Kurt Busch	5635	-142	—

112 laps and appeared to be a contender to take the victory, but he spun his Ford and brushed the wall. The damage to his car was not severe enough to keep him from returning to the race, but his chances of winning were over.

Like Sadler, Stewart had a fast car and established himself in the lead five different times for a total of 61 laps, but he, too, spun and made contact with the wall, which took him from winning contention.

Meanwhile, Johnson was battling his own adversity. As if starting near the back of the field was not enough to overcome, Johnson's car developed electrical problems that required a stop on pit road to allow his crew members to replace the battery in his Chevrolet. Later, a flat tire sent him back to the pits for an unscheduled stop.

But Johnson somehow was able to remain on the lead lap, and as the field lined up for a restart with 22 laps remaining in the race, Johnson was in third place behind Ricky Rudd and Joe Nemechek.

When the green flag waved, Nemechek wasted no time and jumped into the lead, leaving Johnson to race with Rudd for second place. Johnson was able to gain the position and set his sights on Nemechek.

With 16 laps to go, Johnson passed Nemechek's Chevrolet to take his first lead of the race. Nemechek, however, came right back and regained the lead on the next lap. Nemechek led five more laps until, with 11 of the scheduled 334 laps to go, Johnson made one last challenge and passed Nemechek for the last time and drove to victory despite a green-white-checkered finish that was forced when Rusty Wallace spun along the backstretch.

"This was an amazing run," Johnson said after the race. "We had to start from the back. We had a flat tire at one point. We had an alternator and battery issue. We just overcame a lot of stuff. The guys (his crew) did an incredible job of keeping their cool in the pits and changed out what we needed.

"To get a fourth [straight] win here, I couldn't pick a better place. I can't believe we did this."

The win, combined with Stewart's 25th-place finish, moved Johnson into a tie with Stewart for first place in the point standings with five races to go in the 2005 Chase for the NASCAR NEXTEL Cup.

SUBWAY 500

The results of a crazy night at Lowe's Motor Speedway had a considerable effect on the point standings. Tony Stewart took a 75-point margin over Ryan Newman into the event, with Greg Biffle, Rusty Wallace, Jimmie Johnson and Carl Edwards all bunched together within 20 points of Newman and waiting for something — anything — to happen to The Home Depot Chevrolet that would give them a chance to make up some ground.

Stewart's cushion deflated as quickly as his tire did after running over a piece of debris while leading the race, an unfortunate stroke of luck that sent him backing into the wall. A few laps in the pits dropped Stewart to a 25th-place finish, and that combined with Johnson's come-from-behind victory left the two rivals in a dead heat atop the standings.

Biffle and Newman also benefited from Stewart's misfortune, both using top-10 finishes in the UAW-GM Quality 500 to pull to within 17 points of the leaders. Mark Martin, who added a fifth-place finish to his win at Kansas the week before, climbed back into contention by gaining four spots and 87 points in two weeks and left Charlotte 51 points behind, while Martin's Roush Racing teammate, Edwards, knocked 41 points off of his deficit and sat just three points behind Martin.

Dale Earnhardt Jr. (8) leans on Scott Wimmer (22) as the two beat-up machines tackle the tight turns at Martinsville. This kind of action was typical in the race that produced 19 cautions for 113 of the 500-lap distance.

Veterans Rusty Wallace (2) and Mark Martin (6) give each other room as they race through the nearly-flat, concrete corners. Bad luck beset both drivers in the Subway 500, and by the end of the day their hopes of winning the championship were nearly extinguished.

TOP 10 QUALIFIERS

Pos.	Driver	Seconds	mph
1	Tony Stewart	19.306	*98.083
2	Ricky Rudd	19.324	97.992
3	Rusty Wallace	19.336	97.931
4	Ryan Newman	19.340	97.911
5	Denny Hamlin	19.355	97.835
6	Jimmie Johnson	19.412	97.548
7	Jeremy Mayfield	19.433	97.442
8	Joe Nemechek	19.455	97.332
9	Elliott Sadler	19.463	97.292
10	Bobby Labonte	19.479	97.212

* Track Record

Denny Hamlin, driving the FedEx Chevrolet in his third career start, challenges Ryan Newman (12) on the inside. Hamlin caught a lot of attention while driving to his second-straight eighth-place finish, while Newman took 10th and moved up one position in the championship standings.

For Wallace, the opportunity to capitalize on Stewart's troubles came to sudden halt just a couple of laps from the end, when a flat tire sent him spinning down the backstretch. Instead of the top-five finish he appeared to have in hand, the Miller Lite driver limped home in 24th place, one position ahead of Stewart. Although he lost only two points to the leaders, Wallace fell three positions to seventh place in the standings. Time was running out, Wallace knew, and he quickly turned his attention to Martinsville Speedway, site of seven career wins and an opportunity to turn things around.

Stewart quashed any inclinations that the stumble at Charlotte was anything more than that when he rolled onto the tight, little half mile in south-central Virginia and laid down a track-record lap to win his third Bud Pole of the season. Stewart's lap at slightly over 98 mph barely edged out that of Ricky Rudd, who was hoping to put the Wood Brothers, based in nearby Stuart, Va., on the pole at their home track.

Tony Stewart (20) gets boxed in behind Scott Riggs (10) while working through traffic, with Joe Nemechek (01), Mike Bliss (0) and Sterling Marlin (40) on the outside. Stewart was the man to beat while running up front, but he couldn't overtake Gordon once the DuPont Chevrolet got the lead.

(Right) Matt Kenseth (17) squeezes Scott Wimmer (22) to the inside, while Jeff Burton (31) applies pressure from behind. Kenseth had his second poor finish in the last five starts and fell out of championship contention, while Burton had a good run to his third top five of the season.

(Below) Bobby Labonte waits for fresh tires and fuel from his Interstate Batteries crew. Labonte, a Martinsville winner in 2002, drove a great race to a very welcome fourth-place finish, his first top five in 13 events.

Wallace, ready to apply his knowledge and past short-track success, lined up directly behind Stewart in third, with teammate Newman on his right. Championship contenders Johnson and Jeremy Mayfield were sixth and seventh behind Denny Hamlin, who had been extremely impressive in his first two starts driving the No. 11 FedEx Chevrolet for Joe Gibbs Racing.

One year had passed since the tragic airplane accident in the nearby mountains of Virginia that so devastated everyone at Hendrick Motorsports, as well as the rest of the racing community. Perhaps no driver was more affected by the tragedy than Jeff Gordon who, over his 12-year career with the organization, had become extremely close to team owner Rick Hendrick and his entire family.

As if Gordon needed another emotional dip on his roller-coaster season that included a stunning end to his campaign for a fifth championship and longtime crew chief Robbie Loomis

Jeff Gordon (24) extends his lead while Jimmie Johnson and Tony Stewart give chase. Neither Johnson nor Stewart, tied in the points at the start of the race, could catch Gordon in the final 100 laps and wound up battling for second between themselves.

(Left) Steve Letarte (right) makes his fist visit to Victory Lane as a crew chief in only his sixth start at the position. For Jeff Gordon (left), the 73rd win of his career was his seventh at Martinsville, tying him with Rusty Wallace with the most wins among active drivers at the Virginia short track.

SUBWAY 500

NASCAR NEXTEL Cup Series Race No. 32

Fin. Pos.	Start Pos.	Car No.	Driver	Team	Laps	Laps Led	Status
1	15	24	Jeff Gordon	DuPont Chevrolet	500	151	Running
2	1	20	Tony Stewart	The Home Depot Chevrolet	500	283	Running
3	6	48	Jimmie Johnson	Lowe's Chevrolet	500		Running
4	10	18	Bobby Labonte	Interstate Batteries Chevrolet	500		Running
5	21	31	Jeff Burton	Cingular Wireless Chevrolet	500		Running
6	14	97	Kurt Busch	IRWIN Industrial Tools Ford	500		Running
7	30	42	Jamie McMurray	Havoline/Texaco Dodge	500		Running
8	5	11	Denny Hamlin	FedEx Freight Chevrolet	500		Running
9	23	5#	Kyle Busch	Kellogg's Chevrolet	500		Running
10	4	12	Ryan Newman	Alltel Dodge	500		Running
11	2	21	Ricky Rudd	Motorcraft Genuine Parts Ford	500	2	Running
12	25	17	Matt Kenseth	DeWalt Power Tools Ford	500	19	Running
13	24	49	Ken Schrader	Schwan's Home Service Dodge	500	17	Running
14	13	45	Kyle Petty	Georgia-Pacific/Brawny Dodge	500		Running
15	29	29	Kevin Harvick	GM Goodwrench Chevrolet	500		Running
16	19	07	Dave Blaney	Jack Daniel's Chevrolet	500	10	Running
17	34	9	Kasey Kahne	Dodge Dealers/UAW Dodge	500		Running
18	20	8	Dale Earnhardt Jr.	Budweiser Chevrolet	500		Running
19	3	2	Rusty Wallace	Miller Lite Dodge	500		Running
20	22	16	Greg Biffle	National Guard/Subway Ford	500	6	Running
21	12	77#	Travis Kvapil	Kodak/Jasper Eng. & Trans. Dodge	500		Running
22	16	41	Casey Mears	Target Dodge	499		Running
23	8	01	Joe Nemechek	U.S. Army Chevrolet	499		Running
24	26	10	Scott Riggs	Valvoline/Herbie Fully Loaded Chevrolet	499		Running
25	36	22	Scott Wimmer	Caterpillar Dodge	499		Running
26	18	99	Carl Edwards	Office Depot Ford	499		Running
27	39	15	Michael Waltrip	NAPA Auto Parts Chevrolet	498	12	Running
28	7	19	Jeremy Mayfield	Dodge Dealers/UAW Dodge	497		Running
29	9	38	Elliott Sadler	M&M's Ford	497		Running
30	43	32	Bobby Hamilton Jr.	Tide Chevrolet	494		Running
31	28	88	Dale Jarrett	UPS Ford	492		Running
32	41	66	Hermie Sadler	Kilgore for Governor Ford	489		Running
33	38	08	Derrike Cope	Royal Admin. Services/EPH Chevrolet	488		Running
34	35	6	Mark Martin	Viagra Ford	468		Running
35	27	4	Mike Wallace	Lucas Oil Chevrolet	448		Running
36	17	25	Brian Vickers	GMAC/ditech.com Chevrolet	425		Running
37	11	43	Jeff Green	Cheerios/Betty Crocker Dodge	409		Engine
38	32	40	Sterling Marlin	Coors Light Dodge	370		Accident
39	37	09	Bobby Hamilton	Miccosukee Resort Dodge	339		Oil Leak
40	40	37	Jimmy Spencer	BoSPOKER.net Dodge	235		Electrical
41	31	0	Mike Bliss	Haas Automation/Best Buy Chevrolet	172		Accident
42	33	7	Robby Gordon	Menard's Chevrolet	115		Engine
43	42	95	Stanton Barrett	Barrett Motorsports Chevrolet	110		Engine

Raybestos Rookie of the Year Contender.

Chase for the NASCAR NEXTEL Cup Standings
(With 4 Races Remaining)

Pos.	Driver	Points	Behind	Change
1	Tony Stewart	5957	—	—
2	Jimmie Johnson	5942	-15	—
3	Ryan Newman	5894	-63	+1
4	Greg Biffle	5874	-83	-1
5	Carl Edwards	5808	-149	+1
6	Rusty Wallace	5791	-166	+1
7	Mark Martin	5787	-170	-2
8	Kurt Busch	5785	-172	+2
9	Matt Kenseth	5785	-172	—
10	Jeremy Mayfield	5741	-216	-2

leaving to rejoin Petty Enterprises, the six-time Martinsville winner climbed behind the wheel of his DuPont Chevrolet with the memories of close friends lost weighing heavy on his mind. Starting 15th in the Subway 500, Gordon knew the best medicine he could give his team and the whole HEDRICK organization would be a return trip to Victory Lane this weekend.

Stewart took control of the race on a beautiful Sunday afternoon and appeared to have things well in hand, leading 283 laps until the event's 13th caution flew on Lap 343. That's when 26-year-old Steve Letarte — calling the shots in only his sixth race as a crew chief — made the decision for Gordon to forego a stop on pit road, a move that put the Hendrick driver out front for the first time in the race.

With track position at his advantage, Gordon led all but six of the remaining 157 laps — including the last 141 — on the way to an emotional and very satisfying victory.

"That's all him," Gordon said of the critical choice by Letarte. "He's the one that said stay out, and it's up to the crew chief and the guys in the pits to see the big picture. I knew we needed track position. We were just phenomenal once we got out front."

Behind Gordon, Stewart and Johnson provided most of the drama over the closing laps. Running third with 11 laps to go, Stewart closed on the Lowe's Chevrolet in Turns 1 & 2 and gave Johnson enough of a nudge from behind to move underneath and take the runner-up spot.

With Johnson third and Stewart taking the 10-point lap-leader bonus, the Joe Gibbs Racing driver moved 15 points ahead of Johnson in their battle atop the standings.

The Subway 500 was far less kind to veterans Martin and Wallace. Martin, driving a backup car after wrecking his primary mount in practice, had to abuse his Ford while trying to climb through the field and eventually lost his brakes.

Wallace ran a smart race and seemed to be headed for a top-five finish but was hit by Jeff Burton with less than 20 laps to go. Although he remained on the lead lap, the 1989 champion fell to 19th as he crossed the finish line.

With four races remaining in the Chase for the NASCAR NEXTEL Cup, the championship hopes of both Martin and Wallace appeared to be over.

BASS PRO SHOPS MBNA 500

Carl Edwards waits for service to be completed before heading back into action in the Bass Pro Shops MBNA 500. Once in front, quick work by Edwards' crew kept him where he needed to be to secure the important win.

The results from last week's race at Martinsville appeared to have narrowed the list of contenders somewhat. Going into the race, Tony Stewart and Jimmie Johnson were deadlocked at the top of the standings, with Greg Biffle just 11 points back and only six points ahead of fourth-place Ryan Newman.

Behind them, Roush Racing teammates Mark Martin and Carl Edwards sat fifth and sixth in the standings, 51 and 54 points behind, respectively. Rusty Wallace was 92 points away from Stewart, followed by Jeremy Mayfield, Matt Kenseth and 10th-place Kurt Busch, who was only 142 out of first place. With five races remaining, all 10 of the Chase for the NASCAR NEXTEL Cup drivers were squarely in the running.

Martinsville, however, cast a whole new light on the championship picture. The battle between Stewart and Johnson became a bit more spirited after Stewart moved Johnson out of the way in the closing laps to take over the second spot, dropping Johnson to third in the final rundown. Stewart also picked up the lap-leader bonus and that, combined with Johnson's

(Above) An Air Force B-52 passes over Atlanta Motor Speedway minutes before the command to start engines. A crowd estimated at 120,000 fans was on hand on a beautiful afternoon in Georgia for the seventh event in the Chase for the NASCAR NEXTEL Cup.

(Right) Jeff Burton (31) and Jamie McMurray (42) work their way toward the top 10. Burton started 41st and gained more positions than any other driver, finishing eighth, while McMurray drove from 28th to sixth and maintained his grip on 11th place in the point standings over Jeff Gordon.

failure to lead a lap, gave The Home Depot driver a 15-point cushion going to Atlanta. With those two drivers finishing second and third behind race-winner Jeff Gordon, everyone else in the championship hunt lost ground to the leaders.

Ryan Newman moved up one position to third place, 63 points behind Stewart, replacing Greg Biffle, who dropped a spot to fourth and was now 83 points behind. Then there was

TOP 10 QUALIFIERS

Pos.	Driver	Seconds	mph
1	Ryan Newman	28.588	193.928
2	Carl Edwards	28.663	193.420
3	Elliott Sadler	28.670	193.373
4	Mark Martin	28.797	192.520
5	Dave Blaney	28.849	192.173
6	Kasey Kahne	28.878	191.980
7	Kyle Busch	28.903	191.814
8	Martin Truex Jr.	28.914	191.741
9	Dale Jarrett	28.917	191.721
10	Tony Stewart	28.922	191.688

a 66-point gap back to Edwards, who was now 149 points away and listed fifth, followed by the remaining five drivers led by Wallace, 166 point back, down to Mayfield, who dropped to 10th place, 216 points out of first place. Still, no one was forgetting how Johnson rallied from an even larger deficit over the final five races last year and barely missed winning the title in the closest point battle in history. So as the Bass Pro Shops MBNA 500 at Atlanta Motor Speedway approached, none of the championship contenders were about to call it quits.

Carl Edwards carried fond memories into central Georgia, happily looking back to March of this year when he edged out Johnson with the checkered flag in sight to gain his first NASCAR NEXTEL Cup Series victory right here at this track. Now, a little more than seven months later, Edwards showed he hadn't forgotten how to get around the fast, 1.54-mile track and turned the second-quickest lap in Bud Pole qualifying, just a tick of the clock slower than Newman's seventh pole run of the season.

Jeff Gordon (24) tries to gain ground on Dale Earnhardt Jr. (8) along Atlanta's frontstretch. Gordon carried momentum from his win last week to a runner-up finish at Atlanta, while Earnhardt led the most laps in the race and picked up his first top five since New Hampshire, six races ago.

(Right) A dejected Rusty Wallace views front-end damage to his Dodge sustained in an accident less than 10 laps into the race. Although he returned to action, accidents in three straight races contributed to his fall to eighth in the championship standings.

(Below) Mark Martin charges across the start/finish line on the way to a third-place finish, his fourth top five in the last six events to help keep his title hopes alive.

Dale Earnhardt Jr. qualified 17th and spent the first 50 laps of the race moving toward the front. In his seventh event since being reunited with crew chief Tony Eury Jr., Earnhardt drove off pit road second behind Martin during the day's second caution but inherited the lead before the restart when Martin was sent to the end of the longest line for an apparent speeding violation.

Once in front, Earnhardt showed the strength of his Chevrolet by leading seven times for 142 of the next 156 laps, to the delight of many among the estimated 120,000 fans on hand. And while the Budweiser driver kept his Monte Carlo glued to the bottom of the turns, Edwards quietly toured the track on the high side while remaining solidly among the top five.

The day's seventh caution at Lap 190 set up a restart with Earnhardt still out front followed by the Roush Racing Fords of Martin, Kenseth, Edwards and Biffle. Ten laps after taking the green flag, Edwards, driving a car that needed several laps to settle in following restarts, arrived on Earnhardt's bumper, ready to challenge for the lead.

Down the backstretch, the two went side by side with Edwards gaining a slight advantage to lead Lap 207, only to have Earnhardt charge back in front the next time around. Edwards, however, answered right back on the following lap and began to take charge of the race. Out front — and into clean air — Edwards was able to open sizable gaps while leading all but 13 of the final 117 laps on the way to his third win of the season.

(Above) Carl Edwards (99) reels in race leader Dale Earnhardt Jr. (8) shortly past the halfway point in the race. Earnhardt dominated the first 200 laps, but Edwards eventually took the top position and was overpowering on his way to the win.

(Opposite Page) Carl Edwards claims victory at Atlanta for the second time this year, thus completing the season sweep. His third win overall moved him to well within striking distance of a championship in his first full year in the NASCAR NEXTEL Cup Series.

BASS PRO SHOPS MBNA 500

NASCAR NEXTEL Cup Series
Race No. 33

Fin. Pos.	Start Pos.	Car No.	Driver	Team	Laps	Laps Led	Status
1	2	99	Carl Edwards	Office Depot Ford	325	115	Running
2	24	24	Jeff Gordon	DuPont Chevrolet	325		Running
3	4	6	Mark Martin	Viagra Ford	325	43	Running
4	17	8	Dale Earnhardt Jr.	Budweiser Chevrolet	325	142	Running
5	23	17	Matt Kenseth	USG Sheetrock/DeWalt Ford	325	1	Running
6	28	42	Jamie McMurray	Texaco/Havoline Dodge	325		Running
7	16	16	Greg Biffle	National Guard/Charter Ford	325	5	Running
8	41	31	Jeff Burton	Cingular Wireless Chevrolet	325		Running
9	10	20	Tony Stewart	The Home Depot Chevrolet	325	1	Running
10	3	38	Elliott Sadler	M&M's Minis Ford	325	10	Running
11	37	15	Michael Waltrip	NAPA Auto Parts Chevrolet	325		Running
12	7	5 #	Kyle Busch	Kellogg's Chevrolet	325	4	Running
13	21	0	Mike Bliss	Best Buy Chevrolet	325	1	Running
14	9	88	Dale Jarrett	UPS Ford	325		Running
15	11	25	Brian Vickers	GMAC/ditech.com Chevrolet	325		Running
16	12	48	Jimmie Johnson	Lowe's Chevrolet	325		Running
17	29	21	Ricky Rudd	Motorcraft Genuine Parts Ford	324		Running
18	27	01	Joe Nemechek	U.S. Army Chevrolet	324		Running
19	25	11	Denny Hamlin	FedEx Ground Chevrolet	324		Running
20	33	40	Sterling Marlin	Coors Light Dodge	323		Running
21	38	41	Casey Mears	Target Dodge	323		Running
22	31	29	Kevin Harvick	GM Goodwrench Chevrolet	323		Running
23	1	12	Ryan Newman	Mobil 1/Alltel Dodge	323	1	Running
24	5	07	Dave Blaney	Jack Daniel's Chevrolet	323		Running
25	39	45	Kyle Petty	Georgia-Pacific/Brawny Dodge	323	1	Running
26	40	77 #	Travis Kvapil	Kodak/Jasper Eng. & Trans. Dodge	322		Running
27	36	22	Scott Wimmer	Caterpillar Dodge	321		Running
28	19	23	Johnny Benson	Challenger Farm Equipment Dodge	321		Running
29	14	43	Jeff Green	Cheerios/Betty Crocker Dodge	319	1	Running
30	26	04	Bobby Hamilton	Bobby Hamilton Racing Dodge	319		Running
31	35	18	Bobby Labonte	AsthmaControl.com/Interstate Chevrolet	316		Running
32	20	00	Carl Long	Royal Admin Svc/Kellee Kars Dodge	311		Running
33	34	10	Scott Riggs	Checkers/Rally's Chevrolet	291		Engine
34	42	49	Ken Schrader	Schwan's Home Service Dodge	277		Engine
35	6	9	Kasey Kahne	Dodge Dealers/UAW Dodge	276		Accident
36	30	97	Kurt Busch	IRWIN Industrial Tools Ford	270		Running
37	32	2	Rusty Wallace	Miller Lite Dodge	258		Running
38	18	19	Jeremy Mayfield	Dodge Dealers/UAW Dodge	226		Running
39	43	32	Bobby Hamilton Jr.	Tide Chevrolet	219		Engine
40	8	1	Martin Truex Jr.	Bass Pro Shops/TRACKER Chevrolet	176		Accident
41	22	39	Reed Sorenson	Discount Tire Dodge	133		Accident
42	13	66	Kevin Lepage	Peak Fitness/Vassarette Ford	113		Engine
43	15	37	Mike Skinner	BoSPOKER.net/Patron Tequila Dodge	5		Accident

Raybestos Rookie of the Year Contender.

Chase for the NASCAR NEXTEL Cup Standings
(With 3 Races Remaining)

Pos.	Driver	Points	Behind	Change
1	**Tony Stewart**	6100	—	—
2	Jimmie Johnson	6057	-43	—
3	Greg Biffle	6025	-75	+1
4	Carl Edwards	5993	-107	+1
5	Ryan Newman	5993	-107	-2
6	Mark Martin	5957	-143	+1
7	Matt Kenseth	5945	-155	+2
8	Rusty Wallace	5843	-257	-2
9	Kurt Busch	5840	-260	-1
10	Jeremy Mayfield	5790	-310	—

"There at the end I was having a blast," an elated Edwards said following the victory. "I can't believe we ended up winning the race. That's pretty cool, to say the least."

With the win, Edwards gained 42 points on Stewart, who finished ninth, and was now listed fourth in the standings, 107 points out of first place with three races remaining.

"Absolutely we're making a run," Edwards claimed when asked about his resurgence in the title hunt. "We're going to go out here and make a run for the championship. I did not expect to be able to pick up this many points today and anything can happen in racing, so we're not going to quit until the last lap of the last race."

DICKIES 500

Carl Edwards doesn't own a glass slipper. Jack Roush is no fairy godmother. And the No. 99 Ford is anything but a pumpkin. But put the three together and you have the NASCAR NEXTEL Cup Series' real-life version of "Cinderella."

A few short years ago, Edwards was spending his weekends racing on dirt tracks near his hometown of Columbia, Mo., a welcome diversion from his day job as a substitute teacher. Able to hook up with a part-time ride supplied by a local team owner, Edwards tried his hand in the NASCAR Craftsman Truck Series and immediately got noticed by Roush, who recruited the strapping young man with an infections smile to drive his trucks for the 2003 season. A wave of the wand and a few back flips later, Edwards suddenly finds himself smack dab in the middle of a run for the most coveted title stock car racing has to offer — the NASCAR NEXTEL Cup Series championship.

"The people who know me, the people back home in Missouri, [know] this whole thing is a dream come true," Edwards said. "This is not supposed to happen. I have achieved things in my career that are not at all supposed to happen. Winning this championship is a lot more realistic goal than just the fact that I'm here."

Dale Earnhardt Jr. (8) slips under Greg Biffle (16), who slides down the frontstretch during an early-race spin, the result of a loose wheel. With only six cautions in the race, Biffle was not able to get back into winning contention and suffered a setback in the championship points.

(Right) Veterans Bill Elliott (91) and Terry Labonte, in the Kellogg's Chevrolet, chose to put the Dickies 500 on their season schedules. The pair raced each other to the finish with Labonte, driving his 14th event of the season, finishing 31st, one position ahead of Elliott, in his ninth race of 2005.

(Below) Ryan Newman's crew surveys the damage to their Dodge, sustained during qualifying immediately after Newman's first lap resulted in his eighth Bud Pole of the season. After starting at the rear in a backup car, Newman finished 25th and tumbled two spots in the standings.

TOP 10 QUALIFIERS

Pos.	Driver	Seconds	mph
1	Ryan Newman	27.987	192.947
2	Jeff Gordon	28.067	192.397
3	Matt Kenseth	28.130	191.966
4	Joe Nemechek	28.176	191.652
5	Jeremy Mayfield	28.212	191.408
6	Mike Bliss	28.223	191.333
7	Greg Biffle	28.228	191.299
8	Mark Martin	28.247	191.171
9	Bill Elliott	28.268	191.029
10	Dale Earnhardt Jr.	28.292	190.867

Edwards had every reason to be optimistic. Two weeks ago, after Martinsville, he sat fifth in the Chase for the NASCAR NEXTEL Cup standings, 149 points behind first-place Tony Stewart. A winning performance last week in Atlanta knocked 42 points off that deficit and provided Edwards with a realistic shot at the championship — if things went his way.

So Edwards rode into Fort Worth, Texas, with little to lose and everything to gain. Tied with Ryan Newman for fourth in the points behind Stewart, Jimmie Johnson and Greg Biffle, Edwards took to the track in Bud Pole qualifying and turned a relatively disappointing lap

Mark Martin (right) imparts some of his experience and expertise on teammate Carl Edwards (left) in the Texas garage. Ironically, it was Edwards who pushed past Martin in the closing laps of the Dickies 500 to snatch his second straight win.

(Above) Carl Edwards (99), having just passed Matt Kenseth (17), sets his sights on race leader Mark Martin (6). With two fresh tires taken on the final caution, Edwards' Ford clearly was faster and he closed the gap in three laps and went on to take the victory.

(Left) A very happy Carl Edwards emerges from his Ford after his fourth win in this, his first full season of NASCAR NEXTEL Cup Series competition. The victory moved him up one position to third in the standings and kept him in championship contention.

that placed him 30th on the starting grid. Newman, on the other hand, posted a lap good enough to gain his eighth pole of the season but immediately crashed on his second timed lap. Damage rendered Newman's Dodge useless, forcing him to his backup machine and a spot at the back of the field for the start of the race.

Newman's misfortune pushed third-fastest qualifier Matt Kenseth to the inside of the front row next to Jeff Gordon for the start of the Dickies 500, and Kenseth took immediate advantage and jumped to the early lead.

Biffle took over the top spot after 36 laps, but soon after reported a vibration to crew chief Doug Richert. An unscheduled stop on pit road dropped Biffle off the lead lap. That, combined with a later spin due to a loose wheel, resulted in a 20th-place finish for Biffle, severely diminishing his championship hopes.

DICKIES 500

NASCAR NEXTEL Cup Series Race No. 34

Fin. Pos.	Start Pos.	Car No.	Driver	Team	Laps	Laps Led	Status
1	30	99	Carl Edwards	Office Depot Ford	334	82	Running
2	8	6	Mark Martin	Viagra Ford	334	42	Running
3	3	17	Matt Kenseth	DeWalt Power Tools Ford	334	149	Running
4	35	41	Casey Mears	Target Dodge	334	23	Running
5	11	48	Jimmie Johnson	Lowe's Chevrolet	334	2	Running
6	16	20	Tony Stewart	The Home Depot Chevrolet	334	15	Running
7	14	11	Denny Hamlin	FedEx Kinko's Chevrolet	334		Running
8	10	8	Dale Earnhardt Jr.	Budweiser Chevrolet	334		Running
9	12	38	Elliott Sadler	Combos/M&M's Ford	334		Running
10	18	97	Kurt Busch	Crown Royal Ford	334		Running
11	40	42	Jamie McMurray	Texaco/Havoline Dodge	334		Running
12	29	88	Dale Jarrett	UPS Ford	334		Running
13	20	21	Ricky Rudd	Motorcraft Genuine Parts Ford	334		Running
14	2	24	Jeff Gordon	DuPont Chevrolet	334		Running
15	27	1	Martin Truex Jr.	Bass Pro Shops/TRACKER Chevrolet	334		Running
16	33	29	Kevin Harvick	GM Goodwrench Chevrolet	334	1	Running
17	6	0	Mike Bliss	Geek Squad Chevrolet	334		Running
18	42	43	Jeff Green	Cheerios/Betty Crocker/Narnia Dodge	334		Running
19	21	25	Brian Vickers	GMAC/ditech.com Chevrolet	334	6	Running
20	7	16	Greg Biffle	National Guard Ford	334	12	Running
21	38	45	Kyle Petty	Georgia-Pacific/Brawny Dodge	334	1	Running
22	26	2	Rusty Wallace	Miller Lite Dodge	334		Running
23	39	40	Sterling Marlin	Coors Light Dodge	334		Running
24	37	77 #	Travis Kvapil	Kodak/Jasper Eng. & Trans. Dodge	334		Running
25	1	12	Ryan Newman	Alltel Dodge	334		Running
26	17	18	Bobby Labonte	Interstate Batteries Chevrolet	333		Running
27	19	22	Scott Wimmer	Caterpillar Dodge	333		Running
28	13	07	Dave Blaney	Jack Daniel's "Texas Pride" Chevrolet	333		Running
29	41	49	Ken Schrader	Schwan's Home Service Dodge	333		Running
30	32	31	Jeff Burton	Cingular Wireless Chevrolet	333		Running
31	34	44	Terry Labonte	Kellogg's Chevrolet	333		Running
32	9	91	Bill Elliott	Auto Value/Bumper-to-Bumper Dodge	333		Running
33	23	66	Kevin Lepage	Dickies Ford	331		Running
34	22	10	Scott Riggs	CENTRIX Financial/Valvoline Chevrolet	331		Running
35	5	19	Jeremy Mayfield	Dodge Dealers/UAW Dodge	330		Running
36	43	4	Mike Wallace	Lucas Oil Chevrolet	330		Running
37	4	01	Joe Nemechek	U.S. Army Chevrolet	329		Running
38	25	32	Bobby Hamilton Jr.	Tide Chevrolet	328		Running
39	36	50	Jimmy Spencer	Allied Steel Buildings Dodge	327		Running
40	24	5 #	Kyle Busch	CARQUEST Chevrolet	325		Running
41	31	15	Michael Waltrip	NAPA Auto Parts Chevrolet	294	1	Engine
42	15	9	Kasey Kahne	Dodge Dealers/UAW Dodge	151		Engine
43	28	37	Mike Skinner	BoSPOKER.net/Patron Tequila Dodge	151		Rear End

Raybestos Rookie of the Year Contender.

Chase for the NASCAR NEXTEL Cup Standings
(With 2 Races Remaining)

Pos.	Driver	Points	Behind	Change
1	Tony Stewart	6255	—	—
2	Jimmie Johnson	6217	-38	—
3	Carl Edwards	6178	-77	+1
4	Greg Biffle	6133	-122	-1
5	Mark Martin	6132	-123	+1
6	Matt Kenseth	6120	-135	+1
7	Ryan Newman	6081	-174	-2
8	Kurt Busch	5974	-281	+1
9	Rusty Wallace	5940	-315	-1
10	Jeremy Mayfield	5848	-407	—

Kenseth and Mark Martin shared time leading over the first 300 miles, while Edwards picked his way through traffic before joining his Roush teammates at the front of the field. Leading for the first time on Lap 199, Edwards, along with Martin, established themselves over the next 175 miles as the fastest on the track.

Edwards was out front when the sixth and final caution flew on Lap 319 for debris. He and Stewart, running sixth at the time, elected to pit while the rest of the leaders remained on the track.

Crew chief Bob Osborne called for right-side tires on the No. 99 Ford and sent Edwards back to the track, where he lined up sixth for the restart behind leader Martin, Kenseth, Casey Mears, Sterling Marlin and Rusty Wallace.

The green flag flew with 11 laps remaining and Edwards went to work, dispatching Wallace, Marlin and Mears over the next few laps and pulling up behind second-place Kenseth. With five laps to go, Edwards shot past his teammate and zeroed in on Martin, erasing a 12 car-length advantage over the next three trips around the 1.5-mile track.

With less than two to go, Edwards drifted to the outside of the No.6 Ford and blew past as the pair rolled off Turn 2 to take the lead for the last time, able to open a half-second advantage on the way to taking his fourth checkered flag of the season, his second in a row.

Stewart wound up sixth at the finish, one position behind Johnson in their fight for the top spot in the standings, while Edwards' win allowed him to move past Biffle into third place in the points, closing the gap between him and Stewart to 77 points with two races to go in the 2005 Chase for the NASCAR NEXTEL Cup.

"We're going to try to win these [last two] races," Edwards claimed after the victory. "We probably won't beat Tony Stewart. ... The guy knows how to win championships. He's an unbelievable race car driver with a great team, but that's not going to stop us from giving 100 percent."

With things seemingly going his way, the championship remains a real possibility. One thing's for certain, however: Edwards is not about to run home before the clock strikes midnight.

CHECKER AUTO PARTS 500
PRESENTED BY TECHRON

Part of winning a season-long championship is doing what you have to do, when you have to do it. When it comes to winning a single race, however, sometimes you simply throw the cards on the table and play the hand that's been dealt. In the Checker Auto Parts 500, championship contenders did what they had to do, while the race winner gathered up his cards and played them perfectly.

The top four in the point standings — Tony Stewart, Jimmie Johnson, Carl Edwards and Greg Biffle — got their Phoenix weekends started off on the right foot in Bud Pole qualifying. Johnson grabbed a front-row starting position followed immediately by Edwards and Biffle, while Stewart was a bit more conservative in his timed run but still nailed down a top-10 spot, in ninth.

Bud Pole winner Denny Hamlin (11) brings the field under green to begin the Checker Auto Parts 500 with Jimmie Johnson (48) on his right, followed by Carl Edwards (99) and Greg Biffle. The pole came in Hamlin's sixth career start.

TOP 10 QUALIFIERS

Pos.	Driver	Seconds	mph
1	Denny Hamlin	26.831	134.173
2	Jimmie Johnson	26.965	133.506
3	Carl Edwards	26.975	133.457
4	Greg Biffle	26.980	133.432
5	Bobby Labonte	27.020	133.235
6	Brian Vickers	27.081	132.935
7	Bobby Hamilton Jr.	27.099	132.846
8	Kevin Harvick	27.105	132.817
9	Tony Stewart	27.115	132.768
10	Jeff Gordon	27.116	132.763

Rusty Wallace chases Jeff Gordon (24) into the first turn at Phoenix. Gordon had another strong race to third place, raising his total to three top-three finishes in the last four events.

The surprise of the session was Denny Hamlin. Celebrating his recently signed contract to drive the No. 11 Chevrolets for Joe Gibbs Racing in 2006, Hamlin took to the one mile oval and clicked off a lap at just over 134 mph to win the first Bud Pole of his young career. In five previous starts beginning at Kansas Speedway in early October, Hamlin had already scored three top-10 finishes in a late-season performance reminiscent of Edwards' 2005 run after he took the wheel of the "99" Ford for Jack Roush.

When the green flag dropped for Hamlin on Sunday, five days before his 25th birthday, the driver of the FedEx Express Chevrolet jumped immediately to the lead and paced the field for the first 15 laps and 23 of the first 35 before giving way to Biffle. Fourth in the standings and trailing Stewart by 122 points going into the race, Biffle was determined to maximize his efforts by gaining as many points as possible. To that end, the National Guard driver began a dominating performance that placed him at the front of the field for the next 158 straight laps and 172 of the next 194 trips around the Arizona oval, while Stewart, Johnson and Edwards kept pace among the frontrunners.

Joining the championship contenders in the top 10 were Hamlin, Kevin Harvick and eventually Kyle Busch, who had slowly worked his way up from the 15th starting position. Midway through the race, however, Busch experienced a tire problem that forced him to pit road under green, dropping the Kellogg's driver one lap off the pace.

The unscheduled stop also knocked Busch out of pit sequence with the rest of the field — a fact that he and crew chief Alan Gustafson thought might be their wildcard as the event progressed.

True enough, their opportunity to play it came when the eighth caution flew on Lap 228. Busch remained on the track as the leaders pitted and suddenly found himself in the lead for the first time in the race.

"That tire problem, it gave us an opportunity to be out of sequence with the leaders," Gustafson said. "I thought [the eighth caution] would be a good time to take advantage of it and go for the win."

Armed with fresh tires, Biffle returned to the track 13th for the restart and immediately went to work, weaving through traffic in his pursuit of the leader. And by the time the ninth and final caution appeared for Hamlin's spin in Turn 4, Biffle had already arrived in the top five.

Second and third in the championship standings, Jimmie Johnson (48) and Carl Edwards (99) go at it door-to-door on the one-mile oval. Both drivers hung around the top 10 all day and finished together, with Edwards sixth ahead of Johnson, but both lost ground in the points.

(Right) Tony Stewart (20) slides to the inside of his Joe Gibbs Racing teammate, Bobby Labonte (18), in a fight for position. Stewart edged out Labonte for fourth place in the race, padding his lead in the points.

(Below) Scott Wimmer prepares to restart the field during the ninth and final caution of the day. Wimmer, who had stayed on the track under yellow, managed to hold the lead for 11 green-flag laps before Kyle Busch came whizzing past.

With 57 laps remaining, the leaders rolled down pit road for one final pit stop. "Coming in first gave us an opportunity to get four [tires] and be in front of the guys with four," Gustafson said of the stop that sent Busch out ahead of the others. "So we were the first car with four tires [on the restart] and I think that was the key."

Busch lined up sixth behind Scott Wimmer, Dave Blaney, Brian Vickers, Jeff Gordon and Elliott Sadler, with Biffle four spots back in 10th place, and it took Busch just 12 laps to

reach and pass Wimmer to take his second lead of the day. But as he checked his mirror, Busch could see the No. 16 Ford bearing down from behind. Seven laps later, Biffle pulled up on Busch's bumper and dove to the inside to regain the lead. Busch, however, was not about to give up and was relentless in his pursuit of the leader.

"I just wanted to make sure I kept enough pressure on him (Biffle) to where he was still going to keep overdriving his race car," Busch said.

And pressure he did. For five laps until, with 28 to go, Busch poked the nose of his Chevrolet to the inside of Biffle's Ford and surged ahead for the final time on the way to his second win

(Left) Greg Biffle blasts back into action after receiving a fresh set of tires and a full load of fuel. Biffle led 60 percent of the laps in his bid for the win.

(Below) Kyle Busch (5) stays glued to the bumper of Greg Biffle's Ford (16) after Biffle drove past to take a late-race lead.

(Opposing Page) Busch's tenacity eventually paid off as he was able to get around Biffle one last time and stretch out a 0.609-second lead over the final 28 laps on the way to his second career win.

CHECKER AUTO PARTS 500
presented by TECHRON

NASCAR NEXTEL Cup Series Race No. 35

Fin. Pos.	Start Pos.	Car No.	Driver	Team	Laps	Laps Led	Status
1	15	5 #	Kyle Busch	Kellogg's Chevrolet	312	63	Running
2	4	16	Greg Biffle	National Guard/Post-It Ford	312	189	Running
3	10	24	Jeff Gordon	DuPont Chevrolet	312	22	Running
4	9	20	Tony Stewart	The Home Depot Chevrolet	312		Running
5	5	18	Bobby Labonte	Interstate Batteries/Madagascar Chev.	312		Running
6	3	99	Carl Edwards	Office Depot Ford	312		Running
7	2	48	Jimmie Johnson	Lowe's Chevrolet	312		Running
8	12	7	Robby Gordon	Harrah's Chevrolet	312		Running
9	21	88	Dale Jarrett	UPS Ford	312		Running
10	30	77 #	Travis Kvapil	Kodak/Jasper Eng. & Trans. Dodge	312		Running
11	24	38	Elliott Sadler	M&M's/Combos Ford	312		Running
12	11	12	Ryan Newman	Alltel Dodge	312		Running
13	1	11	Denny Hamlin	FedEx Express Chevrolet	312	23	Running
14	29	6	Mark Martin	Viagra Ford	312		Running
15	25	31	Jeff Burton	Cingular Wireless Chevrolet	312		Running
16	17	97	Kenny Wallace	IRWIN Industrial Tools Ford	312		Running
17	18	01	Joe Nemechek	CENTRIX Financial/U.S. Army Chevrolet	312		Running
18	28	42	Jamie McMurray	Texaco/Havoline Dodge	312		Running
19	38	45	Kyle Petty	Georgia-Pacific/Brawny Dodge	312		Running
20	20	21	Ricky Rudd	Motorcraft Genuine Parts Ford	312		Running
21	40	22	Scott Wimmer	Caterpillar Dodge	312	15	Running
22	34	41	Casey Mears	Target Dodge	312		Running
23	8	29	Kevin Harvick	GM Goodwrench Chevrolet	312		Running
24	39	19	Jeremy Mayfield	Dodge Dealers/UAW Dodge	311		Running
25	13	07	Dave Blaney	Jack Daniel's Chevrolet	311		Running
26	6	25	Brian Vickers	GMAC/ditech.com Chevrolet	311		Running
27	22	9	Kasey Kahne	Dodge Dealers/UAW Dodge	311		Running
28	14	43	Jeff Green	Cheerios/Betty Crocker/Rashas' Dodge	311		Running
29	26	2	Rusty Wallace	Miller Lite Dodge	310		Running
30	33	49	Ken Schrader	Schwan's Home Service Dodge	310		Running
31	32	0	Mike Bliss	Net Zero/Best Buy Chevrolet	310		Running
32	16	17	Matt Kenseth	DeWalt Power Tools Ford	310		Running
33	42	15	Michael Waltrip	NAPA Auto Parts Chevrolet	310		Running
34	41	40	Sterling Marlin	Coors Light Dodge	310		Running
35	7	32	Bobby Hamilton Jr.	Tide Chevrolet	217		Accident
36	23	50	Jimmy Spencer	US Micro/Allied Steel Buildings Dodge	214		Accident
37	27	37	Mike Skinner	BoSPOKER.net/Patron Tequila Dodge	214		Accident
38	31	10	Scott Riggs	Valvoline Chevrolet	205		Accident
39	37	00	Johnny Sauter	Miccosukee Resort Dodge	149		Suspension
40	19	8	Dale Earnhardt Jr.	Budweiser Chevrolet	112		Accident
41	43	78	Jerry Robertson	Furniture Row Chevrolet	51		Engine
42	36	95	Stanton Barrett	Cheetah Speed Sys./Langley Prop. Chev.	24		Accident
43	35	34	Chad Chaffin	Fiesta Inn Resorts Chevrolet	14		Overheating

Raybestos Rookie of the Year Contender.

Chase for the NASCAR NEXTEL Cup Standings
(With 1 Race Remaining)

Pos.	Driver	Points	Behind	Change
1	Tony Stewart	6415	—	—
2	Jimmie Johnson	6363	-52	—
3	Carl Edwards	6328	-87	—
4	Greg Biffle	6313	-102	—
5	Mark Martin	6253	-162	—
6	Ryan Newman	6208	-207	+1
7	Matt Kenseth	6187	-228	-1
8	Rusty Wallace	6016	-399	+1
9	Kurt Busch	5974	-441	-1
10	Jeremy Mayfield	5939	-476	—

of the year and a virtual lock on the Raybestos Rookie of the Year title.

Of the title contenders, Biffle did the best with his runner-up finish and closed the gap between himself and Stewart to 102 points, keeping his championship hopes alive.

Stewart drove a methodical if unspectacular race, staying among the top 10 for most of the day before charging to a top-five finish — good enough to widen his margin over second-place Johnson by another 14 points. The Home Depot driver now had 52 points to play with in the final race of the year.

Edwards' two-race winning streak ended at Phoenix, but a solid top-10 run cost him only 10 points in the standings, where he remained in third place, 87 back of Stewart.

For Mark Martin and Matt Kenseth, fifth and sixth in the championship standings headed to Phoenix, the results were decisively bad. Finishes of 14th and 32nd, respectively, mathematically eliminated both from the title hunt, leaving four drivers left to battle it out in the final race of the year at Homestead-Miami Speedway.

FORD 400

Exactly nine months had passed since the season-opening Daytona 500, 35 races ago. Now, only the Ford 400 remained to be run in the 2005 NASCAR NEXTEL Cup Series season — and there was plenty on the line for a number of competitors.

Tony Stewart, Jimmie Johnson, Carl Edwards and Greg Biffle remained in the championship hunt, and each arrived in South Florida knowing exactly what he needed to do.

For Stewart, the formula was simple: finish ninth or better and the championship would be his, regardless of what anyone else did.

After two straight seasons finishing runner-up in the final point standings, Johnson was as determined as ever to take that last step up to the season title. Second to Stewart with a 52-point deficit, Johnson's best chance was to win the race and hope that Stewart finished out of the top 10. Whether Johnson needed Stewart to finish 11th, 12th or 13th depended on how many laps, if any, The Home Depot driver could lead in the race, but Johnson was confident he could do his part based on his record of two top fives and three top 10s in four career starts on the 1.5-mile track.

The Home Depot team works diligently in the Homestead-Miami garage in preparation for the final event of the season. Although their driver, Tony Stewart, held a 52-point advantage, all were aware that a single flaw in their Chevrolet could cause the margin to evaporate in an instant.

(Above) Rusty Wallace climbs aboard his Miller Lite Dodge for the last time. Wallace, who finished 13th in his final race, leaves the series eighth on the all-time wins list with 55 victories and a championship.

(Right) The crew from Penske Racing South gives their driver a thumbs-up salute as Rusty Wallace pulls away for his 706th and final career start.

The scenarios for Carl Edwards and Greg Biffle were much more complicated, but like Johnson, each knew his best hope was to go out and win the race, lead the most laps if possible, and look for the other challengers to have problems of one sort or another.

The rest of the Chase for the NASCAR NEXTEL Cup competitors were mathematically locked out of winning the championship, but good performances in the Ford 400 could move them up in the final standings — an important point when it came time to hand out bonuses at the annual Awards Ceremony in New York City.

Carl Edwards (99) tries the inside alone in an early-race challenge for the lead on Ryan Newman (12), followed closely by Jeff Gordon (24), Kasey Kahne (9) and Dave Blaney (07). Edwards and Newman started together on the front row and led 127 of the first 169 laps, with Gordon leading another 39 during that span.

Money was also an issue for Jeff Gordon, Jamie McMurray and Elliott Sadler, all within 41 points of each other in their battle for 11th position in the final points and the guaranteed $1 million check that came with the position.

Edwards got the jump on everyone in Bud Pole qualifying by nailing down his second inside front-row start of the season. Biffle turned the seventh-fastest lap, while Stewart and Johnson did little to help themselves by qualifying 20th and 32nd, respectively, placing them in the middle of traffic for the start of the race.

Tensions in Stewart's garage tightened even more during post-qualifying practice when the orange-and-white Chevrolet spun, causing the engine to over-rev. After much consultation within the team, the decision was made not to change motors, which would have relegated Stewart to a starting position at the back of the field.

The afternoon sun was low in the sky at the drop of the green flag on Sunday, and that seemed to suit Edwards and Ryan Newman the best. Newman took early control of the race, but gave way to Edwards before the 50-lap mark. Once out front, Edwards led 93 of the next 124 laps — enough to wrap up the lap-leader bonus for the race.

TOP 10 QUALIFIERS

Pos.	Driver	Seconds	mph
1	Carl Edwards	30.673	176.051
2	Ryan Newman	30.675	176.039
3	Kasey Kahne	30.700	175.896
4	Kyle Busch	30.759	175.558
5	Mark Martin	30.809	175.273
6	Casey Mears	30.818	175.222
7	Greg Biffle	30.859	174.989
8	Jamie McMurray	30.863	174.967
9	Dale Jarrett	30.917	174.661
10	Joe Nemechek	30.927	174.605

(Above) Jimmie Johnson's race — and season — ended here, on the Turn 4 apron after the Lowe's Chevrolet broke loose near the midpoint of the race. Johnson could only watch as Tony Stewart (20) passed by on his way to winning the championship.

(Right) Casey Mears (41) takes the point from Carl Edwards (99) as darkness descends on the speedway. Mears led 75 laps in the second half of the Ford 400 and brought his Dodge home fifth for his second top five in the final three races.

(Above) Greg Biffle (16) rolls off the fourth turn in an early-race restart as the sun sets behind the Turn 1 grandstand. While the early leaders found their cars less suited for the night-time conditions, Biffle continued to move up in the running order.

(Left) Greg Biffle lights up the tires in celebration of his series-leading sixth win of the season. Although Biffle ended up tied in points with Carl Edwards, he was credited with second place by virtue of having two more wins than his Roush Racing teammate.

Johnson carefully worked his way through traffic and into the top 10, but then began to feel a problem develop in his Lowe's Monte Carlo. Trying to keep from pitting under green, Johnson continued until, on Lap 127, the right-rear tire let go, sending Johnson into the fourth-turn wall, where his hopes for a championship abruptly ended.

FORD 400

NASCAR NEXTEL Cup Series Race No. 36

Fin. Pos.	Start Pos.	Car No.	Driver	Team	Laps	Laps Led	Status
1	7	16	Greg Biffle	National Guard/Post-It Ford	267	9	Running
2	5	6	Mark Martin	Viagra Ford	267	2	Running
3	17	17	Matt Kenseth	DeWalt Power Tools Ford	267		Running
4	1	99	Carl Edwards	Office Depot Ford	267	94	Running
5	6	41	Casey Mears	Target Dodge	267	75	Running
6	11	07	Dave Blaney	Jack Daniel's Chevrolet	267	6	Running
7	2	12	Ryan Newman	Alltel Dodge	267	33	Running
8	14	29	Kevin Harvick	GM Goodwrench Chevrolet	267	1	Running
9	12	24	Jeff Gordon	DuPont Chevrolet	267	39	Running
10	13	19	Jeremy Mayfield	Dodge Dealers/UAW Dodge	267		Running
11	27	22	Scott Wimmer	Caterpillar Dodge	267		Running
12	19	0	Mike Bliss	NetZero/Best Buy Chevrolet	267		Running
13	37	2	Rusty Wallace	Miller Lite Dodge	267		Running
14	39	7	Robby Gordon	Jim Beam Chevrolet	267		Running
15	20	20	Tony Stewart	The Home Depot Chevrolet	267		Running
16	3	9	Kasey Kahne	Dodge Dealers/UAW Dodge	267		Running
17	9	88	Dale Jarrett	UPS Ford	266		Running
18	8	42	Jamie McMurray	Texaco/Havoline Dodge	266		Running
19	40	8	Dale Earnhardt Jr.	Budweiser Chevrolet	266		Running
20	24	4	Todd Bodine	Lucas Oil Chevrolet	266		Running
21	36	97	Kenny Wallace	IRWIN Industrial Tools Ford	266		Running
22	34	49	Ken Schrader	Red Baron Frozen Pizza Dodge	266		Running
23	23	38	Elliott Sadler	M&M's Ford	266		Running
24	10	01	Joe Nemechek	U.S. Army Chevrolet	266	2	Running
25	16	31	Jeff Burton	Cingular Wireless Chevrolet	266		Running
26	26	40	Sterling Marlin	Coors Light Dodge	265	3	Running
27	35	45	Kyle Petty	Georgia Pacific/Brawny/Gators Dodge	265		Running
28	15	09	Reed Sorenson	Miccosukee Resort Dodge	265		Running
29	41	15	Michael Waltrip	NAPA Auto Parts Chevrolet	265		Running
30	29	43	Jeff Green	Chex Party Mix Dodge	264		Running
31	33	50	Jimmy Spencer	Allied Steel Buildings Dodge	263	2	Running
32	30	77 #	Travis Kvapil	Kodak/Jasper Eng. & Trans. Dodge	263		Running
33	42	11	Denny Hamlin	FedEx Express Chevrolet	263	1	Running
34	21	18	Bobby Labonte	Interstate Batteries Chevrolet	263		Running
35	28	66	Kevin Lepage	Cabela's/Ranger Boats Ford	263		Running
36	38	32	Bobby Hamilton Jr.	Tide Chevrolet	263		Running
37	25	21	Ricky Rudd	Motorcraft Genuine Parts Ford	262		Running
38	31	10	Scott Riggs	Checkers/Rally's Seminoles Chevrolet	259		Running
39	43	37	Mike Skinner	BoSPOKER.net/Patron Tequila Dodge	156		Engine
40	32	48	Jimmie Johnson	Lowe's Chevrolet	124		Accident
41	4	5 #	Kyle Busch	Kellogg's Chevrolet	115		Accident
42	22	39	David Stremme	Commit Dodge	87		Accident
43	18	25	Brian Vickers	GMAC/ditech.com Chevrolet	82		Accident

Raybestos Rookie of the Year Contender.

Chase for the NASCAR NEXTEL Cup Standings
(Final Standings)

Pos.	Driver	Points	Behind	Change
1	**Tony Stewart**	6533	—	—
2	Greg Biffle	6498	-35	+2
3	Carl Edwards	6498	-35	—
4	Mark Martin	6428	-105	+1
5	Jimmie Johnson	6406	-127	-3
6	Ryan Newman	6359	-174	—
7	Matt Kenseth	6352	-181	—
8	Rusty Wallace	6140	-393	—
9	Jeremy Mayfield	6073	-460	+1
10	Kurt Busch	5974	-559	-1

Things were not going all that smoothly for Stewart, either. After starting the race with a car that was a bit too tight, the point leader found himself chasing the setup as track conditions changed with the disappearing sun. The good news for Stewart, however, was that with Johnson out of the race, his margin for error increased to needing only a finish among the top 20 to nail down the championship.

As darkness fell over the track, Edwards, too, found conditions not quite as favorable for his Ford, while Casey Mears felt his Dodge picking up speed. Mears assumed the point at Lap 170 and asserted himself for 75 of the next 84 laps, looking very much like he might be on the way to his first NASCAR NEXTEL Cup Series victory until the eighth and final caution flew with 15 of the 267 laps remaining.

Edwards pitted for four fresh tires under the caution, which dropped him back in the field, while Stewart lined up 14th for the restart needing only to remain on the lead lap the rest of the way.

Dave Blaney, who had stayed out on the track, led on the restart with 10 laps to go, but was passed by Biffle three laps later. Biffle would not simply drive off to the win, however, as Mark Martin made a late-race charge, pulling alongside his teammate as the white flag waved. Side-by-side the two remained over the final 1.5-mile distance, each able to gain ground, only to give way moments later. Off the fourth turn fender-to-fender, the two Fords raced to the stripe, with Biffle able gain only the slightest edge as the checkered flag fell.

Matt Kenseth and Edwards followed Martin across the line, making it a 1-2-3-4 sweep by the powerful Roush Fords. But that was little consolation for them, as Stewart fell only one position over the final laps to finish 15th.

When the points were totaled, Biffle and Edwards wound up tied, 35 points behind Stewart, with Martin in fourth, 105 back. Johnson, who was listed 40th in the final rundown, fell to fifth place, 127 points behind Stewart, the 2005 NASCAR NEXTEL Cup Series champion.

Jeff Gordon finish ninth in the Ford 400 and locked up the 11th position, while Kyle Busch, despite finishing 41st due to an accident, wrapped up the title of 2005 Raybestos Rookie of the Year.

REFLECTIONS
NASCAR NEXTEL Cup Series 2005

Dusk settles in on Phoenix International Raceway during the NASCAR NEXTEL Cup Series' first-ever springtime visit to the Arizona desert.

(Above) In his 12th full season, Jeff Burton nearly returned to the winner's circle with a runner-up finish at Bristol and a third-place run at Phoenix in the spring. His team from Richard Childress Racing had several other solid runs and gained momentum for the 2006 season.

(Above Right) The highlight of Dale Earnhardt Jr.'s up-and-down season came at Chicagoland where he and interim crew chief Steve Hmiel (pictured with Earnhardt) celebrated a well-deserved victory. A few weeks later, Earnhardt was reunited with former car chief Tony Eury Jr. and posted several more strong runs before the end of the year.

(Right) Competition on pit road was furious in 2005 with teams regularly able to complete four-tire stops in less than 14 seconds. Work on pit road was decisive in the outcomes of a number of events during the season, emphasizing the importance of teamwork in NASCAR NEXTEL Cup Series competition.

(Left) Casey Mears (left) finished the season on a strong note with five top-10 runs in the last nine events. Mears moves to the Texaco/Havoline car in 2006, vacated at the end of the year by Jamie McMurray (right), who finished 12th in the 2005 standings and signed with Roush Racing for 2006.

(Lower Left) Kyle Busch takes the checkered flag at California Speedway in early September to post his first NASCAR NEXTEL Cup Series victory and become the youngest winner in series history. Busch scored another win at Phoenix and sewed up Raybestos Rookie of the Year honors.

(Below) Reed Sorenson made his NASCAR NEXTEL Cup Series debut at Atlanta in late October, driving for team owner Chip Ganassi. In his first full year of NASCAR Busch Series competition, Sorenson proved himself as one of the sport's up-and-comers with a record of two wins and 19 top 10s on the way to fourth in the 2005 point standings.

(Above) Kasey Kahne celebrates his win at Richmond in May after a late-race duel with Tony Stewart that yielded the young talent his first NASCAR NEXTEL Cup Series victory in his 47th career start. Kahne nearly won again at The Brickyard, where he finished second to Stewart in another late-race battle.

(Above Right) Ricky Rudd announced late In 2005 hls Intention to cut back from a full season schedule, winding down a career that has spanned three decades. Rudd holds the NASCAR NEXTEL Cup Series record for consecutive starts with 788.

(Right) Mark Martin scored a hugely popular win at Kansas Speedway, the fourth race in the Chase for the NASCAR NEXTEL Cup. Martin's win, along with five other top fives in the final 10 events, helped him to a fourth-place finish in the final championship standings.

Twenty-two full seasons, 706 starts, 55 wins and the 1989 NASCAR NEXTEL Cup Series championship — and we loved every minute of it.

Thanks Rusty, for one heck of a run. You're our kind of racer.